THE
POWER
OF
DIFFERENT

THE
POWER
OF
DIFFERENT

THE LINK BETWEEN
DISORDER AND GENIUS

Gail Saltz, M.D.

FLATIRON
BOOKS
NEW YORK

THE POWER OF DIFFERENT. Copyright © 2017 by Gail Saltz. All rights reserved.
Printed in the United States of America. For information,
address Flatiron Books, 175 Fifth Avenue, New York, N.Y. 10010.

www.flatironbooks.com

Library of Congress Cataloging-in-Publication Data

Names: Saltz, Gail, author.
Title: The power of different : the link between disorder and genius /
    Gail Saltz, M.D.
Description: First Edition. | New York : Flatiron Books, 2017.
Identifiers: LCCN 2016045031| ISBN 9781250060013 (hardcover) |
    ISBN 9781250060037 (e-book)
Subjects: LCSH: Children with disabilities. | Creative ability in children. |
    BISAC: FAMILY & RELATIONSHIPS / Children with Special Needs. |
    PSYCHOLOGY / Creative Ability.
Classification: LCC HV888 .S25 2017 | DDC 305.9/084—dc23
LC record available at https://lccn.loc.gov/2016045031

e-ISBN 9781250060037

Our books may be purchased in bulk for promotional, educational,
or business use. Please contact your local bookseller or the Macmillan Corporate
and Premium Sales Department at (800) 221-7945, extension 5442, or
by e-mail at MacmillanSpecialMarkets@macmillan.com.

First Edition: March 2017

10   9   8   7   6   5   4   3   2   1

CONTENTS

||||||||||||||||||||||||||||||||||||||||||||||||||||||||||||||||||||||||

Introduction   1

1. LEARNING DIFFERENCES
DYSLEXIA   17

2. DISTRACTIBILITY
ADD, ADHD, AND OTHER ATTENTIONAL DISORDERS   47

3. ANXIETY
**GENERALIZED ANXIETY DISORDER, OBSESSIVE-COMPULSIVE
PERSONALITY DISORDER, PANIC DISORDER, AND PHOBIAS**   79

4. MELANCHOLY
DEPRESSION, DYSTHYMIA, AND DYSPHORIA   109

5. CYCLING MOOD
BIPOLAR DISORDER   131

6. DIVERGENT THINKING
SCHIZOID PERSONALITY DISORDER, SCHIZOPHRENIA, AND SCHIZOAFFECTIVE DISORDER   153

7. RELATEDNESS
AUTISM SPECTRUM DISORDERS   173

8. THE FUTURE OF THINKING DIFFERENTLY   203

Notes   219
Acknowledgments   233
Index   237

THE

POWER

OF

DIFFERENT

INTRODUCTION

I spent so many years wanting him to succeed and wanting him to be happy,"[1] Noah, the father of Ethan, a sixteen-year-old who had been diagnosed as a young child with ADD and Asperger's, said to me once. With those words he was articulating the desires all parents have for their children: *to be happy and to succeed*. Those goals, while so simple sounding, can be difficult to achieve—for anyone. But for children and adults with diagnosed brain differences, the path can be even more perilous and uneven.

In the early years of Ethan's schooling, his personal challenges emerged as behavioral difficulties. There seemed to be a disconnect between Ethan's intellectual brightness and his inability to control himself physically and to engage socially in appropriate ways. Ethan himself remembers "jumping around in classes. I might throw tantrums. The usual not knowing when to be quiet, basically behavioral issues that made it hard for me to work with teachers. Teachers would have to take too much time to deal with me, and sometimes I would crawl under the table and read and ignore them."[2] Noah describes Ethan as having "lacked a filter."

This disconnect within Ethan is one that parents and educators are often forced to grapple with: what to do with a child who has intellec-tual gifts but behavioral challenges. Often these are children who lack what is called "executive function"—that is, the ability to contain their emotional and behavioral impulses. A special education environment can eliminate the stress of having to conform to the standards of a crowded mainstream classroom, but it can be educationally uninspiring for a bright child. Noah chose to place Ethan in a special environment to deal with the behavioral aspects of his difficulties—after all, if a child can't sit still and pay attention, a child can't exercise his or her intellectual gifts.

Eventually, via a combination of maturing communication skills, his own remarkable perseverance, and judiciously prescribed Adderall (for his ADD), Ethan decided that he was ready to get out of the protected environment of his special school and put himself in the much more aca-demically rigorous environment of one of Manhattan's most competitive public schools. This was not the recommendation of the special school that he attended. Educators there believed that once a student was catego-rized as having a particular problem, then he or she would always need extra help for that problem; they felt Ethan would flounder if he didn't receive that special attention. It's not that they didn't think well of Ethan as a student—they did. But they failed to see that their labeling of Ethan had also become limiting. They did not recognize he'd developed the strengths, skills, and tenacity to succeed elsewhere.

Noah says, "There's something [in Ethan's] nature to be very curious and inquisitive, very friendly, bright, and creative. And when the condi-tions are right, extremely hardworking and very generous. A lot of those aspects of him must have helped him to become more self-aware." Entirely of his own volition, Ethan applied himself to studying for the New York City specialized high school exam. Noah says, "For a couple of summers he would take the train every day out to Flushing for test prep classes. It totally came from him." It's remarkable to consider that this level of disci-pline existed in the same child who had once been considered a disruption in mainstream classes. Ethan describes his drive to enter a mainstream high school as coming from a "fear for my future and wanting to do more." His father says, "Ethan became extremely focused on proving everyone wrong, by not only getting into a specialized high school, but getting into exactly the one he wanted to attend. He sought some advice from us, but really he only wanted support, which we gave him absolutely. He wanted to prove to himself he could do it and be successful. My role was as en-courager." The challenge of adjusting academically to a New York City specialized high school would be daunting for any student, but Ethan's family was also concerned about how he would transition socially. But while it hasn't always been easy, Ethan has excelled and thrived.

Now that Ethan has learned how to manage the impulsiveness of his younger years, the positive flipside of his ADD has emerged more clearly, and Ethan has flourished creatively. He's transfixed by technology and shows enormous ingenuity in using technology to solve problems. One fea-ture of ADD is what is called "hyperfocus" (single-minded attention) on a task of particular interest. In Ethan's case, what particularly interests him is programming. His ability to hunker down and lose himself in a partic-ular task—which is a direct offshoot of his ADD, as I will go on to describe in chapter 2—contributes greatly to his ability to creatively problem-solve. He wanted to build his own computer, so for his sixteenth birthday he received the parts as gifts. Then he not only built the computer, but also created a remote desktop on his iPad, so that no matter where he was he'd never have to worry that he was missing something he needed for his studies. Noah says, "He'll go on and on about this forever—he's so into technology and turned on by problem-solving." Ethan began coding at the age of ten using the MIT program Scratch, but soon exceeded its limits and has been writing his own computer code ever since. In high school, Ethan has found that he's been able to connect with other bright kids with their own quirks. "My school has a bunch of weird students, which is great for me. There's very little judgment. Almost my entire school is this quirky cast."

Ethan's story is one of ultimate success, and certainly Ethan comes across as being as close to happy as one expects an adolescent boy to be. But his success story was hard won—both by him and by his devoted father. The key to success for Ethan was not simply to mitigate his weakness, however. If that had been his and his father's approach, he might have remained in special education throughout his schooling. Rather, in Ethan's case—and for so many others with brain differences—the key was to mitigate the weakness *and* thereby provide an opportunity to magnify the strengths. The flipsides of Ethan's challenges are also his brightest sparks of genius. This is the mystery and wonder of how the human brain works—a mystery that we are at the very beginning stages of unlocking.

WHAT IS GENIUS, and how can it coexist with what we would consider a mental flaw in the form of a brain difference? For that matter, what is a brain difference? For many of us, Einstein comes to mind as the quintessential genius. Even without the benefit of IQ testing, we can empirically observe that he, like Leonardo da Vinci or Isaac Newton, clearly had intellectual gifts several standard deviations above the person with average intelligence. There are also many high achievers among us who might not be geniuses of this order—geniuses with a capital G, if you will—but who have accomplished above-average things in all fields. It's these high achievers, who have performed in arguably genius ways, on whom I'm most focused in this book.

Oxford Dictionaries defines genius as "exceptional intellectual or creative power or other natural ability."[3] The purity and simplicity of this definition help to clarify the coexistence of gifts and weaknesses within these high achievers. Most of us intuitively understand that while we are exceptionally good at one thing, we might be exceptionally poor at another. The absentminded professor stereotype exists for a reason—as does that of the tortured artist. This book explores the ways in which the unique wiring—some aspects of which might be considered weakness in certain contexts—of many high achievers has directly contributed to their abilities and achievements.

In order to apply names—or diagnoses—to the wide variety of brain differences that exist in humans, clinicians and medical insurers have relied on the *Diagnostic and Statistical Manual of Mental Disorders,* published by the American Psychiatric Association. The newest edition of this manual—the *DSM-5,* as it's popularly known—lists 157 diagnoses.[4] These classifications range from various forms of learning differences, such as dyslexia, to more severe mental illnesses, such as schizophrenia. While the manual isn't what anyone would call scintillating reading, the launch of the *DSM-5* at the American Psychiatric Association's annual meeting in May 2013 incited a firestorm of criticism. The diagnostic manual has always been an imperfect tool. Its neat categorizations of constellations of symptoms into discrete psychiatric disorders are often arbitrary, and the human brain defies such black-and-white definitions. But the manual is a necessary evil for practitioners as well as patients—insurance companies require such categorization in order to cover the costs of treatment.

One of the most vocal critics of the *DSM-5* was psychiatrist Allen Frances, who had been chair of the *DSM-IV* task force. In an article he wrote for *Psychology Today,* he called the APA's approval of the new set of guidelines "the saddest moment" of his long professional career.[5] He felt that the *DSM-5*'s continued expansion of the number of diagnoses served to pathologize too much of human behavior, and he argued the research criteria didn't exist to validate each one of those diagnoses. Thomas Insel, director of the National Institute of Mental Health (NIMH) from 2002 to 2015, also questioned the validity of the *DSM-5*'s diagnostic criteria and objected to its combining of disorders that he felt deserved their own designations. He wrote, "While *DSM* has been described as a 'bible' for the field, it is, at best, a dictionary, creating a set of labels and defining each."[6] And he concluded, "Patients with mental disorders deserve better."

Indeed, they do, and the labeling of disorders is itself a source of significant pain and suffering. The heated debate surrounding the *DSM-5* reveals just how sensitive an issue labels can be, and not just in the medical and scientific communities. Labels are, by definition, limiting, and if they are suggestive of mental illness, they can be downright terrifying. Such was certainly the case for parents of children with Asperger's, who learned that the *DSM-5* folded Asperger's into the autism classification. Those whose children had been diagnosed with the softer-sounding disorder of Asperger's were dismayed to find out that medical experts now placed their children in the same category as people whose symptoms seemed far more extreme and potentially devastating. Such is the power of labels.

While medical professionals, health advocates, and concerned parents have been debating the language we use to diagnose people with brain differences, new initiatives in neuroscience might soon render these arguments moot. Nearly simultaneous with the launch of the *DSM-5,* President Obama announced the Brain Research through Advancing Innovative Neurotechnologies (BRAIN) Initiative, which will create a map of the human brain. Far beyond a purely intellectual exercise, the initiative is a first step in discovering new ways to treat, prevent, and eventually cure brain disorders ranging from Alzheimer's to schizophrenia. We can't begin to solve problems that we can't see, and it's astounding—and arguably tragic—that medical science has thus far been attempting to navigate diseases and disorders of the brain while lacking something as fundamental as a map. For centuries, prior to the discovery of psychotherapy and psychopharmaceuticals, treatment of the mentally ill largely consisted of chaining up patients in institutions that were more like prisons than hospitals, submerging them in freezing water, inciting diabetic shock, and performing lobotomies. Thankfully, we are past such horrors, but nonetheless medical professionals have been operating much like the blind men and the elephant, each of us desperately trying to understand our portion of the larger mystery.

At this writing, the Obama administration has announced that more than three hundred million dollars in public and private financing is pledged to the BRAIN Initiative's efforts. While he was at the helm, Thomas Insel indicated that the initiative would break entirely free of the *DSM*'s labels, his theory being that a pioneering effort shouldn't be constrained by potentially wrong and archaic assumptions. Insel believed it was important to take the old rubric entirely off the table and start from scratch, and all indications are that the BRAIN Initiative will continue in that direction.

The idea of a clean slate is enormously appealing. A new vocabulary would be helpful as well. Advances in our understanding of brain science and the spectrum of conditions have caused an evolution in popular attitudes toward mental illness. But the terms we use are just one hint of the degree to which we have a long way to go in overcoming shame and stigma. Think how often the word *nuts* is used with derision to describe someone with a diagnosed mental condition. The word *retarded* is finally being driven out of our vocabularies, but it's still relatively commonplace to hear someone with a mental illness referred to as *crazy*. While those with mental illness are far more likely to be the victims of crime than the perpetrators, the very few crimes that are committed by those with diagnosed mental illness are too often sensationalized and heralded as exemplary of all of those with mental illness.[7]

It was therefore refreshing when President Obama announced in his introduction of the BRAIN Initiative, "There should be no shame in discussing or seeking help for treatable illnesses that affect too many people that we love." The emphasis in that sentence should be placed on the word *many*. It's estimated that nearly half of all Americans will experience a mental disorder at some point in their lives.[8] Given that statistic, it's arguable that what we call mental disorder—as if it were an aberration—is in fact a natural part of our diversity as a species. And it is entirely possible that the more we come to understand about the brain, the more we will come to realize that there is no such thing as a normal brain. In his blog for *Scientific American,* Scott Barry Kaufman, scientific director of the Imagination Institute in the Positive Psychology Center at the University

of Pennsylvania, writes, "Every single healthy human being lies somewhere on every psychopathology spectrum (e.g., schizophrenia, autism,
mood disorders). What's more, we each show substantial fluctuations on
each of these dimensions each day, and across our lifespan."[9]

Mental disorders are not only prevalent, they're overlapping. There is
no such thing as a single, neat diagnosis. In the past, we have lumped
individuals into tidy buckets—this one has anxiety, that one has depression; this one has autism, that one has dyslexia. However we are becoming
increasingly aware that brain differences and the symptoms associated
with them are not discrete. Many, if not all, of us fall into multiple categories of brain differences. A full quarter of American children have been
diagnosed with anxiety, and anxiety itself can be a symptom of other brain
differences, from attention deficit disorder (ADD) to dyslexia to depression.[10] The narrow labels that we try to apply can be simplistic at best and
erroneous at worst.

A fog of negativity often settles in around a diagnosis of mental disorder. We understand very little about brain differences and what causes
them, and we fear what we don't understand. We dread the stigma, the
judgment, the sense of failure and loss of normalcy. Parents are terrified
for their children, mournful that a diagnosis is a sentence that will inhibit
their future success and potentially doom them to unhappiness. Many
adults have spent much of their lives suspecting that their brains don't
work quite the same way as other people's, and have suffered terrible blows
to their self-esteem—and their relationships—as a result. Often, it's not
until their children are struggling that parents are forced to confront their
own issues. It's now a cliché of ADD treatment that the father of the child
who has been diagnosed will at some point have a lightbulb moment and
say, "I think I have that, too."

The negativity that surrounds brain differences creates an atmosphere
in which our approach is either to ignore symptoms or to attempt to make
them go away. Certainly, judiciously prescribed medication can be a genuine salvation for many individuals with more severe forms of mental dis-

order. However, medicine's overwhelming focus on alleviating symptoms has distracted from an equally important cultural discussion about the unique abilities, strengths, and insights that are a part of these same constellations of symptoms.

There is now ample clinical evidence that brain differences do not solely present us with challenges to be overcome—and this book offers an overview of these studies as well as what this kind of delicate balance between strength and hardship looks like in individual lives. The subject of genius and mental illness has been discussed and debated on a scientific level for decades. Our cultural awareness of the link between mental disorder and genius is as old as philosophy. Plato wrote of what he called "divine madness," and Aristotle recognized that creative people tended toward melancholia. It is no coincidence that such a high percentage of American Nobel and Pulitzer Prize–winning writers are also alcoholics.[11] We're perhaps less aware but not surprised to learn that the most creative individuals are at higher risk for mental illness than are the less creative.[12]

Nancy Andreasen, neuroscientist and neuropsychiatrist at the University of Iowa, conducted a decade-long, highly influential study of thirty writers at the renowned University of Iowa Writers' Workshop,[13] famous for attracting highly creative and talented individuals like Ann Patchett and John Irving. Andreasen compared the writers from the Iowa workshop with a control group of thirty individuals of similar age and IQ who worked in fields that are not overtly creative. She found that 80 percent of writers reported some incidence of mental illness, compared to 30 percent of the control group. While Andreasen's findings are based upon individual case studies as opposed to the kind of randomized controlled study that is typically considered the gold standard for scientific rigor, her work has subsequently been backed up clinically and scientifically by many of the researchers cited throughout this book.

The world is full of fascinating people who didn't achieve such success *despite* their brain differences, but rather in large part *because* of their brain differences. Researchers Darya L. Zabelina, David Condon, and Mark

Beeman of the Department of Psychology at Northwestern University reported in *Frontiers in Psychology* that real-world creative achievement—that is, among healthy individuals without clinical diagnoses—was significantly more likely among those who exhibited greater tendencies toward psychoticism (particularly associated with impulsivity and sensation seeking) and hypomania (an elevated mood state that results in rapid thought processes).[14]

But what does acknowledging the link between brain difference and genius get us? As parents, as educators, even as people who might have been diagnosed with a brain difference ourselves, what are we supposed to do with the evidence that shows that the very things that can cause our lives to be difficult (our inability to relate easily to others, or learning differences, or mood disorders, for example) often come with unique skills and aptitudes (artistic abilities, creativity, a knack for remembering numbers or names, or an ability to visualize data in a unique way)? And is it possible that if we focused not on the diagnoses or labels, but on all the potential—the *spark*—that comes with our brain differences, we could access our unique abilities to contribute to our families, communities, and the world in a new way?

For this book I conducted over fifty interviews with experts in the fields of psychiatry, education, creativity, and child development, as well as exceptionally high-achieving individuals who have openly struggled with symptoms of brain differences. I spoke with several schools to identify children who exhibited great intellectual and artistic gifts while also struggling with psychiatric diagnoses and/or learning differences. I spoke with many of their parents to identify the constellation of factors that goes into nurturing a child with brain differences. I also spoke with the recent head of the National Institute of Mental Health and other leaders who are guiding the future of the fields of adult and child psychiatry and neuroscience. And I performed an exhaustive review of scientific literature and current studies as they relate to the science of understanding the correlations between symptoms of brain differences and particular strengths. The goal of this book is to cast a light on this correlation between genius and brain difference, and to help both individuals with brain differences and their families and communities to foster and support the exceptional abilities that accompany difference. This isn't to say that all of those with brain differences are or have the potential to be geniuses with a capital G. Not everyone with obsessive-compulsive disorder will turn creation on its head like Charles Darwin did. However, anyone who seems to experience a heightened attention to detail can be encouraged to channel that ability to create their own highly successful outcomes and to exhibit their own sparks of genius. Similarly, not all children with ADD can grow up to become revolutionary thinkers like Albert Einstein. However, it is nonetheless true that ADD is strongly associated with flights of fancy and ingenuity, and Einstein could not have made his historic scientific breakthroughs were it not for his daydreamy, distractible mind. Once parents release some of their anxiety about their children's diagnoses dooming them to failure, they can invest more of their energy into identifying what will grab their child's imagination and create opportunities for them to shine in their own areas of strength. In the words of psychologist Scott Barry Kaufman, "I don't think everyone [with a brain difference] has the potential to achieve greatness in every field, but I think everyone has the potential to achieve greatness in some field."[15]

There is, of course, more to achievement than an atypical brain. And there are extremes of illness that are deleterious to any expression of creativity. It's as important to note, however, that in the absence of any brain difference, there is also a comparatively lower frequency of above-average creativity. This phenomenon is referred to as the *inverted U-shaped curve,* and it applies across the brain differences discussed in this book. This means that there is in fact a sweet spot for expressions of the special strengths and abilities, or spark, associated with any brain difference. This ideal range exists between the extremes of average brain function and acute illness. Therefore, the person with mild to moderate bipolar disorder is likelier to be creatively productive than is either someone without bipolar disorder or someone with severe bipolar disorder.[16] This also means that individuals with brain differences are far more capable of displaying their spark productively when their symptoms are moderated via appropriate treatment.

In addition to the neurology of individual brain differences, this book will explore the other special qualities that distinguish high achievers with brain differences from those who haven't been able to cope as well. It will address how those positive qualities can be fostered within us, and also tended by parents and educators. A complex host of factors that contribute to success—from support networks, to proper treatment, to sheer grit and determination—can enable people with brain differences to harness their unique skills and points of view to contribute invaluably to our culture. Through stories of individuals, families, and educators who have contributed invaluably to the success of people with all sorts of brain differences, we will see what it is that can make the difference between a diagnosis dooming one to a life of insecurity and unhappiness or a diagnosis that helps someone access their unique gifts and opens up a world of opportunity.

In my twenty-three years in private practice as a psychiatrist and on the faculty of Weill Cornell Medical College and New York–Presbyterian Hospital, I have always paid particular attention to the ways in which successful people manage to incorporate their shortcomings with their gifts. The irony is that while my patients are focused on getting past the obstacles that exist between them and their larger goals, it is very often the case that there is great strength to be mined from those obstacles, and brilliance to be observed in how my patients both utilize their struggles and maneuver around them. This was the inspiration behind my development of the *Strength of Mind* series at the 92nd Street Y, which delved into the impact of psychological makeup on personal achievement, and the *Psychobiography* series, which examined the correlation between mental disorder and brilliance in renowned artists, authors, and historical figures.

As a practicing psychiatrist, I have seen firsthand the wells of emotional intelligence and insight exhibited by my patients with brain differences. Treated properly, with the right therapy or medication, the positive aspects of depression, for example, do not go away, but can be drawn upon. Even one of our country's leading intellectuals, Andrew Solomon, the National Book Award–winning author of *Far from the Tree* and *The Noonday Demon,* among other highly regarded books, attributes his acute sensitivity to the empathy he has gained via his own experience with severe clinical depression. His awareness of an arguably beneficial side to what might otherwise be considered a purely negative diagnosis was echoed among the many experts and high-performing individuals whom I interviewed for this book.

I have interviewed multiple successful and supremely creative individuals with brain differences for this book, and in each case I have asked them if, given the choice, they would eliminate their brain difference. To a person—and no matter how much pain their difference has caused them—they said that they would not. Each of my interviewees couldn't imagine separating their strengths from their weaknesses.

Science bears out their instincts. Medical experts used to conceive of a sort of phrenology of the brain—that you could segment it into parts in which each piece of the brain is responsible for a highly specific function. But that old-fashioned view has now been debunked. Our brains are not filing cabinets. We can't pluck out what doesn't serve us or identify exactly what does. Rather, our brains are more like coral reefs in which even the most seemingly distinct species (or parts of the brain) are highly interconnected and interdependent.

Brain function isn't tidy. There is a tidal flow back and forth between parts of the brain, and deficiencies in certain areas allow for acuities in others. For example, in the case of the ADD brain, there is a dysregulation in what is now known as "executive function." Contrary to popular belief, the person with ADD isn't incapable of paying attention, rather the individual can't always control when they focus and what they focus on. Yet it is this very dysregulation that lessens thought inhibition, encourages daydreaming, and yields creative thought.

It is the tension and interplay between order and disorder in the brain that create the ideal conditions for genius. According to neuropsychologist and brain imaging researcher Rex Jung, genius can be directly attributed to the nature of the dynamic flow between the two networks in the brain—the cognitive control network and the default network. The cognitive control network is in charge of solving problems in the external world (also called convergent thinking), and the default network is responsible for internally generated thoughts (also called divergent thinking). In the neurotypical brain, these networks are in balance with each other and there is a less pronounced ebb and flow. In the atypical brain, there is more dramatic, rapid, less hindered ebb and flow.[17] It's important to note that in high-performing individuals with brain differences, there is still some degree of balance between the two networks. The person with bipolar disorder, for example, may experience flights of creative thought while swinging into a more manic phase; however, without proper treatment—for example, the regulating influence of medication—the thinking becomes too disordered to be productive. Creativity may originate to some degree in the default network, but it needs the orderly influence of the cognitive network in order to be expressed well.

This interplay of inhibition and disinhibition—the way that some parts of the brain suppress others, and the way that a deficit in one part of the brain can create an amplification in another—is a new and rapidly emerging field of discovery. We're also just beginning to get a glimpse of the sophistication of this interplay. For example, while *less* gray matter in the left lateral orbital frontal region is associated with higher creative achievement, a *higher* volume of gray matter in the right angular gyrus is also associated with greater creative output. In other words, a deficit in one area of the brain is as responsible for genius as is a pronounced asset in another part of the brain. This is a powerful and inspiring discovery: strength cannot exist without weakness.[18]

But this discovery only takes us so far. The goal of this book is to explore this fascinating link from the perspective of real people and what that connection has meant in their lives. We will examine the science behind this remarkable correlation, and we will delve into the lives of adults and children from all walks of life who have contended with some degree of mental disorder yet who have thrived and achieved extraordinary things.

When the new *DSM-5* launched to such a hue and cry, many of my colleagues and I just shrugged our shoulders. As Tom Insel noted, the *DSM-5* is, quite simply, a list of labels. It is helpful in that it allows doctors to assign names to conditions so that insurance companies can classify them and cover the patients' treatments and prescriptions. But labels aren't the way that those of us in the mental health field actually treat our patients. We treat symptoms, not diagnoses. For example, melancholy is a constellation of feelings, and can be an aspect of numerous conditions—if, for instance, you have suffered from untreated anxiety for many years, it's very likely that you will go through depressed periods. When exploring an individual's potential, the label is less important than the way the brain actually expresses itself.

For this reason, *The Power of Different* is organized according to major symptoms as opposed to conditions. Beyond diagnoses and classifications, the most important questions this book asks and answers are: What are the traits—learning differences, distractibility, anxiety, eccentric thinking, melancholy, cycling mood, and lack of relatedness—associated with the most common brain differences? What are the potential gifts, talents, tendencies, and particular sparks of brilliance or insight that often accompany those traits? How have others with those same brain differences applied their own sparks of brilliance and made the most of traits that might otherwise have caused real difficulty in their lives? What can we as individuals, parents, spouses, family members, and educators do to help people with brain differences access their own unique potential?

I chose these seven constellations of traits because they encompass the vast majority of people with brain differences while also being the most strongly associated with creativity. Readers will potentially find themselves and loved ones in multiple chapters. The parent of the child with ADD might recognize her son in the chapter on distractibility, but she might also find some interesting common ground in the chapter on learning differences. Similarly, the person who experiences episodes of melancholy will likely recognize their own bouts of obsessional thinking in the chapter on anxiety. It is the symptoms—not the labels—that impact how we engage with the world and how the world engages with us.

I will reveal—to the degree that current scientific knowledge allows—not only the mechanics of these correlations, but also the inspiring stories of real people with remarkable, atypical brains. These are people just like you and me, just like our children, spouses, parents, colleagues, and friends, who have struck a delicate balance among their seeming flaws and their apparent gifts. I will address exactly how these individuals—from award-winning scientists to celebrated artists and performers, to children and adults with less fame but no less drive—have learned to fully utilize their exceptional minds. And they will illuminate how all of us can learn to do the same.

1.

LEARNING DIFFERENCES

COMMON DIAGNOSIS

DYSLEXIA

"They aren't testing my knowledge, but how well I can not be dyslexic in that moment."

—SCHUYLER, AGE SIXTEEN

Schuyler is a bright and wise-beyond-her-years sixteen-year-old attending high school in Manhattan. When she was just two years old, she told her mother, Erica, that she couldn't see. Yet every doctor to whom Erica took her said the same thing: Schuyler had perfect vision. One doctor went so far as to suggest that Schuyler was an attention-seeking middle child and gave her a pair of fake eyeglasses to wear, telling her that they were "magic." Schuyler wasn't fooled, nor was she attention seeking. She told her mother that the magic glasses were broken.[1]

When Schuyler entered kindergarten, her perceived inability to "see" became an inability to learn to read. Because Schuyler was so bright, she managed to hide this deficit until second grade. Using her intuitive powers, she was always able to discern story and meaning from the pictures in books. However, as the reading became more complex, the strain began to wear on her. When asked to rate all the subjects in school using the faces

that we associate with pain levels in doctors' offices, Schuyler wrote a smi-
ley face next to every subject except for reading, which she labeled with a
frowning, crying face. Her teacher was stunned—she considered Schuyler
one of her best students in reading. When the teacher asked her about it,
Schuyler replied, "I have a secret. I can't read."

It wasn't until fourth grade that Schuyler was given a name for why
she couldn't read: dyslexia, a neurologically based learning difference that
occurs in 5 to 10 percent of school-age children.[2] Dyslexia can present in
many different forms—some people have difficulty reading but not deciphering numbers, others have more difficulty with numbers, and still
others have difficulty with both. And the nature of the difficulty is also
varied—two people with dyslexia might describe their experiences differently, based upon subtle variations in how their brains process visual information. Some people with dyslexia describe letters as being reversed
and seemingly disconnected. Others describe the letters moving or vibrat-
ing on the page. Some see all the letters correctly, but cannot see the groupings of letters within a word, which form the phonemes that are the
building blocks of words (for example, *garage*=*gar*+*age*). As a result, the
word seems like a collection of symbols rather than an immediately rec-
ognizable word. Some experience similar issues with numbers. Some
children have difficulty with their sense of left and right, others with clum-
siness and coordination, still others with their sense of time and advance
planning.

Researchers are still at the very early stages of understanding how this
process works. In any case, and despite these variations in symptoms, difficulty deciphering words and/or numbers at a speed commensurate with
one's intelligence falls under the umbrella classification of dyslexia. It is the
most common of the learning differences, and in fact children diagnosed
with other conditions very often have dyslexia as well. ADD (attention
deficit disorder) is the most common brain difference associated with
dyslexia. Twenty-five percent of people with dyslexia also have dyscalculia
(difficulty learning or understanding mathematics), and some degree of

impaired motor development affects nearly 50 percent of all dyslexics.[3] Other, less common learning differences that can exist separately from or along with dyslexia include dysgraphia (difficulty writing and forming letters), dyscalculia (difficult comprehending mathematical concepts); dyspraxia (a speech disability involving impairment of the area of the brain that tells the muscles how to move in order to correctly pronounce sounds); and finally auditory, memory, and processing disabilities, which affect the individual's ability to understand language despite normal hearing and vision.

As Schuyler's experience illustrates, despite how common dyslexia is, it can often go undiagnosed, and many people grow to adulthood believing they aren't good readers, when in fact they have dyslexia. (It is such a common brain difference that it could be argued that it is not so much a "difference" as a trait.) One reason that well-behaved, smart girls often slip through the cracks when it comes to identifying their learning differences is that for decades dyslexia was thought to be more prevalent among males. Girls (and boys) with dyslexia who don't disrupt the flow of the classroom and who manage to struggle through with passing grades are thought to be merely average students. Instead of being average, however, these students with dyslexia are working much harder than others just to keep up.

Dyslexia can vary widely in severity, and Schuyler's is on the severe end of the spectrum. For Schuyler, reading is a process of inference. "I skip words when I read, but then I fill them in in my mind." When she read aloud as a child, her mother pointed out to her, "Four of those words don't exist on this page." But even when Schuyler inferred a different word than the one written, the meaning that Schuyler derived from the passage was the same. "I would turn them into words that made sense to me." Not only this, Schuyler felt she was often improving on the text. "I would say that my way made more sense."[4]

Schuyler is frustrated with the educational system, which she doesn't think caters to her abilities or to others like her. In particular, she objects to the way most tests are structured. She finds "they aren't testing my knowledge, but how well I can not be dyslexic at that moment." It's anxiety provoking for her, this feeling that she has to leap through hoops that aren't made for her. "I wish I could just jump to my future career and learn what I need to know for that."

Even children without learning differences can be overwhelmed by academic expectations and a fear of not measuring up, and for a child like Schuyler this is magnified tenfold. Schuyler's mother, Erica, recalls the deep sadness that her daughter brought home with her from a very young age. Once Schuyler confessed to her teacher that she couldn't read, she was placed in remedial reading classes three times a week. "They tried to drum [reading] into her. She got really upset and would say to me, 'Why me, why me?' The teachers would put baby books in the classroom baskets so she would have something she could read. It was humiliating." Any parent who has soothed a child's anxiety over homework can easily imagine how Schuyler's struggles with dyslexia spilled over into her home life. In Schuyler's case, Erica says, she often "ate her problems," and she has struggled with her weight as a result.

In high school, Schuyler took a class with a teacher who was particularly inflexible. While Schuyler has learned to advocate for herself, in this teacher's class, Erica says, "she was intimidated. It was torturous. She just cried and cried." When Schuyler explained her learning difference and how it impacted her ability to take in information, the teacher told Schuyler that she "didn't believe in dyslexia." Erica went to the administration and successfully transferred Schuyler out of that class. Parents of children with learning differences not only absorb their children's pain, they can experience their own challenges—practical and emotional—in advocating for their children. This requires enormous investment of time at all stages, and a willingness to persist in the face of rejection and exhaustion. Erica recalls that when Schuyler was learning vocabulary, "she would make flash cards, but she wouldn't read them, she would hand them to me and then say let's talk about them. She will spend ten minutes discussing a single flash card, whereas my other kids will [memorize thirty in the same amount of time] and be like, I got it, I got it." Rote memorization doesn't work for Schuyler. In social studies, for example, "she has to understand the peasants, the serfs, the feudal system, the monarchy. She could write for two hours on something, but don't ask her thirty vocabulary words."

For her career, Schuyler would like to change things for other people with learning differences. "In my rampages with my mom I would say I want to change the schooling for dyslexic kids. I don't find [it's fair] to be graded against kids whose strengths are my weaknesses and vice versa. I have always said that dyslexia is an ability, not a disability. I know in the real world I am going to be more successful than the girls who can regurgitate information. I have all these ideas that are not even explored yet, and so I feel as if I am going to do something in this world that is going to matter."

Schuyler has tremendous internal drive, and this will help her enormously in overcoming the challenges she has yet to face. It's a shame, however, that so many interesting minds are crammed into a cookie-cutter idea of what a good student should look like and should be able to do. National Book Award–winning author John Irving, who is dyslexic, was considered "lazy" and "stupid" by teachers in school. In response, he says, "I simply accepted the conventional wisdom of the day—I was a struggling student; therefore, I was stupid." If it hadn't been for his love of wrestling and the support of his coach, Irving might have dropped out of school altogether.[5]

While there is a nationwide conversation about how the United States can become more innovative and competitive, some of the most original thinkers among us aren't at all well suited to the regimented academic expectations (measured by standardized test scores) and requirements to excel across all subject areas that our educational system demands. And many of those original thinkers are—not coincidentally—highly dyslexic.

Testing often feels like the measure of our lives—and of our lives' potential. From earliest childhood—and particularly so in the most competitive school districts around the country—we are judged based upon a set of external rules and standards. Some of us excel. Many of us,

particularly those with dyslexia, do not. And while we might console ourselves with the thought that we, or our children, aren't "good test takers,"
nonetheless the judgment is made, or at least implied: those who do well
on the test are smarter than those who do not. And thus a child who struggles to decipher words is labeled as not as bright or gifted as her peers, and
she's put into a classroom or school that is thought to better match her
abilities.

For many students with learning differences, the challenge isn't simply
that they don't test well, it's that they perform unevenly. Our educational
system was designed around an expectation of uniformity that leaves no
room for the angular thinker—the person whose performance is jag-
ged, with strong aptitudes in certain areas and disinterest or outright
deficiency in others. And yet, when we look at the geniuses who have
accomplished the greatest things, and who have made the most revolutionary contributions to the world, we see—almost without exception—a
group of what I call very "angular" thinkers. Among those geniuses you
would find individuals who were not simply better at some things than
others, but who exhibited genuine deficits in certain areas. These were
not students who had mostly A's but lapsed into a B or a C in one or two
classes. These are individuals who simply failed in certain—sometimes
most—areas; individuals whose brains did not work in the way that those
subjects, or styles of teaching, demanded.

The net label *learning difference* catches within it an enormous amount
of individual variation. The choice of the word *difference* over *disability* is
intentional and substantive. Whereas *disability* is used to make a qualitative statement about the individual learner's intelligence, *difference* is
stripped of value, emotional content, and, most important, shame. The
latter is why it takes, on average, two years from the first appearance of a
learning difficulty for parents to bring their child to an expert for evaluation. Because we focus so much attention on the negative aspect of a learning difference—the qualitative judgment of a disability—we become
afraid of the implications of a diagnosis, and we resist it altogether. The

result is children who suffer through feeling stupid, sometimes for years, and who grow into adults who may learn to compensate for their differences, but who still carry a load of embarrassment and self-loathing.

This isn't the whole story, of course. There are many individuals with learning differences who, through strength of mind and character, and with some key interventions, have been able to persist past labels and pigeonholes. They have been able to make their way through years of schooling often by working twice as hard as everyone else, and have eventually achieved the freedom to pursue what they really love. And this is when they truly thrive. These individuals include scientists, writers, artists, and entrepreneurs. And the exciting—and inspiring—characteristic that they have in common is the degree to which their talents are a direct result of their differently thinking brains.

WHAT IT MEANS TO HAVE A LEARNING DIFFERENCE

Learning differences take myriad forms, many of which are complex and haven't yet been fully studied or understood, because they occur in such small segments of the population. However, researchers estimate that among all those who are thought to have a learning difference of some kind, fully 80 percent present most significantly with dyslexia. According to Matthew Cruger, senior director of the Learning and Development Center at the Child Mind Institute, "learning disorders as a category is the largest group of all kids receiving special education services. More than autistic students by a huge margin, and far more than kids who have emotional disturbances. [Children with learning disorders] are about 45 percent of the population of kids receiving special education services. And the majority of LD kids have dyslexia."[6] It's entirely possible that most, if not all, other learning differences either include or are permutations of the central diagnosis of dyslexia.[7]

Despite how remarkably common dyslexia is, there is generally very little understanding of what it means, even among educators. If you ask most people to define the disorder, they might say that it involves a visual shuffling of letters and digits, and that those with dyslexia have difficulty reading. This idea of dyslexia as letter reversal dates at least as far back as 1887, when Rudolf Berlin, a German ophthalmologist, first coined the phrase.[8] In 1889 W. Pringle Morgan wrote an article for the *British Medical Journal* describing the perplexing phenomenon of an otherwise bright patient who was unable to learn to read.[9]

Very little changed for well over a century after that original observation. By the 1990s, advances in neuroimaging definitively proved the neurological basis of dyslexia. In 1998, Sally Shaywitz, one of the foremost experts on dyslexia, and her colleagues in the Department of Pediatrics at the Yale University School of Medicine studied dyslexic and nondyslexic readers using a functional MRI, which produces computer-generated images of the brain as it performs activities. They found that dyslexic readers "show less activation in a brain region linking print skills to the brain's language areas. Specifically, dyslexic readers showed reduced activity in a large brain region that links the visual cortex and visual association areas (angular gyrus) to the language regions in the superior temporal gyrus (Wernicke's area)."[10] While this illustrates that dyslexia is a disorder of language acquisition and not of sight, the perception of dyslexia as a visual disorder persists. In the past, some dyslexic children were even given eye training, as if dyslexia were a mechanical as opposed to a neurological phenomenon. Today, children who are diagnosed with dyslexia are still often thought to need hours of extra reading instruction, as if more rote drilling might finally teach them to decipher written words and to spell properly.

This confusion is somewhat understandable since the dyslexic brain does take in visual information differently from the nondyslexic brain. Adding to the complexity, dyslexia can present in ways that are subtly different, and if you ask two individuals with dyslexia to describe their experiences, they will have some areas of overlap, but not necessarily all.

For example, some people with dyslexia excel at math and others struggle. Some people with dyslexia always find reading to be a painful chore, and others eventually love to read. But there are neurological commonalities that have been proven to exist. Shaywitz and her husband, Bennett A. Shaywitz, of the Yale Center for Dyslexia & Creativity, have spent decades researching the particular strengths and weaknesses of people with dyslexia. As Sally Shaywitz writes, "reading ability is taken as a proxy for intelligence; most people assume that if someone is smart, motivated and schooled, he or she will learn to read. In dyslexia, the seemingly invariant relation between intelligence and reading ability breaks down."[11] In a 2010 study published in *Psychological Science,* Shaywitz and her colleagues charted definitively how IQ can be high in a dyslexic, while reading ability can be very low. The two are "uncoupled" in a way not found in the non-dyslexic individual.[12]

Dyslexia is a disorder of the language system—according to Shaywitz, "more specifically, within a particular subcomponent of that system, phonological processing."[13] In simpler terms, this is the memory system we use when we need to write down a telephone number or copy an instruction in school. This is most likely at the root of the misconception that dyslexics reverse letters and numbers—in actuality, they are simply misremembering details of what are to them arbitrary symbols. For this reason, many experts consider traditional intelligence testing, which requires word deciphering, to be grossly inaccurate when measuring the abilities of the person with dyslexia.

Functional brain imaging shows that there is a disruption of the left hemisphere posterior neural systems in dyslexic children and adults while they are performing reading tasks. In practice, this means that the dyslexic brain looks at words and the phonemes that make up words (the individual sounds that are the building blocks of language) and sees random and arbitrary symbols. For those without dyslexia, the recognition of words is automatic; in the person with dyslexia, all of those symbols must be memorized (whether or not the person with dyslexia is aware of this). Deciphering meaning in written language is a constant effort. It's no wonder then that those with dyslexia read more slowly. It's nearly impossible for those without dyslexia to comprehend the stamina required for the person with dyslexia to keep up with the standard reading load of a regular workday, much less an academic day.

Clinicians don't currently scan children's brains in order to diagnose them with dyslexia; rather they have developed sophisticated, multipart tests. According to Matthew Cruger of the Child Mind Institute, "it is always important for us to listen to children read aloud. Reading rewires the language areas of the human brain so that one can sound out and automatically recognize words, and we like to hear the capacity of every child to sound out the words they see and to show that they can quickly recognize the words in front of them. Slow, choppy, or robotic reading might signal problems in this area."[14] Cruger notes that evaluators look for "phonological awareness (hearing the sounds in spoken language and making them); rapid word retrieval (being able to quickly recall word labels); single word reading and spelling ([reading and spelling words ranging from simple to more unusual in terms of spelling and number of phenomes in the word]: *my, they, into, guess,* to *custodian, soliloquy, gherkin*); nonsense word reading ([reading words such as] *mib, quantric, millimegnalian*); reading speed and fluency (measuring the speed and accuracy of a child reading aloud); reading comprehension (answer[ing] multiple choice or open-ended questions about short passages)." Evaluators then compare how the child measures against the accepted norms of their own cohort (age and grade).

As sophisticated as this testing has become, it can only measure so much in the individual child with dyslexia. Two other elements of dyslexia also significantly impact the ability to read and accurately recall what has been read. Studies show that dyslexics are far more able to recognize letters in the periphery of their vision rather than at the center of an image or the page.[15] Imagine the brain of the person with dyslexia who is reading around the edges of the page. This is akin to assembling a jigsaw puzzle from the outside in, which might work well in a puzzle but is incompatible with left-right, top-down reading. Second, those with dyslexia have been shown to have poor short-term (or what is called "working") memory. This is the memory system that we use when we need to write down a telephone number or copy an instruction in school. This is most likely at the root of the misconception that dyslexics reverse letters and numbers—in actuality, they are simply misremembering these arbitrary symbols.[16] If you combine all of these brain differences—difficulty deciphering, a focus on the periphery, and poor working memory—the challenges of the dyslexic child in a traditional academic setting become poignantly clear.

What also becomes clear is the way in which these challenges camouflage the real talent and intelligence of the person with dyslexia. While the dyslexic individual might have difficulties with short-term memory, long-term memory is in no way affected, nor is the ability to comprehend complex meaning or to draw deep understanding from written and spoken material. In Schuyler's case, her mother, Erica, observed that while Schuyler struggled to memorize vocabulary words, she had a deep and sophisticated understanding of the larger concepts reflected in that vocabulary (for example, when she studied the feudal system in school). The more expansive net that the person with dyslexia casts isn't just visual and cognitive, it's also auditory. According to a 1987 study published in the *New England Journal of Medicine,* there is some suggestion that people with dyslexia are able to interact with their auditory environments while drawing upon their wider spatial attention—that is, they are able to pick out sounds and vocal nuances that others cannot.[17]

A University of Wisconsin study found a strong association between dyslexia and "speed of recognition of impossible figures."[18] The use of "impossible figures" is a common feature of intelligence testing—typically they are renderings of complex stairways, for example, that might or might not be logistically possible. Tests often reveal that people with dyslexia are able to do the required mental calculations more quickly than those without dyslexia. The nondyslexic brain, when regarding such intricate designs, tries to break the pieces down into what appears to make logical sense, and often does so inaccurately. However, the person with dyslexia, who takes in the entire image at once—using their strong peripheral vision—immediately and correctly assesses what is and isn't possible. This study further posited that the deficits that exist in the left hemisphere (the language center) of the dyslexic brain are directly linked to the strengths that exist in the right hemisphere (the spatial center). Given these acuities for discerning pattern, it's not surprising that there is such a strong association between artistic creativity and dyslexia. A Goteborg (Sweden) University study found a significantly higher percentage of dyslexics among students enrolled in an elite art program compared with the general population.[19]

Individuals with dyslexia and other learning differences can succeed—and succeed brilliantly—in an extraordinary number of fields. And we will explore the ample science that supports this claim. Beyond the increasing load of neurological evidence arguing for a link to giftedness, there are other keys to the success of people with learning differences that are harder to measure, yet are no less important. These are the traits of grit and resilience—qualities that those who have had to face constant struggle to understand, and to be understood, need to have in abundance.

THE EXPERIENCE OF HAVING A LEARNING DIFFERENCE

The individuals with dyslexia who were interviewed for this book share many common traits and experiences, no matter their age or particular interests. These fall into four categories. First, they each experienced significant, and at times traumatizing, difficulty in school. Second, they consciously or unconsciously developed "work-arounds" that allowed them to navigate academia and the larger world. Third, they have gifts of creativity and insight that directly correspond with their brain differences. And fourth, they display tremendous drive and determination to put these gifts to use.

CHALLENGES OF LIVING WITH LEARNING DIFFERENCES

Beryl Benacerraf, a clinical professor at Harvard University, is a world-renowned expert in radiology who discovered an important fetal indicator for Down syndrome.[20] She then developed a genetic sonogram that revolutionized the way pregnant women are screened. She's the recipient of numerous awards for her work, and, not coincidentally, she's also highly dyslexic.

She recalls her experience in school as being "very shameful" and remembers struggling for a long time. Part of her shame stemmed from having such highly intellectual and accomplished parents—her father was a Nobel laureate in medicine, Baruj Benacerraf. Her parents and teachers originally thought that Beryl's difficulty with reading was due to being multilingual; she was thrust into an English-speaking classroom as an eight-year-old, when her parents moved to the United States from Venezuela. However, when her reading skills didn't improve, her parents came to believe that she was simply being lazy and careless. She continued to receive this message all the way through her admission to medical school. She felt blamed for her deficit. This was terribly wounding to Beryl's self-esteem. Hopeless at standardized tests, she attended a medical school that didn't require the MCAT. And thanks to her father making a few phone calls on her behalf, she was accepted to Harvard Medical School as a second-year transfer—a feat almost unheard of. This pulling of strings left Beryl feeling even more ashamed. She was in medical school, but she felt like a failure—as if she had slid in through the back door and didn't really deserve to be there.

Carol Greider, professor of molecular biology and genetics at Johns Hopkins University and winner of the 2009 Nobel Prize for Medicine, diagnosed herself as dyslexic when she was in her late teens.[21] Like Beryl

Benacerraf, she never did well on standardized tests, so although she worked hard to get good grades in school, she did poorly on the SAT and GRE. She recalls feeling embarrassed to be taken out of class by the special education teacher in grammar school. Looking back on her old schoolwork now, it's obvious to her how severely dyslexic she was, but she suffered through school feeling like, in her words, "a stupid kid." She recalls, "I had this remedial help, and all of my friends were in advanced classes. I just figured they were smarter than I was. So I worked harder to get the grades." Despite her tremendous gifts, which are now quite obvious, she did so poorly in early math that in seventh grade her math teacher wouldn't recommend her to advance to algebra. Her father insisted that they put her in the higher-level class anyway.

This sense of not measuring up, of feeling stupid—and the accompanying loss of self-esteem—is extremely common among adults with dyslexia, largely due to misdiagnosis or ignorance of what dyslexia means. Among younger generations, now that evaluations and individual educational plans are far more common, the blow to self-esteem can be lessened. However, this very much depends on how informed educators and parents are about what dyslexia does and does not mean, and how successfully they support the child with dyslexia. And of course, adolescence can be challenging and stressful whether or not a child has a learning difference. For that reason, it can be difficult to separate the effects of a brain difference from other environmental and developmental influences.

Sidney is a sensitive and artistic sixteen-year-old who has moved nine times in her life.[22] At this point she finds it "reassuring when I know that something will be the same when I return to it." Her father is dyslexic as well, so when her mother noticed that Sidney was memorizing books as a child rather than reading them, she immediately intervened and had Sidney evaluated. In third grade, despite her remarkable brightness, Sidney was reading at below a second-grade level. Her mother moved her to a school for children with learning differences, and by the time she left in eighth grade to enter a highly competitive mainstream high school, she was reading at a twelfth-grade level. Still, despite her success in school, she suffered considerable anxiety over the years—not an uncommon experience among children with learning differences.[23] The strain of having to work so much harder than everyone around you just in order to keep up can be overwhelming. "I see words mix up as I'm reading. My eyes will be five words behind my brain. One word becomes another or they slur together." While she hasn't been diagnosed with attentional problems, she does find it difficult to stay organized. "I just move my mess from place to place. If I ever had a break I would spend a week organizing myself." She also struggles with time management, mostly due to how much longer it takes her to read, which is an added stressor at a school where an hours-long homework load is common. When Sidney gets too frustrated and overwhelmed while working on an assignment, her mother encourages her to walk away and come back to it later.

Similarly, Schuyler points to the anxiety-provoking impact of the status-focused college application process. "When kids were talking about Harvard, the idea was that the better-known the school is that you attend, the better a person you are. The school is correlated with you. I try to refrain from that idea, but sometimes the society pressure does get to me. Colleges see statistics, not who you are as a human being. They don't know how much you engage in class. An essay can be created or tutored for any kid, but there's no one pushing your hand and pencil during a test." Schuyler finds it deeply unfair that nondyslexic children who find memorization easy (and who will forget that material within days of acing the test) can do better than she does, while they actually have less of a grasp on the material.

Even though Schuyler attends a prestigious private school in Manhattan, she has also encountered ignorance among teachers. "My biology teacher said, 'She speaks so well in class, I was shocked by her first test grade.'" The teacher told Schuyler that she needed to work harder at the class since it didn't come as easily to her. "I wanted to explain to her that it's not that I don't get the concepts, it's the way her tests are constructed.

But you can't say that to a superior—that, 'no, it's you and not me'—because that's insulting." Children with dyslexia can feel like abstract-thinking aliens in a foreign, concrete landscape.

DEVELOPING WORK-AROUNDS

Many, many children with dyslexia do go on to very successful adult lives—as the examples of brilliant and high-functioning adults such as Beryl Benacerraf and Carol Greider illustrate. One of the primary keys to success for people with any brain difference is to develop work-arounds—ways of not cheating the system, but trying to fit their abstract selves into a regimented environment. Because reading continued to be tremendously difficult for Benacerraf, in college she attended a school that required only one English class. She made sure she took poetry, because of the low word count. Once in medical school, she found that she didn't need to read every word of textbooks; in fact, she had a much easier time studying graphic (rather than textual) representations of information and found she could glean everything she needed to know from the images, graphs, charts, and associated captions in her course material.

Now that she has her own ultrasound practice, Benacerraf still takes advantage of strategies that help her skate around her reading and writing deficits. She dictates most of what she writes and has staff to proof and vet anything that goes out under her signature. While some dyslexics, like Carol Greider, find spell-check programs to be very helpful, Benacerraf is so severely dyslexic that she often can't get close enough to the correct word spelling for the program to recognize what she's trying to say. She has to try retyping the word from scratch, over and over. She has a tendency to mix up words, and certain word counterparts are perpetually problematic for her, so she avoids them—*exacerbate* and *exasperate*; *circumscribe* and *circumcise*. "When I start saying a word, I sometimes don't know what's going to come out. Each person with dyslexia has their tough words they can't use in speech."

Because Sidney is so highly visual, she has developed a fascinating work-around that she calls a "mind map." It began as doodling, which her mother had read can help some people focus. Now the doodles are more complex and are inextricably linked to her thought process. "As I'm thinking of something, I feel like I'm drawing out an idea. I stretch my brain until I can think of a word or idea. It really helps on tests if I can't think of a word or spelling. I start drawing and building off each letter if I don't remember a word. It helps with math, too." Listening to music also helps her. In class, she finds it easier to focus on what the teacher is saying when she has classical music playing in an earbud in one ear. Her mother lobbied for the school to allow it.

Schuyler has also developed visual methods of retaining what she needs to know. When studying for a biology test, for example, she will see the information in the form of a diagram. Instead of recalling the words for the parts of a cell, she will see the cell in her mind, along with the labels. The labels are not words—they are images of words, like drawings. The one downside of this visual thinking is that sometimes the thoughts and images can "overlap and collide in my head." And this process can become even more abstract, involving turning ideas themselves into shapes. "I close my eyes and make the shapes form a roller coaster, or a pleated sheet that I can control." For her English class, she might transform a character into a physical object as a way of better understanding it. A particular personality type might strike her as "a house in a mask form to suggest his self-loathing." Or "a block with a bunch of bookshelves. The block is stern and the bookshelves are the house itself." This process isn't conscious or intentional for Schuyler. "That's just how they [ideas and words] appear to me."

Sidney is highly self-aware—of both her strengths and weaknesses, which is also important in developing coping strategies. "I always feel like no matter when I start something I never have enough time to finish. That's why I like to start projects ahead of time. I can't do anything quickly, but I put a lot of effort into them." Recently, she's learned that a very good way of staying organized is to restrict herself to only a small bag—the less space she has for mess, the better.

Sidney and Schuyler are lucky to have involved parents who have actively sought out the best schools and programs for their children, and who don't hesitate to speak up when they feel that accommodations need to be made. As children get older, however, it's also important for them to learn to advocate for themselves. While Schuyler has experienced the frustration of not being able to overtly criticize a teacher's testing methods, she has learned how to make herself understood with faculty. Since her intelligence doesn't always come across in written work, "I talk to my English teacher after class, or in physics I will talk to my teacher about a concept we haven't discussed yet. In class I raise my hand a lot and don't feel self-conscious. It's a method of communicating to them that I do understand."

Julie Logan, professor of entrepreneurship at the Cass Business School in London, calls these coping strategies (including organizational systems, visualizations, self-advocacy, temperamental qualities such as tenacity, and myriad other highly individual techniques) "compensatory skills."[24] Logan surveyed 139 business owners in the United States and found that more than 35 percent self-identified as dyslexic. In a *New York Times* article about her findings, she remarked, "We found that dyslexics who succeed had overcome an awful lot in their lives. . . . If you tell your friends and acquaintances that you plan to start a business, you'll hear over and over, 'It won't work. It can't be done.' But dyslexics are extraordinarily creative about maneuvering their way around problems."

These strategies and methods are essential for success in a world that doesn't cater to the dyslexic mind. And when they are implemented, the results can be astounding.

THE GIFTS OF THE BRAIN WITH DYSLEXIA

Beryl Benacerraf, who felt like a failure because she needed her father's help to get into Harvard Medical School, eventually discovered her remarkable gifts only because she had managed to struggle her way past all the hurdles of academia. Benacerraf had already learned that she was more successful at retaining information when she studied the charts and graphs in her textbooks, rather than the written text. But when she was a medical resident at the end of her radiology rotation, her professor said to her, "I've never seen a gift in imaging and pattern recognition like you have. It's uncanny. You should really think about going into radiology." Discovering that she had a true genius for something particular changed Benacerraf's life. Still, it took time for her to accept that she was gifted. "When I looked at images the abnormality just jumped out at me, like a neon sign. It was a new world. It was amazing. I never realized I was special that way. I kept thinking that the other students would catch up with me. It took a decade for me to realize it wasn't luck."

It wasn't luck at all—it was Benacerraf's exceptionally acute peripheral vision, a gift she has almost certainly *because* she is dyslexic. "When I look at an image I'm not looking at little parts of the image. I take in the whole thing all at once as a pattern." In other words, the same neurological process that makes it difficult for her to read text enables her to almost effortlessly find abnormalities on a scan. She also believes that ideas and conclusions come to her more quickly because she thinks visually. "Images are faster than speaking to yourself in words. Sometimes images come so fast I lose my train of thought." Benacerraf's highly visual brain works in business as well. She finds that she's quite good at running her private imaging practice, a large, multipart enterprise. "I don't get mired, I take in the big picture and delegate details to others. Putting together ideas that others wouldn't think of plays out entrepreneurially in this area."

Benacerraf has also found that discovering her gift has gone a long way toward healing some of the injuries her self-esteem suffered over so many years of feeling stupid. At the beginning, "I was this crazy lady who could diagnose Down syndrome in a fetus. I knew I was right, it was just a question of proving it." Now, she has "supreme confidence." When a family member needs an important scan, she does it herself, and it brings her great pleasure to feel competent.

Carol Greider knew that she wanted to major in biology when she was a senior in high school. Whereas some dyslexics might find biology challenging because of all the naming and labeling and the extensive vocabulary, Greider turned her reading deficit into a strength in a way that is very common among dyslexics. As a child, Greider "couldn't spell at all even if they sounded out the words, so I learned to memorize the whole word." Because of this learned compensation, "senior year doing anatomy in biology it was super easy for me to remember vocabulary."

Later, in graduate school and beyond, Greider noticed that she had another heightened ability that was far more central to becoming the scientist she is today. "I am able to read ten complex research papers and then distill from them all the pertinent points, homing in on the key issues. That is very important for moving ahead in science. I think maybe more so than others, I can quickly see what the most interesting next question is." In the competitive scientific environment, many researchers are simultaneously racing toward the same discoveries, and in that race Greider sees herself as having an advantage in being able to identify the most interesting line of investigation among myriad possibilities, and then following that. Sidney and Schuyler both exhibit analytical gifts comparable to what Benacerraf and Greider depict. Even more fascinating, both girls use very similar terms to describe their love of abstract concepts. Schuyler says, "The more abstract the idea, the easier it comes to me." Unlike Greider, Schuyler finds the naming involved in biology difficult since to her it requires arbitrary word labeling and recall. However, the concepts behind those labels are highly comprehensible to her. She understands on a fundamental level what the parts of the cell are, what they do, and how they work, whether or not she can immediately retrieve the name for each part of the cell. She also finds that abstract work is easier because she's more engaged with it. "If you ask me what a thing is called, I won't know because I just don't care enough." Ironically, considering the difficulty most dyslexics have with reading, English is now Schuyler's favorite subject. "I might not be able to read as fast as everyone, and I may not structure my essays the way others do, but I love reading something and finding an idea through dialogue, or a theme throughout the book. There is no concrete answer to a person, no one side to a story, and that's why I find it the most interesting." She acknowledges that she can't truly know if she possesses greater than average analytical skills, but she notices in class other students—the type of students who read faster and do much better on tests—will go back repeatedly to the same idea in class. "But I take the idea and elaborate and create a new argument and a new idea." This is part of why she is so exceptionally gifted at debate (she attended a Cambridge University summer debate program and won all the major awards). She says that she immediately sees all the pros and cons of opposing arguments. Whereas others might get stuck—or inaccurately predict the other team's plan of attack—because they are only able to see their one side of the argument, Schuyler can see all sides. Similarly, Sidney says, "I do better with abstract concepts and ideas as opposed to solid things that require huge amounts of knowledge stored." Like Schuyler, Sidney very much enjoys debate. Sidney says, "Words are ways to build new ideas or thoughts. I like building off of other people's ideas."

Sidney shows tremendous artistic promise as well as manual dexterity. She's gifted at drawing and painting, and once made a dress freehand out of a large bolt of cloth, with no instruction or pattern. She also loves to invent solutions for household problems—a latch or a fastener for a picture frame, for example. Schuyler, on the other hand, exhibits the kind of bird's-eye organizational ability that Benacerraf describes. She has shown great facility for stage management, and has an exceptional ability for grasping the entirety of what a production requires, from practical elements such as sets and props, to what actors fit into which roles.

There is something else that many individuals with dyslexia share, although some of their strengths and weaknesses may differ: empathy. It's impossible to pinpoint how much of the sensitivity evident in many people with dyslexia is rooted in having suffered with a learning disability, versus being a product of divergent thinking. But in either case, both Sidney and Schuyler exhibit great wells of empathy for others who have dealt with similar challenges. Based upon her vast clinical work with individuals, Sally Shaywitz considers "exceptional empathy and warmth, and feeling for others" to be among hallmarks of people with dyslexia.[25] Sidney is considering a career in museum exhibit design for children, and speaks in glowing terms of the rewards of working with young children and instilling in them a joy of learning. She says, "My goal in life is to become a better person, and part of growing up is improvement and change." Schuyler says that she rarely thinks of a villainous character in literature as a villain. "I can see what would have happened, if some traumatic event hadn't happened. When I place them on the other path, I can see how that different set of choices might have changed the path they were on." She also has the ability to summon the emotions that the text elicited, which speaks directly to the issue of working versus long-term memory in people with dyslexia. She feels that her recall of the text, and her ability to put herself back into the text, is more acute than that of her nondyslexic peers. In addition, she says, "I have always been a good friend. I think that's because I'm able to put myself in other people's positions. I used to get embarrassed a lot as a kid; I think all kids probably have that. I would be mortified that I sat down weirdly or shook with the wrong hand. So I made sure that nobody felt weird around me, everyone felt as if nothing they were doing was wrong."

While people with dyslexia might sometimes have difficulty identifying the individual trees in a forest, they are arguably better able to grasp the pattern of and interrelationships within such a complex landscape. In the case of someone like Beryl Benacerraf, her ability to detect minute changes and flaws in a big picture allows her to read what others can't in ultrasounds. Dyslexic scientists, engineers, and astrophysicists find this ability allows them to pick out or notice deviations from patterns, giving them an advantage in their fields. This concept is also in operation more metaphorically among dyslexic entrepreneurs who report being able to see the big picture, both creatively and organizationally, thus giving them a business edge.[26]

As much as we hate to see our children suffer, there is something to be said for the strength of character one can derive from being tested and from having to adapt to a challenging environment. Similar to the dyslexic entrepreneurs studied by Julie Logan who refused to accept failure, critically acclaimed and bestselling author John Irving insists that the roadblocks he's faced have helped him enormously. "I'm more persistent. Persistent and stubborn. I have to apply myself to get anything done at all. I have to put in twice as much effort and I can't be lazy. Problem-solving, yes. Because when I am organizing my thoughts or coming up with alternative solutions, I may have to think of ten billion before I get to a good one. Like taking a photo: you might take a thousand but only ten will be good. That's how I feel—if I think of enough different ways something will work then one eventually does. It's become an advantage. In writing a novel, it doesn't hurt to go slowly. It doesn't hurt anyone as a writer to have to go over something again and again. I have the stamina to go over something again and again no matter how difficult it is—whether it is for the fourth or fifth or eighth time. This is something I would ascribe to the difficulties I had to overcome at an early age."[27]

Evan, a seventeen-year-old senior in a highly competitive public school in Manhattan, is confident, good-looking, athletic, and immediately comes across as being self-possessed. His first memory of being behind his peers in reading occurred in second grade.[28] The books that the children could choose to read were classified by difficulty from A to Z. Sitting next to two classmates, he noticed that the child to his right was reading letter O and the child to his left was reading X. Evan was on F. When he finished his book, the teacher sent him down to a first-grade classroom to find one that matched his reading level. The belief that he was not as smart or as fast as his classmates struck Evan very deeply in that moment. Although he wasn't told that he was dyslexic, this difference between him and his classmates was not at all lost on him.

Evan wasn't able to read with any degree of fluency even as recently as eighth grade. Despite that, he is now in AP English, which is "tough and rigorous." He has dysgraphia (an impairment in the ability to translate thoughts to the written word, often associated with handwriting that is difficult or impossible to decipher), so while he thinks he would do better in class if he took notes, it's pointless—he can't read his own handwriting. Instead he listens, and he has a remarkable capacity for taking in and remembering disparate facts and then analyzing them down to their essence. He takes German, which he doesn't enjoy, and the requirement for which he could have waived, but instead of quitting, he persists. "The colleges want to see a challenge." He speaks about his classes with no particular passion. Certainly some he likes more than others, but he doesn't experience the joy of learning for its own sake that Schuyler and Sidney exude. For him, school is a chore to be gotten through, and a necessary means to the end of playing soccer for a division 1 college team, and eventually to playing professionally.

Despite his ambivalence toward school, he does very well and works tremendously hard. There doesn't seem to be anything that Evan does that he doesn't commit himself to fully. He's hesitant to say for sure whether he differs from his classmates in terms of comprehension, but he has noticed that he seems to be able to absorb more than average. He also tends to go above and beyond instructions. When the other students were asked to build a robot for engineering that accomplished A, B, and C, that is exactly what they did. Evan's robot did all of those things, but then his robot "might do D along the way also. The others maybe took the path of just what the teacher wanted them to do." Evan doesn't express strong preferences among his classes, but he does particularly warm to physics, which enables him to study seemingly abstract universal laws. "I feel like I've often thought about stuff, like the way something falls, that others haven't thought about. And I realize now that forces apply." He quickly adds, "My grade in that class is not where I want it, but it will be."

Evan doesn't shy away from pursuing a singular mission. "I'm ambitious and competitive. I've always been that way. I want to show that I'm

dyslexic and doing well." This persistence to the point of defiance is characteristic of Evan. He went to a school for students with learning differences, but found it too easy. When considering high schools, he was advised
to choose a less competitive one, but instead he chose one of the top specialized high schools in Manhattan—which required excellent test scores,
something that isn't easy for any student, much less one with dyslexia. He
says he chose the more academically rigorous school because he "didn't
want anybody telling me that I couldn't do what everyone else could. I just
set my mind to it, I'm going to do this."

Originally, he thought of becoming a doctor—not because he loved science, but because the prestige appealed to him. It's as if he chose the most
difficult possible field in order to prove himself. Now he thinks he may go
into business, because the idea of fourteen more years of school in order to
become a doctor does not appeal to him. In any case, he says, much like
John Irving, "I wouldn't change my dyslexia because I've seen how I've
been able to do well." And succeeding is of enormous importance to Evan.
"If I'm going to do something, I'm going to do it well."

HOW PEOPLE WITH
DYSLEXIA CAN FLOURISH

Robert Cunningham, current head of school at the Robert Louis Stevenson School in Manhattan and advisor on learning and attention issues for
Understood.org, feels strongly that what differentiates the high-achieving
person with a learning difference from the one who does not succeed can
be laid at the feet of educators.[29] "Whatever clarity or caring that [success-
ful] person was exposed to made that change. If that were available to more
kids, then you would see more extraordinary success." He also cautions
against "wanting every kid to be able to do everything."

Insisting that children perform well across the board is setting up
children with brain differences to fail. In addition, the demand that

children progress through remedial levels prior to being able to engage with abstract concepts is dulling and discouraging to the lively dyslexic mind. Cunningham notes, "We get bogged down a lot in skill development and progression, and there is an intractable belief that if you don't master X you can't proceed to Y. In most cases that isn't accurate. Kids whose minds would function incredibly well with more complex concepts never get to reach them. It's possible to grasp calculus without being proficient at addition. You have to understand the concept, but performing the calculation is not necessary." Similarly, "your lack of proficiency in reading skills can stagnate language comprehension, but it doesn't have to. If you are limited in skill development in reading, you spend all your time at the building block levels and you never get to character analysis, to complex plot points, to foreshadowing. How many of us think that a lifelong love of learning is instilled by focusing on stuff that kids hate? At some point an educator and parent have to be courageous enough to say, that [remedial skill] is no longer so important."

For the child who is struggling with these rigid expectations, there is hope. Although work and reading loads increase, in high school and college there is more opportunity to specialize. This is what angular thinkers need—the chance to go full bore into what excites them. In the meantime, parents can help by advocating for their children, creating a dialogue with teachers, and enlisting their help in figuring out ways for the child with a learning difference to shine. The problem, Cunningham points out, is that most schools teach to the middle, with a focus on the group over the individual. The child with a learning difference needs a more individual focus, if only to enable them to find the things they are good at. Cunningham often says to teachers, "When you use a term like 'dyslexia,' what you are really talking about is a pattern in the way a kid's brain is working, and that pattern is within a much larger context. If you step back and look at that pattern along with all the others, you tend to get a better impression of what that kid is going to latch onto and excel at. The same characteristic can be either a strength or a challenge depending on the context."

Sally Shaywitz says, "I worry when schools don't differentiate creativity and imagination from spelling and grammar. In dyslexia, higher thinking and reasoning are intact even though spelling and grammar may not be. It's not higher-level math, it's memorizing the times tables. What happens in dyslexia is that the numbers are stored as words, so kids with dyslexia have huge problems with multiplication or division memorization. I don't usually diagnose [the deceased], but I believe that Einstein was dyslexic. He did have the kinds of problems that we would think of as dyslexia." And of course, he was also monumentally creative. It's helpful to have someone like Einstein—or Benacerraf, Irving, and Greider—for Shaywitz to point to when she makes an initial diagnosis of dyslexia in a child. "One of the most important things you can do when you make a diagnosis is to sit down with the parents and the child and draw a bell-shaped curve." While the areas negatively impacted by dyslexia are often "average or perhaps slightly below average," very often in other conceptual areas, the child is at the ninetieth percentile or more. "I think it's very important for an objective outsider to say this."

The question of accommodations and special schools for people with dyslexia and other learning disabilities is controversial. Shaywitz points out that it can be isolating and damaging to self-esteem for students to be in an environment where their intelligence is misunderstood. On the other hand, life outside of school doesn't cater to our brain differences, and we need to learn to adapt.

There are ways that schools can do better, though, and there is no education-based reason for them not to. William DeHaven, head of school at Winston Preparatory in Manhattan, notes that at his school it's not necessary to give children with dyslexia time and a half on tests, because the tests are structured with the students in mind.[30] Robert Cunningham also questions the more-is-more approach to testing. He argues that schools offer extra time on tests to students with learning differences because "it's easy. It's much trickier to reduce the number of expressions. How many times does a kid need to do the same thing before I am ready to say that

I am convinced? Am I more convinced by forty-six problems than four? No, I'm not. Either you can do it or you can't." He adds, "There is still a large percentage of the population that believes that 'learning disability' is a fancy way of saying lazy or stupid." This impacts how teachers speak to students. "With language processing, most teachers just talk more at the student," which is analogous to "speaking more loudly at someone who speaks another language." Instead, particularly with younger and newly diagnosed students, it's important to communicate information in "smaller chunks. Pause longer. Add visuals."

Most people with dyslexia do take much longer to read, and therefore offering children with learning disabilities more time on tests that require reading is an important accommodation. However, it's not a blanket cure for what ails the testing system. Schuyler says that extra time on tests is not necessarily a help to her. Compared to classmates with attention issues, "I'm very different from them. It's not about my attention. I have difficulty focusing on small, minute details, because I think about the big picture. The bigger the idea, the more it devours in our world, the more intrigued I am by it. If something is a small speck in a book, I'm not going to find that as interesting as a chain that goes throughout a book. No matter how small the idea, no idea is isolated. There is no such thing as something without associations. I want to understand the world and how everything connects to everything else. From city to country to continent to world."

Some parents, educators, and even employers worry that the accommodations offered to students have become excessive, and that we are bringing up a generation of students who won't be able to perform under time pressure—or who aren't suited to fields that expect it—but Shaywitz dismisses that concern. "It's not the thinking or knowing" that's a problem for dyslexics, "it's the reading. When people say 'I would never want to be brought into an ER where there are dyslexic doctors,' my response is that if you have a heart attack and you're brought in not breathing and your doctor has to go read about your symptoms, then you're dead. If your doctor knows what to do and can react quickly, you're going to be okay." She works with a dyslexic pediatrician who says, "I can't read quickly, but I can think quickly." With dyslexia, it's important to disassociate reading and thinking. At the Yale Center for Dyslexia & Creativity, Shaywitz and her colleagues did a study of Yale graduates five or more years after graduation, half of whom were dyslexic. "We asked the alums about their experiences at Yale and currently, in the workplace, and they were doing fantastically well. Many of those who were dyslexic said it made them look at things more carefully and gave them more perseverance."

Shaywitz offers multiple examples of high-functioning people in jobs that require monumental amounts of reading who also have dyslexia. One high-powered attorney told her, "I read slowly but I get so much out of it, and I am ahead of others who read faster but understand less." Another attorney she spoke with, a partner in a law firm, doesn't charge for the extra time it takes her to read. Both are, according to Shaywitz, "highly sought after because they are so brilliant in their thinking. "I always say there are very few things people with dyslexia can't do, but they wouldn't make good file clerks."

It's not uncommon that the most distinguished physicians and scholars in their fields make appointments to visit Shaywitz in her office at Yale. "It's always the same scenario. They will set up a time and my secretary will make sure there is a box of tissues." Within a few minutes of arriving, the visitor will say, "You probably never heard this before, but I can't read well." Once Shaywitz received a call from a highly regarded business mogul and philanthropist, whom she assumed was contacting her about one of her grandchildren. In fact, her questions were about herself. She was about to receive an important appointment with enormous responsibility attached, and she feared that her dyslexia might be an impediment. She was genuinely fearful that she might embarrass herself. Shaywitz and her colleagues evaluated her using their standard measures and she turned out to be both highly intelligent and highly dyslexic. When they told her the news, which Shaywitz intended to be reassuring to her—that is, proof that she was certainly smart enough to handle the job—she was initially unwilling to be reassured. She said, "You gave me one of those dumbed-down tests. We give those tests to prospective employees to see who's most able." Shaywitz told her it was ironic that she was unwittingly weeding out job applicants who had the same qualities of genius that she possessed.

Since self-doubt and some degree of self-loathing commonly occur in people who are diagnosed with a learning difference, it is all the more re-markable that so many people who experience those differences say they wouldn't want to rid themselves of their dyslexia. Schuyler says, "I find that my inability to read will not hinder me in my future." Moreover, she be-lieves the gifts that come with her dyslexia are far greater than the chal-lenges. "Dyslexia is such a huge part of me, not just a factor of me. You can't isolate it from the rest of me. All of my interactions are based on my mind, and if you take a part of me away you'll take me away little by little."

Beryl Benacerraf, who struggled so painfully with shame prior to dis-covering her gift, says that she wouldn't trade her dyslexia. "I don't know if I hadn't had dyslexia if I'd have done something important in another area. I was dealt a deck of cards, and I did my best with it." And to others with dyslexia, parents, and educators, she has this advice: "I think they have to realize how the mind works. That you can't just hit your head against a wall and try to make yourself do what you can't do, and put a square peg into a round hole."

For Benacerraf and Greider, as well as for Sidney, Schuyler, and Evan, the answer to living and succeeding with dyslexia isn't to read faster or to fit in better. It's to find their own path, their own way of expressing their brilliance. Each of us can do the same—and can help make it possible for our children to see their own angular brains as endlessly fascinating terrain, full of potential to be explored.

2.

DISTRACTIBILITY

ADD, ADHD

"What's a box?"

—STEVEN STANLEY,
AWARD-WINNING PALEONTOLOGIST

When Steven Stanley was growing up, he was considered "pretty bright," but certainly not gifted.[1] Steven always had difficulty paying attention. He'd look at the clock in school and think, "20 percent of the class is over. Now 40 percent. I couldn't wait for the bell to ring. It was hard to focus." This might sound like typical day-dreamy child behavior, but Steven's problems continued on into college. "Sitting through lectures, it was fatiguing just trying to follow and take notes."

Ambitious by nature, Steven had a powerful desire to do well, but in order to do so he had to strategize. In high school, his strategy was to devote far longer to completing assignments than anyone else. By spending five hours a night studying, he managed to pull a B+ average, while his classmates—whom he assumed were smarter than he was—seemed to sail through with A's. "It was degrading . . . and I could see that other students didn't work as hard as I did." In college, he says, "It was triage. I'd have to aim to get a C in one class so that I could get an A in another." This caused him extreme anxiety and even feelings of depression. He made it into Princeton University, which he considered a stroke of pure luck, and immediately feared that he wouldn't be able to keep up. "I'd go to the university store and get all these books for the term and I would think, How am I ever going to manage this? It was daunting. I was worried all the time."

It wasn't until Stanley was in his late forties that he sought out a name for the set of challenges that he had faced since childhood. He was by then an award-winning paleontologist, internationally recognized for his exceptional brilliance and contributions to the field. However, he still felt plagued by his difficulties with focus, and by the degree to which simple things that came easily to others were painfully difficult for him. In particular, his recollections of having been thought academically lazy and socially obnoxious were sources of great humiliation and even anger for him.

The diagnosis of attention deficit disorder changed Steven's life. Certainly one immediate benefit for him was to be prescribed Ritalin, one of several drugs that can facilitate focus in those with ADD. Even more powerful was the professional, expert acknowledgment of what he'd gone through. The doctor who diagnosed Stanley noted how extreme his symptoms were, and in comparing them to his string of professional accomplishments he said, "I don't know how you managed to do this." Finally, someone had told Stanley what he'd needed to hear since childhood—that he wasn't less smart than others, nor was he stupid. This was a fear he held that no amount of accomplishment could dispel. He wanted to weep when he learned that he was certifiably highly intelligent, and that he simply had an atypical brain.

ACCORDING TO THE CENTERS FOR DISEASE CONTROL, in 2012 more than 8 percent of children between the ages of three and seventeen received a diagnosis of attention deficit disorder (ADD)—more than 11 percent of all boys in that age group—making it possibly the most diagnosed of disorders among American schoolchildren.[2] The name itself confuses—while ADD and attention deficit hyperactive disorder (ADHD) have been used interchangeably in the past, many of those with ADD exhibit no physical hyperactivity. For the purposes of this book, I will use the more commonly accepted abbreviation ADD to refer to all who have been diagnosed with ADD or ADHD.

Despite its prevalence, we still have multiple misconceptions about the symptoms of attention deficit disorder and what a diagnosis means in the long term. The most common characteristics of the disorder, and those with the most far-reaching effects into adulthood, are impulsivity and attention inconsistency. The former can take the form of an inability to curtail one's behavior—in a child that might mean that any urge is acted upon immediately, whether it's speaking out of turn in class or being physically rambunctious. Once chastised, the child will understand that such behavior is inappropriate, but in the moment they aren't able to restrain themselves. The child with attention difficulties comes across as the typical daydreamer—this is the child who is criticized by teachers and parents for not being able to stay on task, or seeming not to listen when they are being spoken to.

Most of us have a clear picture in mind when we think of the child with ADD, and it's rarely positive. Words that come to mind are impatient and scatterbrained. Children with ADD, particularly when they are left undiagnosed and untreated, are subjected to a near constant flow of negative messaging, particularly in the classroom. The child with ADD can be a disruption—speaking out at the wrong time, fidgeting, interrupting the flow of class, and generally contributing to a chaotic environment for other students. It's easy to sympathize with the frustration of teachers trying to keep a herd of children on task. The unfortunate impact on the child who is the recipient of so much negative feedback, however, can be injury to self-esteem and squelching of any kind of love for learning. These lively children feel they're constantly being told, "No—what you are doing, thinking, and feeling is wrong: *don't do that, sit down, calm down, be quiet.*"

Steven Stanley would have had an easier time of it if he'd been born in 2015 instead of 1941. Educators today are much more likely to urge an evaluation for a child with behavior issues, rather than to punish children who can't control their ability to stay on task. Nonetheless, it's difficult for many to believe that the symptoms of ADD are the result of a neurological difference, rather than misbehavior. Critics of the diagnosis argue that difficulty paying attention and sitting still are no more or less than inherent characteristics of childhood.

This speaks to a key misconception about ADD—namely that those with the disorder can on some level control their powers of attention, or that they will mature out of their difficulties. It's true that we all occasionally struggle to maintain attention to important tasks—to hold a thought, finish a project, remember where we left our keys or what our homework assignment was—but the child or adult with ADD has a physiological inability to control their focus to the same degree as the rest of the population. They are clinically more distractible and impulsive than those who fall into the average center of the bell curve. The admonition to "pay attention" is hopeless for the person with ADD. As psychiatrist, leading ADD expert, and author Edward M. Hallowell noted in the introduction to the most recent edition of his book *Driven to Distraction,* "telling someone with ADD to try harder is no more helpful than telling someone who is nearsighted to squint harder. It miss[es] the biological point."[3]

One of the difficulties in accurately diagnosing children and adults with ADD is that it's often assumed that the person with ADD must, by definition, be incapable of concentrating. As a result, those who exhibit selectively excellent—if wavering—concentration or those who have noticed it in their children often don't consider ADD as a possible diagnosis.

In reality, the person with ADD is apt to lock in with an exceptional degree of focus when she is genuinely interested. If you asked the person with ADD to apply that same degree of attention to, for example, a dense biography of someone in whom she has no interest, her mind would wander uncontrollably. This is not proof that those with ADD are willfully undisciplined. Rather, according to Michael P. Millham, senior research scientist at the Child Mind Institute, it's a direct result of their physiological lack of impulse control, specifically characterized by what he calls *delay aversion*.[4] While all of us would prefer to spend time doing activities we enjoy rather than with drudgery such as paying bills or studying, people with ADD have a clinical disadvantage in trying to stay focused on the latter. Neuroimaging illustrates that long-term incentives simply have less impact on the brain's reward circuitry in those with ADD.[5] So, for example, the child with ADD might know on some intellectual level that if she studies for her science test, then she will get a better grade on her report card in a few months' time. Nonetheless the temptation—and immediate reward—presented by an intensely interesting video game is nearly impossible for her to resist. The child with ADD simply can't control the more attractive impulse without considerable training and intervention such as behavioral therapy and one-on-one coaching.

There is a movement among clinicians to rename ADD "executive function disorder," and when we consider ADD from the standpoint of biology—rather than from the subjective observation of seemingly unruly schoolchildren—that name change makes a great deal of sense. What is actually happening in the brains of people with ADD or executive function disorder is a veering from the norm in the communication between the portions of the brain that execute goals and tasks and those that ponder ideas and look inward in less specifically goal-oriented ways. This miscommunication yields exactly the sort of inability to pay attention and to stay on task in the moment that plagued Steven Stanley as a schoolchild. Using functional MRI (fMRI) and electroencephalography (EEG), researchers can see the differences between those with ADD and those without when moving between tasks.[6] Think of executive function as a switch in the brain that controls where the electrical current (or focus) flows. In the person with a so-called normal brain, that switch is fairly hard and fast. For the most part, the current flows where the individual wants it to, and turns off when directed. However in the person with ADD, the switch is loose—it wobbles, and the current flows indiscriminately and unpredictably.[7]

That wobbling is the source of a great deal of pain and distress in the person with ADD. There is a strong correlation between ADD and anxiety and self-esteem issues like those experienced by Steven Stanley.[8] More than 40 percent of men and 50 percent of women with ADD have multiple anxiety disorders. Approximately a third of children with ADD also have an anxiety disorder. While it's easy to understand how this is related to the unconscious yet very real stress of lacking control over one's focus, there is also some indication that the coexistence of ADD and anxiety is not cause and effect, but rather a result of the way the ADD brain works. Imagine the ADD brain as being a highly tuned antenna that points itself in not always predictable or controllable directions, and imagine that same brain being unable to switch off unpleasantness or stress triggers.

However, as with other brain differences, the story of ADD is not all about challenge. It's also about exceptional ability—the kinds of abilities that have allowed Steven Stanley to make revolutionary discoveries in his field. An exciting amount of research now suggests that uncontrolled wavering of attention (and the lapses into freethinking that occur simultaneously) is also the key to the exceptional originality and creativity exhibited by many of those with ADD. It's very possible that without the ADD brain's dysregulation, we'd never have the flights of fancy that have yielded an enormous amount of human achievement.

WHAT IT MEANS TO HAVE ADD

The concept of hyperactivity in children has appeared in clinical literature since the nineteenth century.[9] It wasn't until the twentieth century that clinicians began to experiment with pharmaceutical treatment of symptoms of hyperactivity. In 1937, physician Charles Bradley essentially landed by accident on the discovery that stimulants could improve the behavior, focus, and school performance of children whom we might today diagnose as having ADD. By the 1970s, our modern definition of ADD was beginning to take shape. In 1980, the American Psychiatric Association's *DSM-III* first named it attention deficit disorder. Still, as Edward Hallowell recounts in *Driven to Distraction,* as late as 1994, when that book was first published, "few people had even heard of ADD. . . . Those few who had heard of it didn't really know what it meant. It conjured up stereotypical images of hyperactive little boys disrupting classrooms and turning life at home into chaos. It was considered to be a condition found exclusively in children, almost all of whom were male. It was thought that children 'grew out of' ADD so that it disappeared by adulthood. Only a rare few doctors knew that ADD could continue on in adults and that females could have it as easily as males."[10]

Today we understand that the neurological differences in the ADD brain are very real, and can be seen visually. Although controversial among some clinicians, in 2013 a brain wave test was approved by the Federal Drug Administration to assist in the diagnosis of ADD.[11] In MRI scans comparing the brains of children with ADD to those without, researchers at Columbia University noted less coordinated brain activity between the two regions of the brain involving decision making (the prefrontal cortex) and controlling impulses (the caudate) in children with ADD.[12]

The tension and dysregulation between the brain centers for decision making and impulse control are at the heart of the ADD diagnosis, and are central to the experience of those with ADD. Millham is actively delving into the interworkings of brain networks in children with ADD. While decades of neuroimaging research have focused on the dorsal and ventral attention networks—the goal-oriented portions of the brain— newer research has uncovered a subtle counterpart called the "default network." This is the portion of the brain that is more active during rest and more directly involved in one of the activities that we strongly associate with those with ADD: daydreaming, or what Dr. Millham calls "spontaneous cognition." Increasingly, he and other researchers are clarifying the ways in which ADD is a result of abnormalities in the regulation between those two networks.

From a practical standpoint, the sensation seeking that is associated with the ADD brain has significant upsides. In an article published in *Frontiers in Psychology*, Darya L. Zabelina, David Condon, and Mark Beeman of Northwestern University reported that there is a real creative advantage to impulsivity.[13] The same study found that those with low impulse control have a stronger tendency to act on their creative urges, rather than simply to think about them. In another study conducted at Ruhr University in Germany and published in *Child Neuropsychology*, researchers found that children with ADD showed an enhanced ability to overcome "constraining influences."[14] This might otherwise be described as "out of the box" thinking, and could explain why people with ADD often exhibit startling originality.

In her 1995 study "The Coincidence of ADHD and Creativity," Bonnie Cramond of the University of Georgia compared the scientific data for people considered to be creative to those with ADD/ADHD.[15] She found strong correlations in brain structure as well as outward temperament. Both types found repetitive tasks excessively dull and unpleasant, and both were engaged by novel tasks to a higher than average degree. Both types responded better to being able to dictate their own process rather than having to follow rules.

The many studies on ADD and creativity mirror this finding. Holly White, a researcher at the University of Memphis, tested creativity among adults with ADD and without, and found that while those with ADD showed higher levels of creative thinking, those without ADD were better at "problem clarification and idea development."[16] In school as well as in workplace environments where team efforts are valued, the person with ADD can mesh beautifully with the person without, and the results when they coordinate efforts can be much greater than the sum of their parts.

THE EXPERIENCE OF HAVING ADD

Across the spectrum of children and adults diagnosed with ADD, there is one common factor: an irregularity of executive function. This irregularity emerges in ways that begin to feel quite familiar the more one learns about the experiences of those with the ADD diagnosis. Child Mind Institute neuropsychologist Michael Rosenthal says, "Part of the disorder is that you have trouble modulating your attention. It's not an inherently good or inherently bad thing, but it is just what it is and it can be used for good things and it can be used for bad things. There is a part of the brain, the frontal lobe, that is underperforming in [those] with ADHD and as a consequence their reward systems are a little bit funky. So they'll get into something and that thing is so rewarding to them that it's hard for them to shift their attention to something else."[17]

Dominick Auciello, also a neuropsychologist at the Child Mind Institute, compares the wavering attention in those with ADD to a flashlight. "The focus can be strong or weak, it can be broad or narrow, it can point this way or that way."[18] In the person without ADD, "there is an executive—your hand—controlling that flashlight and regulating these things." In the person with ADD, the executive hand is erratic, so the light doesn't always go where it should. And particularly in the rule-bound, structured world of mainstream academia, with its often overcrowded classrooms, such wavering of attention can be a very difficult challenge to overcome.

CHALLENGES OF LIVING WITH ADD

Einstein famously said, "If my theory of relativity is proven successful, Germany will claim me as a German and France will declare that I am a citizen of the world. Should my theory prove untrue, France will say that I am a German and Germany will declare that I am a Jew."[19] Given the success of his theory, it would therefore not surprise Einstein at all that numerous groups—including people with ADD and the clinicians who work with them—have been eager to claim him as one of their own. While we have concrete evidence of Einstein's superlative intellect, we have only anecdotal evidence, and his own self-reporting, to suggest the deficits that might have coexisted with his gifts. Thus, we can't scientifically confirm that his impatience and inattention to detail were the result of the kind of dysregulation we've now seen in the brains of children and adults with ADD. Nonetheless his biography offers multiple opportunities to draw lines of correlation between his attentional difficulties—particularly in rigid academic settings—and his genius.

Even as a very young child, Einstein could build a house of cards to fourteen stories, and by the age of twelve he threw himself wholeheartedly into mathematics. He spent one summer vacation plowing through his school's entire math curriculum, and also immersed himself in philosophy. He later described his voracious reading as "fanatic freethinking." In a way that is highly familiar to anyone with ADD—or to anyone who knows, treats, or teaches someone with ADD—when Einstein was interested in something, he was completely enraptured, but when he was disengaged, nothing could encourage him to focus. His Greek professor at Munich's Luitpold Gymnasium told him in front of his entire class that he would never amount to anything. Later, his sister recalled that Einstein was considered lacking in intelligence when he was young.

Einstein loathed school, and he particularly hated the German teaching system, which was largely devoted to rote learning. He found memorization pointless, and later in life he wouldn't bother to learn his own telephone number (after all, he said, what was the point of memorizing something that you could look up). Incapable of keeping his disgust to himself, Einstein was equally disliked by the school's administration, and finally, at the age of seventeen, he was asked to leave. Einstein was thrilled to oblige. His family had moved to Switzerland for his father's work, so he joined them there and enrolled in a second-tier school. When it became apparent that he excelled in math and science but was utterly unprepared in practically every other subject, he was sent back to secondary school. His Swiss teachers were more patient with him than the Germans had been, however, and some of them even seemed to appreciate his freethinking ways. On a geology trip, Einstein was asked by his professor, "Now, Einstein, how do the strata run here? From below upwards, or vice versa?" Einstein replied, "It's pretty much the same to me whichever way they run, Professor."[20]

In the present age, when children are expected to excel across all subjects in order to gain admission to college, it's remarkable to consider the degree to which Einstein was utterly unmotivated to apply himself to anything that he considered boring. Einstein found practical and earthbound subjects painfully uninteresting, so he simply ignored them. While his father wanted him to study engineering, Einstein chose the abstract subject of theoretical physics instead. He couldn't get excited about how to light up buildings, but he was enchanted with the essential nature of electromagnetism.

Of course, as discussed in the introduction, Einstein was a genius with a capital G, and therefore he is, by definition, exceptional. Nonetheless, elements of his story can be meaningfully applied to many children and parents coping with the same erratic attention and up-and-down academic performance. Reading can be particularly agonizing for the child with ADD. When faced with a pile of academic reading for school, many children with ADD will read a sentence, or a paragraph, or a page, and realize that although their eyes were scanning the words, their brains were utterly disengaged. Adding to these children's difficulties, some researchers believe that as many as 40 percent of children with ADD also have dyslexia.[21] Students with ADD describe their experiences reading in subjects they find dry or uninteresting in language that mirrors that used by people with dyslexia; they often say that when reading something in which they're not interested, their minds wander and the words swim on the page. However, for those with ADD who are not also dyslexic, the problem is not one of language processing, rather it is purely one of wavering focus. If the student is actively interested in what they are reading, then focus isn't a problem and attention can be laser-beam intense.

Ethan, who was diagnosed with ADD as a young child, is a handsome and thoughtful sixteen-year-old in one of Manhattan's most competitive public high schools.[22] While he exhibits remarkable drive and determination, he admits "it takes me a little while to do homework. More than the usual futzing around that every kid does sometimes. Especially with math it takes me a long time. During a computation my brain freezes. There's some [part of my mind] off free." At these times, and without being aware he's doing so, Ethan finds his mind wandering. Often he's "trying to figure out something else, anything really. It's almost like my brain is occupied with something else and I'm not sure exactly what."

Related to the issue of focus is the considerable challenge of organization. Most people with ADD have difficulty with executive function, which is housed in the prefrontal cortex of the brain and is responsible for planning. Assessing the time and steps needed to complete a task as well as multitasking can be negatively impacted by poor executive functioning. Derogatory descriptives for the child or adult with ADD abound— scatterbrained, forgetful, airy. Ethan says, "I feel like I'm always running behind on something." These challenges—attentional and organizational—are built into the experience of having ADD. They can be mitigated, but will always be a part of the person's neurological makeup.

The challenges that people with ADD face are not only academic; often their greatest struggles are emotional in nature. As all-encompassing as the school experience is for children and young adults, it's therefore difficult to separate the challenges of academia—keeping up with workload, for example—and the attendant emotional stresses that are often apparent in children with ADD and other brain differences. It's unclear if the strong incidence of anxiety in children and adults with ADD is due to a difference in the brain that causes both problems, or whether some perception of falling behind because of one's ADD leads to anxiety. Anxiety alone can lead to inattentiveness, because a child is preoccupied with worri-some thoughts. But if the child has ADD, then even once the anxiety is treated they will still be inattentive. Children with both anxiety and ADD tend to be more inattentive but less impulsive than those with ADD alone. There is a strong association between ADD, risk-taking, and lack of im-pulse control. This makes great sense when we think of ADD in terms of the previously discussed deficit in executive function. Imagine the person with ADD as having a brain that's like a classroom. Ideally there should be a teacher in charge who draws all eyes to her. In the ADD brain, that authority figure is weak and inconsistent, and the children run amok. Not only does the child with ADD have difficulty staying on task, he can have difficulty sitting still and thinking before speaking. Children with ADD can be the squeaky wheel in any given classroom. They crave intellectual stimulation, and when they aren't engaged they become restless—and reckless. As a very young child, Einstein was known to have a terrible tem-per. His sister Maja described how his whole face would turn yellow when he became angry, and the tip of his nose would pale to white. Once he threw a bowling ball at her. He also hit her with a hoe.[23] She wasn't his only target—he once threw a chair at his tutor.[24]

Not all children with ADD exhibit difficulties with physical and be-havioral impulse control, but it's not uncommon. Ethan, who is tall for his age and looks older than his sixteen years, was often a source of frustra-tion for teachers and adults who thought he was older—and believed he should be more mature—than he was. At age ten he looked like he was fourteen, but emotionally, according to his father "he was even less devel-oped. He lacked a filter" in social interactions, and could often be inap-propriate, both with children and adults.[25] For example, he'd engage verbally with adult strangers in a way not typical for a young child. As his father recalls, these adults were often impressed by Ethan's intelligence, but at the same time they were taken aback by his forwardness and lack of inhibition. On such occasions, Noah didn't stop Ethan from engaging, but he would stand by to "monitor." In school, his acting out could be severe—hiding under tables, engaging in tantrums and other disruptive behaviors. When Ethan was evaluated, he was diagnosed with Asperger's as well as ADD. Ethan's father, Noah, then placed him in a special school for students with behavioral issues, and the focused support he received there helped Ethan through the most intensely stressful years.

By the time Ethan was in eighth grade, he felt held back academically. His maturity level was catching up to his age, and he felt able to make the jump to an intensely academic, mainstream high school. Increasingly, he has found himself to be "pretty self-aware, less restless." His father says that what had seemed inappropriate as a young child now seems more appropriate. That is, the verbal precocity of his early years has evolved into verbal fluency. In combination with therapy and coaching, children with ADD who suffer from social awkwardness and difficulties with impulse control can find that the outward appearance of these traits naturally lessens over time thanks to the calming effect of age and maturity. Moreover, as children mature, their peers do as well, and there can be considerable relief in discovering that it's no longer as necessary—or desirable—to be a perfect clone of one's friends.

The calming effects of growing up aside, these traits and tendencies toward spontaneity of speech and action don't just disappear—they are always a part of one's temperamental makeup. Ethan continues to feel some awkwardness with other young adults, an experience not uncommon to any child who has a brain difference. Often, these children get along better with adults, since adults tend to have more outward patience with eccentricity and with thought processes that are perceived as outside the norm.

Steven Stanley has struggled with his lack of verbal filter throughout his life. As a young child, he was often chastised by his mother for blurting out insensitive remarks. Even as late as age fifteen, he was chided by her for his inappropriateness. "Steve," she said to him far more than once, "I thought we had sorted this out with you a long time ago. Think before you speak." As an adult, he's worked hard to become a more respectful listener, but to some extent he recognizes that his tendency to speak unedited and off the cuff is part of who he is as a person, and is a direct result of his essentially lively, impulsive mind. "My mind does jump away from things. I have had to learn not to interrupt people when they're talking. I learned during my professional life to hold back sometimes. I start to say something, and then I realize that someone else is still talking, so I stop."

Edward Hallowell, author of *Driven to Distraction,* was diagnosed with both dyslexia and ADD and is quick to point out that ADD is, generally speaking, a disorder of disinhibition. Simply put, the ADD brain is not tied down. This looseness affects the person with ADD in any rule-bound environment, including during social interactions. Hallowell says that he used to think his own tendency to blurt out words prior to thinking them through was "weird. Then I realized, yes, you're different, but different isn't bad. I'm not always appropriate, but that doesn't mean I'm bad." Hallowell recalls being at a party with his wife, Sue, and a female artist friend of his wife's. "The artist was a very attractive woman. When she said, 'That's my sister there in the blue dress across the room,' I looked over at the sister, and before I could stop myself I said, 'But you're so beautiful and she's so homely.' Pregnant pause, wherein Sue stared daggers at me and the artist simply paused, but then burst out laughing. 'I love how honest you are,' she said. 'Thank you,' I said, 'but I really didn't mean it the way it came out.' 'Sure you did,' the artist said, 'but it's old news. My sister and I laugh about it.' Of course, I was mortified. The last thing I wanted to do was insult the woman's sister. That's the hard part of disinhibition: unintentionally hurting someone else's feelings." As another example, he adds, "I can't tell you how many women I asked to marry me on the first date. Fortunately, they were more restrained."[26]

Hallowell is quick to point out that the vast majority of the time, he manages not to offend, but nonetheless when offense does occur, it causes him great shame and embarrassment. This is the price he pays for having, as he describes it, "a race car brain and bicycle brakes." The process of learning to live with ADD—and simultaneously coming to maximize one's potential—involves using all the power of one's brain while also learning to build up one's internal controls.

DEVELOPING WORK-AROUNDS

All people with brain differences, including children and adults with ADD, can develop techniques that mitigate the challenges of their particular neurological makeup while emphasizing their considerable creative gifts. Hallowell wants to reframe the entire discussion of ADD traits, explaining, "We cast everything in the realm of pathology." He argues instead for a strength-based model. "ADD is a gift that's very hard to unwrap. And I would go further than that and I would say it's a talent." Taking his race car analogy one step further, he says, "A Ferrari without brakes is dangerous, but the Ferrari with brakes wins the race. If you strengthen those brakes then the sky's the limit." People with ADD can learn to harness their power. "Like Niagara Falls. Until you build a hydroelectric plant, it's just a lot of noise and mist. If you build a hydroelectric plant you light the state of New York."

One of the most powerful work-arounds for the person with any brain difference is simple self-awareness. Knowledge of one's weaknesses and one's strengths can not only help us make better choices for ourselves, but can help us align ourselves with people who compensate for us in the areas in which we're less capable. For children with ADD, the surrounding adults need to take responsibility for fulfilling that role. Supportive parents are key, as is the parents' willingness to advocate for children in school. Adults with ADD can more proactively find people in the workplace as well as in their personal lives who can help them stay on track.

In their own age-appropriate ways, both children and adults with ADD can benefit from strategic partnerships. In school, that might involve pairing the creative, impulsive child with ADD with other children who are more organized by nature. In the workplace, Hallowell points out the enormous potential in combining the strengths of the person with ADD tendencies and someone with complementary strengths. Someone who is impulsive by nature can "make a lot of mistakes in business. So hook up with someone who is by nature methodical and looks at all the possibilities. You may not like that person, but you need that. That's a wonderful pairing—the euphoric person and the implementer who can help grow the idea."

Robert Cunningham, former head of Gateway Schools, current head of Robert Louis Stevenson School, and founder of Understood.org, has had a long and illustrious career in educating children with brain differences.[27] He makes special note that the most supportive parents understand their children's strengths and not just their weaknesses: "The better parents understand what is going on with their kid and how to look at the child as more than a set of deficits. If you can move a little away from that and take time to explore those strengths, and if you effectively communicate that to teachers, that creates a dialogue. Then teachers will work to find opportunities within their school programs that will give your kid the opportunity to shine." Not every child with a learning issue or brain difference will attend—or should attend—a special school. But within the parameters of a mainstream school, parents who "make it their mission to spot what their kid might have an aptitude for" can help guide teachers in carving out the space that these children need to flourish.

This involves effort on the part of parents both in the home and in the school. By necessity, parents often spend more time attending to their children's difficulties. But Cunningham says that in order to find what a child is good at, the parent should spend more "time with the child on things other than what is most difficult." He recommends the same for educators. "I often say to teachers, how many of you think a lifelong love of learning is instilled by focusing on stuff that kids hate?" He gives the same advice to parents, particularly since schools by definition are set up to value the needs of the many over the few. The child who falls outside of the average, middle area of performance needs a parent advocate to help ensure they are actively encouraged to find their special talents and abilities.

Ethan has two powerful things going for him—his own remarkable internal motivation and the support of a very involved father. On his own, Ethan has found solace in applying himself to subjects that matter to him. In those areas, he has no difficulty hyperfocusing. Meanwhile, in subjects that he finds boring, he consciously looks for an aspect of the subject that interests him, or he finds a way to explore that subject through the prism of an area of interest. Ethan's father says, "I encouraged him to express himself however he wanted, whether through technology, filmmaking, drawing, or writing stories. I was also a huge advocate for getting him all the outside support I could get him."

Ethan's father exemplifies the kind of positive focus that Cunningham encourages. And his determination to seek the right additional help for Ethan has also made an enormous difference. Hallowell points out that the "real disabilities of ADD are shame, fear, and believing that you're disabled. That's what really disables a person. There are so many examples where people turn these [deficits] into wonderful stuff, but if you believe you can't, you can't. That's where the damage is done. So I will take a kid and make him really glad he's got ADD, but I will say that part of getting your brakes is accepting a coach, accepting a tutor, and they can help you do things that don't come naturally to you."

This combination of being offered help, accepting that help, and also embracing one's strengths and weaknesses is key to developing the work-arounds one needs to master living with ADD. Hallowell likens this to the rhyming constraints of a poem. "Find a structure to work within and embrace it as your friend. Once you have that structure, you can create beauty."

Hallowell also embraces the reality that while going through school you have to do things that you're not good at. "It's important not to give people permission to blow off [the harder subjects], because if you do, you're restricting their options later on." This is where the quality of grit becomes an important determining factor in success. As Hallowell notes, "There is good suffering and there is bad suffering. Good suffering is working at something, bad suffering is humiliation, depression, and isolation. There is a myth that excellence occurs in direct proportion with suffering. Well, excellence occurs in direct proportion with good suffering, but inverse proportion with bad suffering."

He wouldn't describe it this way himself, but Ethan has certainly mastered the art of good suffering via hard work. After having spent several years in a special school geared at students with learning differences, he decided that he wanted to go to a mainstream high school. At the age of thirteen and totally on his own, he prepared for the New York City specialized high school exam, and scored so well that he was placed in one of the top schools in the city. His ambition is what drove him to work so hard. While he appreciated that the special school he attended had helped him tremendously with his behavioral issues, he says, "I worried about what colleges would think. 'Oh, you're special ed? That's cute, goodbye.' Also the academics weren't the best, because [the special school] was mainly focused on behavior. So I was afraid I wouldn't be prepared. Fear for my future and wanting to do more is what drove me to want to leave special ed."

Once in his competitive high school, he chose to major in math, even though it was his worst subject, because he wanted to challenge himself to be the best. He says that he finds solace in applying himself to things that matter to him. His father points out that he is also capable of finding some interesting angle even in the subjects that don't interest him. "All of the really heavy lifting comes from Ethan. He wanted to build a computer and I said great, so for his sixteenth birthday, everyone pitched in the parts. Then he built a computer and created a remote desktop on his iPad so [none of his schoolwork can be] lost now. [If you ask him,] he'll go on and on about this forever. He's so turned on by technology and problem solving."

Ethan takes the perhaps cliché idea of turning one's weaknesses into strengths yet another step further. He applies his strengths—in his case his extraordinary ability and obsession with computers—into coming up with a solution to one of his biggest challenges, organization. As his father says, "he turned perseverating into persevering."

Beyond the intangible qualities of grit and determination, and the support of parents, educators, tutors, and colleagues, there are of course more concrete ways to address some of the symptoms of ADD. The first is via extra time in school, particularly on standardized tests. As noted in chapter 1, there are educators and clinicians on either side of the argument for extra time. Some argue that offering extra time is an artificial remedy, since the real world doesn't offer extra time. Robert Cunningham argues that the issue isn't whether people with ADD should be given extra time, the issue is why we all aren't given as much time as we need. "I don't buy the pedagogical argument for a time limit. So many surgeons have ADD. They may have trouble with their paperwork, but they are super focused in the OR.

"I think this notion of speedy versus nonspeedy is overrated. What you really want to find out is how much a person knows. The time limit is an artifact of administrative convenience." It also measures "a fairly narrow skill: being fast. But usually what you give up when you acquire speed is depth. And I think our speeded-up culture is sacrificing a lot of depth."

An even more controversial subject is the question of whether to medicate children and adults with ADD. There is real and justified concern about the possible overprescribing of a variety of powerful drugs, among them Adderall and Ritalin, for children with milder forms of ADD who might be helped by behavioral therapy alone. Coaching has been shown not only to be beneficial, but also to change the individual's behavior in the long term. While the effects of drugs wear off, coaching in valuable skills such as organization and setting timers, as well as traditional talk therapy to help with anxiety, impatience, and frustration, can mitigate some of the symptoms of ADD without medication. The unique benefit of behavioral therapy is that in time, and thanks to the wonderful plasticity of the brain, these new behaviors can become permanent skill sets.

The decision to prescribe is one that should be made carefully with doctors, and there should be no shame attached to medication if it's required and if it helps. Certainly for children who exhibit extremes of hyperactivity, medication can be particularly helpful in calming the body and focusing the brain enough so that real learning can take place. However, drugs should always be prescribed in conjunction with therapy and/or ADD coaching. No prescription on its own can address the repeated blows to self-esteem that children and adults with ADD suffer after years of feeling less intelligent than their peers. Nor do drugs teach the behaviors that will help those with ADD function in the world and the workplace as they grow older.

Ethan takes Ritalin for his ADD, and he noticed something interesting about when he needs it and why. He observed that when he was doing a challenging summer internship during which he was put to work on an intensive project, he worked nearly nonstop from nine to five every day and never needed his medication. However, "If I don't have my pills at school, I'm a disaster." He says that the difference is so marked in school that if he forgets to take his pill his teachers notice it immediately. So why didn't he need the medication during his internship? Ethan's theory is that at school "I'm not free to manage myself." During his internship he was working on computer code for an app, and he started the summer with a very steep learning trajectory before him. The work was difficult but fascinating to him, and he was supervised very little. Ironically, when he was given the least structure, he was able to better discipline himself.

Ethan has mixed feelings about taking Ritalin. On the one hand, he acknowledges that he needs it during his school day. On the other hand, "I hate to admit it helps. I don't like relying on something else to focus and perform in school. It makes me feel infantile. I want to be able to control myself even with my ADD, because it's who I am. I shouldn't have to rely on drugs to control myself." Ethan isn't alone in his ambivalence, but it's important to stress once again that if hyperactivity and wavering focus are hindering learning to the extent that a child or adult's true brilliance cannot emerge, then there is and should be no shame in taking advantage of pharmaceutical help. Steven Stanley says that he has benefited tremendously from being prescribed Ritalin, and he notices immediately when the effects wear off. ADD medications, just like any drugs, can be of enormous benefit—when prescribed correctly.

THE GIFTS OF THE BRAIN WITH ADD

The term *Renaissance man* is worn out and overapplied, but in the case of Mario Livio it is more than apt.[28] Livio is an astrophysicist and author of multiple books that span subject matter from the hard sciences to the fine arts. He's also a great lover of classical music and he's the scientific advisor to the Baltimore Symphony Orchestra, having worked with composers to create two contemporary classical pieces inspired by Hubble images. In addition to being diversely talented, Livio has led a dramatic life. He had an excruciatingly difficult upbringing, having been raised by extended family and in institutional settings when his parents became political exiles. He also served as a medic in the Israeli army during three separate—and often highly traumatic—military actions. In addition—and although he was never formally diagnosed with it as a child—Livio is exemplary of someone with ADD who exhibits genius-level ability.

Livio didn't struggle academically in school, largely because he is so intelligent, but there were years during which he found academics "extraordinarily boring." School was so dull to him, in fact, that he often didn't do his homework. From his earliest years he was rambunctious and found it nearly impossible to sit still in class. He was so hyperactive, in fact, that he has "broken almost every bone in [his] body," including his femur when he was four years old. His physical impulsivity and distractibility have lasted into adulthood—not long ago he smashed two fingers in a car door. His early years were spent in Romania, which, at that time, was a communist country with strictly enforced academic discipline. On his first day of kindergarten, he got up from his desk and launched into a Romanian folk dance. When asked later why he would do such a thing, he said, "I was just bored to tears." But as we have seen in others with ADD, when Livio was interested in the subject material, his attention was riveted. While he was unable to sit still in school, he was nonetheless a voracious, self-directed reader at home.

Livio's scientific area of expertise is theoretical particle physics. According to Livio, this means, "I don't do observation. I barely know through which side of the telescope one looks. I look at the observations [of the other scientists] and come up with theoretical models to explain what they see." His attraction to the highly theoretical is a direct result of his brain's embrace of the abstract—a characteristic of creativity that is not at all uncommon among those with ADD. He describes his most creative thinking in words that suggest brain activity even more unconscious than what we might call creative flow. "I have the distinct feeling that I have come up with some ideas not just during daydreaming, but during sleep. I would sort of wake up in the middle of the night and think, Aha, that's what I really should be doing. It doesn't happen a lot, but occasionally, when a problem really bothered me," and he was thinking about it a great deal during the day, "then sometimes during sleep I would wake up and say, Aha, I think maybe that's the way."

Over the course of his career, Livio has developed a style and rhythm of work that keeps his lively mind interested while minimizing distractions. Perhaps because he loves music so much, he has learned that he can't have it on while he works. However, he's also noticed that unlike his colleagues who can sit at their desks for hours at a time, he needs to take breaks to walk around and release some pent-up physical energy. "A few of my colleagues, I see them able to sit in front of their screens from 8 a.m. to 5 p.m. without hardly getting up at all. I can concentrate on a problem at my desk for half an hour, but then I have to get up and walk in the corridor. Maybe I am still thinking about the problem, but I'm not sitting in the chair."

Age alone has minimized many of the more challenging traits associated with hyperactivity that Livio exhibited as a child. While he thinks he would certainly have been diagnosed as having ADHD back then, he's unsure if he would be diagnosed today. However, "I am restless. And yes, my mind is restless. But this does not mean that I cannot focus. I can." One way in which Livio satisfies his restless mind is by keeping exceptionally busy in his primary career (he has published an extraordinary number of papers in his field) and also by cultivating and pursuing his multiple interests outside of astrophysics. His work with the Baltimore Symphony is one example. And his books—the latest of which is *Brilliant Blunders,* about the mistakes genius scientists have made on their road to discovery—touch on many different subjects, allowing him to delve with curiosity into all the areas, scientific and otherwise, that fascinate him. That conscious strategy "has worked for me for years."

Mario Livio's story brings to mind what Edward Hallowell has called "impulsivity gone right. You don't plan to have a creative thought. If you're not a little bit disinhibited, you're not going to be creative." For himself, Hallowell notes that high energy and large output are important parts of any creative endeavor, and both are qualities built into the person with ADD. Highly creative people such as Mario Livio and Edward Hallowell generate a high number of thoughts, many of which are discarded prior to hitting upon a breakthrough. Hallowell says, "For every thousand 'she's so homely' comments, there's one gem. And I think, Oh, that's a good one. But there are always more useless or embarrassing ones than good ones." Hallowell describes this as being "cursed blessed."

Hallowell's particular talent, which he directly attributes to ADD and dyslexia, is a "sixth sense and ability to see through people. I read people in a way that is almost a liability. Hypocrisy I can spot a mile away, and I can always see the phony ulterior motive." This intuitiveness is exceptionally acute, and he notes that he shares it with others who have been similarly diagnosed. "What we [with ADD and dyslexia] see as obvious is something that others don't see at all. Meanwhile, we struggle with things that they find easy—organizing ourselves, reading quickly. They think we should just get our acts together. But we say, it's not that easy. "

Paleontologist Steven Stanley describes a similarly uncanny ability to make connections that others do not. "I have a tendency right away when something comes up to think about how it relates to other things. Things just come to me. I see things that are comparable or similar to a very different area. I see the analogies. I'm also quick to put [my thoughts] into action. I'm fundamentally a creative person, always wanting to solve problems, and I will never hold back. It's hard for me to know what compels me to make these connections. They sort of just naturally come to me."

What Stanley describes is representative of disinhibited creative thought. The brain with ADD, when released from the typical bounds of logic and preconceived notions, naturally and unconsciously links thoughts that others might find unthinkable—and unlinkable. Stanley was struck quite powerfully when the expert who first diagnosed him as having ADD said, "When you gave a wrong answer as a child, you just answered the wrong questions." Stanley's brain, typical of someone with ADD, is often leaping ahead of where everyone else's thoughts are resting, but he feels that the image of the lightbulb going off over one's head is misleading. In his view, his revolutionary thoughts are not inexplicable flashes, but instead are purely logical. "It's logical solutions to things. Logical solutions to problems I've thought about." This enables him to "connect disparate things in my research." In contrast with colleagues who exhibit more linear ways of thinking, Stanley's mind "jumps around." One could say Stanley's thinking is not stuck in a box; to that he responds, "What's a box?"

Ethan is a few generations younger than Steven Stanley, but he is another perfect example of someone with ADD who has discovered both exceptional aptitudes and struggles. Because of his remarkably strong will and drive, he has been able to succeed in a highly competitive environment despite his diagnoses. Meanwhile, his creative and naturally obsessive, hyper-focused brain has allowed him to pursue his passion and abilities in computer science far beyond the ken of the typical teenager. He began coding via the MIT-developed program Scratch when he was in fifth grade, and within a few years he transitioned into coding on his own. At his summer internship for the New York City Public School Construction Authority, his task was to create a prototype mobile version of the authority's Web site. He had no experience in mobile development or programming, and for the first two weeks he immersed himself in studying the multiple computer languages that would enable him to move forward with the project. Such intensive and complex study might seem like a recipe for boredom, but Ethan was enthralled despite the difficulty of the job. "I didn't have any problems focusing. If I was bored with one part, I could move to another, so I found that with the freedom to organize my work I was able to focus for extended times through the day. I would even work through lunch. It was difficult, but for me it was enjoyable. I would bitterly complain, but I loved the challenge. I love computers and my boss was really impressed with my work." He knows with certainty that he will make a career from coding. Ethan feels that his uniquely creative abilities in coding are part and parcel of his ADD mind. He also creates highly unusual and quite amazing graphic computer art, which he loves producing. When asked if he would want his ADD to be magically waved away, he answered unequivocally: "No. As hard as it is, I believe it's where my original work comes from."

Finding a field or area of interest that captivates the child with ADD is perhaps the single most important way to ensure future success in life. For Dom, a thoughtful and charismatic senior in an independent high school for children with learning disabilities, that area of passion is music.[29] Dom was raised in difficult financial circumstances by a single mother who continues to be his biggest fan. His first exposure to music was learning to play violin at age three, and it didn't stick. When he was ten, however, in large part to cure his restlessness and boredom, he discovered drums while attending the Boys' Club. Dom describes himself as "not entertained very easily," and the swimming, sports, and pool table that were readily available at the club never held his attention for long. So he wandered into the music department, met his first drum teacher, and "That was it. That was it."

Although he often grew frustrated when he felt he wasn't picking up the drums as quickly as he wanted to, his passion for music kept him going, as did his ambition. When he first heard music that he responded to powerfully, he didn't just enjoy it, he aspired to it. As young as thirteen years old, "I knew, okay, this is what I'm going to do. Jazz fusion. This is it. Just the whole high pace. Beautiful." Certain music and musicians "just kind of gave me a sight of what I wanted to do, who I wanted to play with, what I wanted to compose." It's particularly remarkable to note his discipline and intensity of focus on his goal in the context of his ADD. That kind of determination is diametrically opposite to the stereotype of the scattered kid with attention problems.

In addition to having ADD, Dom also has dyslexia. While he enjoys learning and is inquisitive by nature, "I'm not a big fan of the whole school thing. [The dyslexia] makes it very hard for me to read. It messes with my math skills. It's embarrassing." He doesn't let himself become discouraged by these challenges, however. "It's just a part of who I am for right now. It's a weakness that can be overcome. After a while I said, okay, it's something I have to throw in the trash can, that's all." Music is also harder for him to read, both because of his dyslexia and his ADD. But he is willing to do whatever it takes to move past those difficulties and achieve his goals.

Dom has a difficult time shutting off his brain, and music has become a solace to him emotionally as well as artistically. In particular, it calms him. "I tend to think a lot even when people are talking. I tend to tune them out. It's just me and my thoughts. I overanalyze stuff. The only thing I don't overthink is music." Dom's brain responds to music—and generates its own music—in extraordinary ways. He can compose music in his mind, without writing down a single note. For a long time, it didn't occur to him that this made him special. "I thought that's just how it was done. I can get lost in my thoughts and I can think pretty vividly. I feel like thinking is kind of like dreaming." In addition, Dom exhibits the very rare gift of synesthesia, a neurological phenomenon in which there is a cross-ing over of the senses, so that something heard can be seen in color, and in even rarer circumstances, tasted. For Dom, it's both. "When I hear something really good that I love I start to either see colors or I can taste certain types of food or fruit, just certain tastes, or I can see certain colors or textures almost like a canvas that you can smell." Recently, Dom's drum teacher played an Indian-influenced fusion piece for him and "I started to taste lemon and saw a kind of yellow." This isn't something he imagines with eyes closed, but rather something that he sees.

The experience is highly pleasurable for Dom and borders on medita-tive. Because his brain can be so unquiet, these times when he can shut out noise and thought are precious to him. He describes a desire for noth-ingness in a way that suggests not depression, but rather an absence of dis-traction. When he spent a summer at the Berklee College of Music in Boston, he would occasionally retreat to a practice room, put a sheet over the window, and "I would think about nothing, just nothing. It feels great. My mind is quiet, and it only happens for a certain amount of time." It's much more difficult for him to achieve this kind of peace back home, where there are academic pressures and other demands placed upon him. But when he is free to pursue only his music, he can find that quiet place.

Ned Hallowell argues that when talking about children and adults with ADD, "deficit is a tremendous misnomer. We as mental health pro-fessionals ought to spend a lot more time probing to find areas of talent. Most of the people who come to see us sell themselves short and don't think they have any talent. When you find areas of talent, then motivation will follow."

HOW PEOPLE WITH ADD CAN FLOURISH

Arguably the most important element of Albert Einstein's genius was his exceptional predilection for daydreaming. The story goes that the seeds for his theory of relativity were planted while he was desperately bored in class one day, and he imagined that he was riding a beam of light to the edge of the universe. One thought followed another, and on into infinity. Coupled with his frequent flights of fancy was an extraordinary ability to hyperfocus when he locked into something that captured his imagination. In one single year, 1905, he wrote four papers that changed our conception of the universe—all this while he simultaneously toiled full-time in the Swiss patent office.

This combination of daydreaming and creative output is highly significant to all of us, not just those with genius-level intellect. Researchers at the University of California, Santa Barbara, have theorized the existence of a direct link between daydreaming and complex problem solving.[30] Participants in their study were broken into three groups, and all were given a challenging mental task to perform. After this first task was concluded, one group was given complete rest, another was given a simple, mindless task to perform, and a third was given an equally challenging task. The second group, which was given the mindless task, reported a significantly higher degree of daydreaming than the other two groups, and when all three groups were asked to return to their original challenging task, the daydreamers performed 40 percent better than the others.

The late-nineteenth-century psychologist and philosopher William James, who was the first to develop the concept of "stream of consciousness," was once dismissed as being absentminded. In response, he said that he was actually "present-minded" to his own thoughts.[31] And, arguably, inattention is in the eye of the beholder. What is perceived by a teacher as inattention to the task at hand could actually be quite focused attention to a light beam traveling to the edges of the universe. As Steven Stanley's doctor pointed out to him, he was giving the right answer to the wrong question.

Considering the playful nature of geniuses such as Einstein, Steven Stanley, and Mario Livio, and the clear benefit of self-directed creative time to children and young adults such as Ethan and Dom, it's distressing to note the degree to which unstructured play has been squeezed out of our children's lives—both during the school day and after. When we look at the large body of evidence that daydreaming and freethinking are the source material for so much discovery, we should wonder what we're losing in our race toward numerically measurable achievement.

This relationship between daydreaming and creativity is not a new discovery—Jerome L. Singer first published his major study into that direct link more than half a century ago—and each new study published in recent decades has further emphasized how much we hobble our conscious thoughts when we try to too-strictly control our unconscious thoughts. The fruits of daydreaming are not simply single bursts of creativity. Rather, there is extensive recent evidence that the neurological benefits of daydreaming are expansive and far-reaching.[32] When we consider the various CEOs who describe themselves as daydreamers, it's not surprising to learn that multiple researchers have determined that one of the rewards of freethinking is a heightened ability to plan forward. Retrieving memories, turning them over and pondering them, gives us a foundation on which to build a potential future.

Ethan beautifully articulates the disconnect between what excites him creatively and the expectations of a competitive school environment. Noting the creative problem solving he engaged in during his summer internship, he says, "That doesn't happen as much in school. In school it's a worksheet, and do these three things this way." Ethan experiences greater enjoyment and engagement in more creative assignments at school. Recently assigned to write an article in the style of yellow journalism, he decided to lay out his piece graphically. He also spent hours poring over *The New York Times* archives reading up on the subject; he describes himself as "definitely hyperfocused" in completing that specific project. Interestingly, history is not his favorite subject, but the creativity and flexibility of the assignment drew him in. This again underlines the idea that the parents and educators who love and work with people with ADD can help them work within the lines of academia while finding ways to express their particular genius.

While we can all be absentminded—or present-minded to our own thoughts—it is safe to say that very few of us will achieve what Einstein did, or even Mario Livio and Steven Stanley have. Yet we have myriad other, more achievable models of originality, freethinking, and bits of genius to look to—both for ourselves and for our children.

This is not to minimize the downsides of ADD or to suggest that it can go untreated without ill effect. Even highly intelligent, high-performing children with ADD who do well in lower grades can suffer tremendous blows to self-esteem when their powers of concentration and organization are challenged by the rigors of high school and college. Along with their heightened powers of original thinking, children and adults with untreated ADD are at much greater risk of substance abuse and marital strain. The spouse who can't please bosses, forgets anniversaries and appointments, and becomes so locked into his own exciting thoughts that he can't be pulled away to focus on everyday matters can find it hard to sustain intimate relationships—and those who love and depend on him can feel frustrated and isolated. Without a diagnosis, the person with attentional difficulties can simply appear selfish and irresponsible. It's not unusual for parents to diagnose themselves with ADD in my office. With a diagnosis, whether in childhood or adulthood, can come relief as well as an opportunity to address longstanding conflicts—both external and internal.

But treatment doesn't mean erasure. The mental health field has grown increasingly adept at diagnosing and treating mental illness and mental disorder. However, along with our ability to identify mental illness and disorder has come a new kind of stigmatization—namely the mistaken belief that we can and should make brain differences go away.

Treatment can mitigate the downsides of ADD. Ritalin and Adderall can help children stay in their seats and concentrate on tests, and

behavioral therapy can help patients develop organizational systems and
even to retrain their brains to stay on task when needed. But neither therapy
nor drugs will render the brain permanently "normal." And given the
remarkable linkage between attentional deficits and extremes of originality,
we shouldn't desire to flatten out those differences.

Einstein, who so hated rote learning, once said, "Imagination is more
important than knowledge." We can only conjecture what Einstein would
have thought of our educational system's emphasis on standardized testing, but yet another quote from him offers us a clue: "If you want your
children to be intelligent, read them fairy tales. If you want them to be
more intelligent, read them more fairy tales." Of course, Einstein's version
of reading fairy tales was teaching himself an entire math curriculum in
one summer, so we might take that recommendation with a grain of salt.
Nonetheless, it's worth noting that Einstein didn't study those math books
because anyone was forcing him to do it. To him, solving a hairy math
problem was akin to play—and he remained a playful man throughout
his life.

Teenager Dom described himself as a child as "not entertained very
easily," but once he did find the thing that enraptured him—drumming,
in his case—"That was it." And he wouldn't exchange the challenges of
having ADD for the possible upside of being more uniformly attentive.
"It's a pain, but no. Because it's me."

3.

ANXIETY

COMMON DIAGNOSES

GENERALIZED ANXIETY DISORDER, OBSESSIVE-COMPULSIVE PERSONALITY DISORDER, PANIC DISORDER, AND PHOBIAS

"I figured out fairly early that the world was divided into two groups: the group who pays people to listen to their problems, and the group that gets paid to tell the world their problems."

—DAVID SEDARIS

The bestselling writer David Sedaris was in second grade when his father moved his family from the north to Raleigh, North Carolina.[1] It was 1968, and Raleigh was still very much a southern town. Every time Sedaris spoke, it was evident that he wasn't a local; he was frequently beaten up and called "Yankee" both at school and Boy Scouts. Adding to that stress was Sedaris's private understanding that he wasn't like the other boys. "You don't have a word for being gay when you're in the second grade, you know?" he says. Other boys seemed to play their roles "effortlessly," while Sedaris lived in fear that he would disappoint everyone, including members of his own family, if they ever found out he was gay. He felt constant anxiety from "trying to pass for a normal boy."

It was around this time that Sedaris began showing the first signs of what he now believes to have been a form of juvenile Tourette's. In class, he felt compelled to lick the light switch, for example, or to hit himself in the forehead with his shoe. He also began forcefully rolling his eyes, intentionally causing himself pain, and in a way, that soothed him. In his essay "A Plague of Tics," from his book *Naked,* Sedaris also describes his tendency toward what would clinically be referred to as obsessive-compulsive disorder:

> It was a short distance from the school to our rented house, no more than six hundred and thirty-seven steps, and on a good day I could make the trip in an hour, pausing every few feet to tongue a mailbox or touch whichever single leaf or blade of grass demanded my attention. If I were to lose count of my steps, I'd have to return to the school and begin again. . . . I wanted to be at home more than anything, it was getting there that was the problem. I might touch the telephone pole at step three hundred and fourteen and then, fifteen paces later, worry that I hadn't touched it in exactly the right spot. It needed to be touched again. Bypass that mailbox and my brain would never for one moment let me forget it. I might be sitting at the dinner table, daring myself not to think about it, and the thought would revisit my mind. *Don't think about it.* But it would already be too late and I knew then exactly what I had to do. Excusing myself to go to the bathroom, I'd walk out the front door and return to the mailbox, not just touching but jabbing, practically pounding on the thing because I thought I hated it so much. What I really hated, of course, was my mind. There must have been an off switch somewhere, but I was damned if I could find it.[2]

The behaviors that Sedaris describes in exquisite and painful detail are compulsions that he felt an irresistible urge to perform in response to anxious, obsessional thoughts. People with this kind of obsessive-compulsive response to anxiety may or may not be aware of the feelings that are driving this behavior, but they construe the ritual activities as being protective in some way. For a brief time, this activity can even provide relief from anxiety. However, this short-lived relief becomes the very thing that provides the positive reinforcement to keep the same cycle in place—a cycle of anxious, obsessional thought leading to protective compulsive behavior, leading to relief, and then back to anxious thought again.

Throughout high school, Sedaris exhibited symptoms of anxiety that interfered with his quality of life to an exceptionally painful degree. It's unfortunate and worth noting that the same word we use to describe his condition, we also use to describe our feelings about a high-pressure day at the office. The word *anxiety,* in all of its derivations, is among the most overused in the English language. In urban areas, in high-powered fields, in competitive academic environments, feeling anxious is not only accepted as a matter of course, it's worn as a badge of honor. If you're not anxious, the assumption is that you're not working hard enough. If asked which they would prefer, a child who was utterly calm and unperturbed about taking the SAT or a child who was anxious and worried about taking the test, in my clinical and personal experience many parents would choose the latter. A high level of stress is seen as indicative of caring, and of being likelier to apply oneself seriously to a task.

There is some truth to this perception. The elevated levels of vigilance and concern associated with anxiety do in fact yield a child more likely to study for the test than to blow it off. However, when taken to a pathological extreme, anxiety doesn't motivate, it paralyzes. The child becomes so anxious about the test that she freezes and can't finish it. The performer physically can't get onstage because he's so frightened of failing. Other manifestations of anxiety, such as phobias and obsessional thinking, can so severely interfere with daily life that, like David Sedaris, individuals feel as if they are being held hostage by their own brains. This degree of anxiety is not beneficial in any way, nor should it be equated with non-pathological stress. Lena Dunham, writer and creator of the HBO series *Girls,* devoted an episode of that show to her character's relapse into obsessive-compulsive disorder. In an interview about the episode, Dunham reflected on her own experience with OCD.[3] "It's something that I've struggled with," she said. "So I feel as though I am able to shed a certain kind of light on the experience and do something that doesn't necessarily feel cookie cutter. One of my biggest pet peeves is when people [say], 'I just love it when my room's clean; I'm so OCD!' It's like, actually no, you're just a neat person and not a slob animal."

Most people with a diagnosed anxiety disorder have one or more family members with some type of anxiety disorder.[4] There is certainly an element of genetic loading for anxiety, but this biological predisposition is not an all-or-nothing phenomenon. Early life stressors can increase the likelihood that someone with any predisposition will succumb to an anxiety disorder, especially if they have few methods of coping with the stress being introduced. In Sedaris's case, having a chaotic home environment and fearing the discovery of what seems an unacceptable sexual identity are genuine stressors that could increase the likelihood of the expression of anxiety.

Considering how debilitating the effects of anxiety can be, and how many people suffer from it—by some estimates as much as a third of the population—it's reassuring to note that in my experience as a clinician it is also one of the most treatable disorders. Very often it's treatable via behavioral therapy alone. In addition, it's clearly the case that some common qualities of the person with anxiety—alertness, diligence, attention to detail, perfectionism, drive to perform well—can be distinctly beneficial. While David Sedaris's constant awareness of his differences was painful to him, that same hyperattention to detail is a hallmark of his writing. The key, as with all other brain disorders, is to harness those benefits while mitigating the negatives.

When he was young, Sedaris's obsessiveness was wild and uncontrolled, but as he got older he learned to focus the impulse. So, for example, those wild desires transformed into a rigid need to clean house on a specific day at a specific time—and there was no question of ever doing it on a different day or time. Arguably, cleaning house might interfere with one's social life if taken to an extreme degree, but it certainly has practical benefits as well. Over the years, Sedaris's compulsivity softened somewhat. Now he describes his obsessiveness as "tamed"—and to some degree, tamed obsessiveness is essentially discipline. This discipline could explain how he has managed to write so many successful books while also maintaining a dizzying schedule of performing around the world.

David Sedaris is perhaps the quintessential example of someone who was able to transform his neurologically based irrational impulses into a highly controlled—and effective—ability to stay on task. Moreover, his desire for control didn't only give him remarkable focus, it also drove him to want to be funny. When he was attending the Art Institute of Chicago, he noticed that when other students presented their work to the professor in front of the class, they behaved as if they were talking alone to a therapist, rather than being conscious of the fact that there were at least twenty people in the room also listening. He was astounded that these students weren't more attentive to their audience. So when it was Sedaris's turn, he invariably made it his mission to make everyone laugh. Simply sensing the energy in the room wasn't enough for him. He needed auditory proof that the audience was with him, that he was controlling their responses.

Multiple factors separate the person with clinical anxiety who can ultimately function well from the one who cannot. Severity of symptoms is only one piece of the puzzle. Good treatment is another important piece. Beyond those concrete factors, there are a host of intangible qualities that enable someone with the right combination of talent, drive, and manageable anxiety to perform extraordinarily well under pressure.

WHAT IT MEANS TO HAVE ANXIETY

What we refer to as anxiety encompasses a large number of behaviors and experiences. Because we use the word to connote everything from mild symptoms of stress to pathological conditions, it's important to understand the significant biological differences between a stress response to individual circumstances and an anxiety disorder.

Human beings, like all animals, experience a fight-or-flight response when faced with danger, releasing adrenaline. In biological terms, this rush of adrenaline is called autonomic discharge, and it results in an increase in heart rate, breathing rate, and sweating. When the body senses danger, these physical changes occur first—before any conscious reaction. This is evolution's way of having us act quickly, and without thinking, thereby improving our odds of survival. Only after this physiological response has kicked in are signals of awareness sent back to the brain. At moments of external threat, it may seem to us that we are thinking nervous thoughts first, then experiencing nervousness in our bodies; however, it's quite the opposite.

This is the level at which fear and anxiety can seem similar. The anxious person has the same fight-or-flight response—and in some cases experiences the same physical panic, agitation, cold sweat, and itchiness—that anyone can feel when adrenaline begins to pump in response to a threat. However, the person with anxiety isn't reacting to immediate danger, but rather to worry about what might happen. This is certainly the case for those with generalized anxiety disorder (GAD), who tend to compulsively worry about "what-ifs." People who suffer from GAD can spend the majority of their time obsessively turning over negative outcomes and countermeasures. In milder forms, this kind of worry can be preventive—the student who is worried enough about the test to study harder is likelier to do better than the student who knows she's smart and trusts that she'll do well. However, that same worried student might feel that she has to study all night, thereby hurting her performance the next day. Or she might even freeze and be unable to complete the test at all.

Post-traumatic stress disorder (PTSD) also falls under the umbrella of anxiety disorders, although rather than the free-floating "what-ifs" of GAD, these physical and emotional responses have a specific basis in fear—as in the case of the military veteran whose body and emotions continue to react as if threat is ongoing. In such cases it might be tempting to argue that it is the trauma that causes the anxiety and not the brain's neurological wiring; however, overall, only about 20 percent of adults who experience a trauma will develop PTSD. Women are twice as likely as men to develop PTSD, and the severity of the trauma also impacts whether PTSD will be experienced. For example, 49 percent of rape victims will experience PTSD. For this reason, it can be misleading to assign one figure to the likelihood that trauma will lead directly to PTSD. More often than not, trauma does not result in PTSD.[5] Whether you are particularly at risk for developing PTSD after a trauma is partly due to genetics—in that there does seem to be an increased risk if one or more family members have also experienced it—and partly to environment.[6] Early life trauma can significantly increase your risk of experiencing PTSD in response to adult trauma. A study of Vietnam veterans with PTSD found higher rates of childhood physical abuse (26 percent) than among veterans without PTSD (7 percent). It appears that when a child endures emotional trauma, the undeveloped brain's neurology is altered and primed for fear-based problems later in life.[7] As with many neurological disorders, genes and environment work in tandem.

Panic disorder and agoraphobia are related anxiety disorders. It is possible to have a single panic attack and never develop a panic disorder, and it's possible to have panic attacks or panic disorder without agoraphobia. However in those with a tendency toward anxiety and panic attacks (both of which appear to have a genetic component), the panic attack itself can become a source of dread. The time between attacks can be haunted by fear and worry about having another. If the anxiety of experiencing another panic attack becomes severe enough, the individual can come to fear any kind of public exposure or engagement, and agoraphobia results.

Phobias, including social anxiety disorder, are also anxiety disorders, and taken as a group they are the most common of the anxiety disorders. They range from a fear of spiders, which is not all that life affecting (especially in urban areas), to social anxiety disorder, which can have an acutely negative impact on quality of life. A fear of being in certain social situations can generalize into a cascade of thoughts about being judged negatively and embarrassed in public. This can lead to extremes of avoidance, and a retreat from public life.

Clinically, obsessive-compulsive personality disorder (OCPD) and obsessive-compulsive disorder (OCD) are two separate diagnoses. OCPD is typically expressed as an extreme rigidity with regard to finances and routines. Simply put, the person with OCPD copes with his anxiety by attempting to control his environment. This can have positive impact—a balanced checkbook, diligence at work—but at pathological levels it can be damaging. Think of the spouse, for example, who controls the finances to such a degree that it leads to arguments, or the person who takes diligence at work to workaholic levels. OCD, on the other hand, is associated with repetitive behaviors such as those that David Sedaris experienced. Obsessive checking would also fall under that category. Anyone with mild levels of anxiety might check for his wallet or phone more than once, but the person with OCD will check over and over, well past the point of rationality.

Both OCD and OCPD tend to run in families, suggesting that there may be a genetic component, and functional magnetic resonance imaging (fMRI) shows differences in the communication between the front parts of the brain (where reasoning occurs) and deeper structures in the brain (where fear and anxiety originate).[8] We still do not know what exactly causes this difference in circuitry. There is some disagreement in therapeutic circles as to whether OCPD and OCD belong under the heading of anxiety disorders. The DSM-5 removed OCD from the umbrella of anxiety and now considers it as being an impulse-control disorder. Nonetheless, many clinicians continue to consider OCPD and OCD along the continuum of anxiety. The reality is that what is true of the experience of anxiety is also true of OCPD and OCD. That is, people suffering from anxiety, OCPD, and OCD all experience anxious thoughts in a continuous loop that they find impossible to break.

Many people, especially children, have magical "protective" thoughts that they use as a defense against anxiety. For example, children who say "step on a crack, break my mother's back" and then avoid stepping on any cracks, do so as a way to cope with their conscious or unconscious anxiety about their mother's safety—or possibly, it is an expression of their anxiety about separating from their mothers. Adults do similar things—counting, having "lucky numbers," or adhering to particular random routines that they associate with a positive outcome. In the person without an anxiety disorder, anxious thoughts float away at some point—they dissipate. However, in the person with OCPD or OCD, the thoughts become sticky. So, for example, the fear that robbers might break into the house might cause an anxious feeling, which might then inspire an individual to check the doors and make sure they're locked. Once this is done, the individual experiences a decrease in anxiety, and the thought that robbers might break in is rationally dismissed. However, when anxiety, OCPD, and OCD are present, the thought is not so easily dismissed. In addition, the process of checking the door becomes a positive reinforcement of the original thought loop. That is: "Robbers might break in. I need to check the door. I have checked the door, and now I feel safe. Therefore, I will check the door again, and I will feel safe again." The more this pattern is repeated, the stronger the neurological connection between safety and checking becomes, and the less the original impulse is bound to any sort of reality. In fact, the content of the anxious thought itself is not very important, and may move around and morph—the person suffering from OCD or OCPD may be obsessed by germs and contamination and then move to counting and checking.

Anxiety disorders are the most commonly occurring brain difference. In any given twelve-month period, just under 20 percent of the adult population will experience anxiety, and 23 percent of those cases will be "classified as 'severe.'"[9] Depending on the specific symptoms and the severity, either psychodynamic psychotherapy, behavioral therapy, or pharmaceuticals (or some combination of these three) can have a tremendously positive and almost immediate impact. People with anxiety disorders also tend to be supremely self-aware patients. They recognize the ways in which their anxiety has impacted their lives—that they have begun to avoid social situations that cause them anxiety, or that they have become unable to fly on planes or cross bridges, or that they put off doing important tasks because their perfectionism has tipped over into a pathological fear of failure. While diagnosing other brain disorders can require a great deal of investigative work on the part of clinicians, typically the person suffering from anxiety is able to say, "I feel afraid a lot of the time. I worry a lot, and not always about specific things that I can control." In addition, people with anxiety—including those who are ultimately diagnosed with OCPD or OCD—will readily report that they feel the anxiety in their bodies, and can describe in specific detail the physical sensations of jumpiness and agitation that they experience.

This heightened awareness is at the heart of what can be the greatest upside of anxiety. Across the spectrum of anxiety disorders, one of the primary characteristics of anxiety is hypervigilance. It's basic common sense to assert that someone who is more aware of potential pitfalls can work to prevent them, and this conclusion isn't just anecdotal. Multiple studies have shown that people with anxiety are in fact better able to accurately assess emotion in others, predict outcomes, and even perform to a higher standard at work. A University of Cambridge study found that those with generalized anxiety disorder were not only more capable of reading facial threat than the control group, they were also better able to accurately read happiness in faces.[10] In other words, people with anxiety are more attentive across the board, not just in the areas that particularly worry them.

A State University of New York study of individuals with and without diagnosed GAD found that a high degree of worry correlates positively with intelligence in people with anxiety (in people without diagnosed anxiety, the inverse was true).[11] This means that among those with anxiety, actively worrying does not interfere with the ability to perform well intellectually. Moreover, those with more severe anxiety are more likely to have higher IQs. At the same time, individuals without an anxiety disorder will perform less well on mental tests when they are actively worrying.[12] When examining brain scans, researchers found that both worry and intelligence involved a reduction of metabolic substrate in the brain's white matter. Using a combination of verbal evaluations and other assessments as well as the brain imaging, researchers concluded that intelligence may have coevolved with worry in humans.[13]

Theoretically, a certain amount of worry is not only healthy, but desirable in maintaining a species. According to Barbara Milrod, an expert in the field of anxiety disorders in adults and children, anxiety may also be "something with a selective advantage," in addition to being a troubling set of symptoms.[14] That is, it is evolutionarily advantageous that not everyone in a population is risk-taking. "If you think about population genetics," Milrod says, "if a third of people suffer from this, clearly there's a selection bias that ensures the persistence of anxiety. Otherwise it would die out. There's a reason why it's still around—it imparts a selective advantage."

In addition, giftedness and ability can be sharpened by manageable levels of anxiety. A study conducted among M.B.A. students at UCLA's Anderson School of Management found that those who self-identified as more neurotic (describing themselves as often feeling anxious and guilty) positively impressed others when they participated in team projects as compared with self-identified extroverts.[15] A University of Wales Department of Psychology study found that among individuals with greater ability, the tendency to worry correlated positively with workplace performance. Researchers posited that anxiety is "an important component of motivated cognition, essential for efficient functioning in situations that require caution, self-discipline, and the general anticipation of threat."

As with all brain differences, the degree to which the benefits can be utilized is in direct proportion with how well the downsides are mitigated. On the milder end of the inverted U-shaped curve of anxiety, an individual exhibiting the classically driven, type A personality might be fueled by her anxiety—motivated to perfect her performance, to achieve, and to avoid failure. Even those with more severe symptoms can find ways to cope via therapy, drug intervention, and ingenious work-arounds, while also drawing on the positive attributes of anxiety to perform exceptionally well in school and in their chosen careers. While it's true that severe, untreated anxiety can be debilitating, a diagnosis of an anxiety disorder is in no way a life sentence. Treatment is tremendously effective, and the acute benefits of hypervigilance to potential pitfalls and difficulties are too real to be ignored.

THE EXPERIENCE OF HAVING GENERALIZED ANXIETY DISORDER

While a star athlete might relish the feeling of amped-up excitement that precedes a game, no one with a diagnosed anxiety disorder would claim to enjoy the symptoms. The unbearable feelings associated with extreme stress are what bring the individual with severe anxiety into the doctor's office—the public panic attacks that render the person terribly embarrassed (or worse, fearing the onset of a heart attack), or the desperate feeling that no matter how hard the patient might try, she simply can't turn off or even dim her constant cascade of worries. The experience of anxiety penetrates every part of life—it's as inescapable as our own emotions.

CHALLENGES OF LIVING WITH ANXIETY

David Sedaris hated gym class more than any other part of his school day. "You'd just do anything to get out of it," he says. "You'd throw yourself down the stairs and you'd just pray that you could break a leg. You know, you'd stay home sick, you would invent illnesses, anything to get out of that anxiety of walking into the locker room, and the anxiety of being on the field, or on the court, or anything like that." There is a reason that so many adults look back on high school and shudder. Even for the nonanxious, high school is a minefield. For someone like David Sedaris, it was a minefield in shark-infested waters. "You know, I wish that someone had told me when I was in high school, nothing will ever be this hard again. It's unfair that the hardest moments that you'll have to live with are when you're fourteen to eighteen. But, you know, there it is."

The social component of school is difficult on its own—as is the very experience of adolescence—and when an enormous pressure to perform is added into the mix, it's no wonder that so many teenagers now complain of anxiety. In my clinical experience, many of these are children who are simply overworked. However, when anxious feelings intrude on the child's ability to enjoy life, then the problem has gone beyond having too much homework.

Sixteen-year-old Sidney, who was diagnosed with dyslexia in childhood, also exhibits strong symptoms of anxiety.[16] It's common among children with learning differences to present with anxiety (in fact, this can be the first indication that a learning difference exists). It makes sense that a struggle to keep up with peers would yield distress, but in addition there is some indication that brain differences travel in pairs—what is called, rather ominously, comorbidity. The overall comorbidity between learning differences and other brain disorders is a massive 62.2 percent.[17] The likely reason is that these are all genetically influenced disorders involving dysfunctions in cortical connectivity. *Cortical* refers to the cortex, the outer layer of the cerebrum, which consists of a large percentage of the folded gray matter of the brain and is greatly responsible for higher-level thinking. ADD and dyslexia are the result of differences in how the cortex's neural pathways operate. Although science has not yet pinpointed what either of these pathways is, it appears that the pathways of many learning differences and disorders overlap. Therefore, when a pathway is not functioning as it typically should, it will often affect more than one area of brain activity.

Sidney feels her anxiety in a highly physical way. "When I was a kid, every day before I went to school, I'd throw up in my dad's car. I didn't throw up in any other cars. Just his car, right before school." She still gets terrible stomachaches when she feels particularly stressed. Anxiety, she says, "manifests physically for me, I think, more than it does emotionally. I wouldn't think, Oh, my God, I'm so anxious in my head, I'd feel, Oh, my God, I think I'm gonna throw up." When she felt anxious in class, sometimes her skin would crawl and itch so badly that she'd scratch her forearms until she bled.

The greatest source of Sidney's anxiety now is in trying to keep up. She's aware that it takes her longer than classmates to do her work. "I always feel like no matter when I start something or what I do, that I never have enough time to finish." To make matters worse, like most teenagers, Sidney is running on a constant sleep deficit. She would love to go to bed early, but there simply isn't enough time in the day. She wakes up at 6 a.m. and commutes to school an hour each way. Then she has hours of homework. She also has an after-school job at a museum three days a week. A high school student this busy who works this hard is not unusual. Far too many teens find themselves overscheduled, overextended, overworked, and overwhelmed.

According to John Walkup, director of the Division of Child and Adolescent Psychiatry at Weill Cornell Medical College, one of the central questions to ask when evaluating a child or adolescent for anxiety is whether the child's stress level is expectable and proportionate to his or her situation.[18] So, for example, the child who has multiple finals in a given week is going to quite naturally feel stress. However, if she has the ability to do well, then that stress should remain manageable. Similarly, if the child does not have the ability to perform up to expectations, then that is an entirely logical cause for feeling anxious and overwhelmed, and what needs to be addressed is not the child's anxiety, but rather his expectations. Walkup points out that there is a very clear difference between the child who reports feeling stressed about her workload and the child who freezes in the face of it. "That's why I like to talk about pathological anxiety. Pathological anxiety is disproportionate to the situation. It lies in the background and then is triggered by relatively routine events—going to school, thunderstorms, or ordering food in a restaurant." To some extent, he notes, performance pressure can be motivating. What is not motivating, however, is becoming so flooded with anxiety that we simply shut down. Being flooded by routine events is the characteristic of pathological anxiety. Anxiety is a negative emotion with high physiological arousal, whereas excitement is positive emotional content with the same high arousal. Your body may be feeling the same way, but it is the content in your mind that varies. This is why sometimes it is actually difficult to tell whether you are excited or anxious, and why sometimes excitement, which feels like anxiety, can change into anxiety if you start to think negative thoughts. So, for example, excitement about a date or a party invitation might turn into anxiety if the individual begins to consider possible negative outcomes or sources of insecurity.

Adolescents have many reasons in their daily lives to feel both excited and anxious. Meanwhile, parents of high school students experience tremendous pressure themselves, and this can create an unhealthy feedback loop between parent and child. The last few years of high school can feel like the parents' final shot at seeing their children off into the world well settled and well equipped, and it can be jarring for both generations when parents transition from nurturing caretakers to drillmasters. Parents feel responsible for building their children's college résumés, so instead of encouraging their children to sleep more, as they might have done in grade school or middle school, they are more likely to push their children to study harder and to do more. We drill it into students that they cannot simply be good academically—in order to get into a good college they must be *stellar* academically, and also participate in multiple extracurricular activities, and come up with revolutionary ways to distinguish themselves from all the other college applicants.

This can create a strange tension in the parent-child relationship. John

Walkup notes that some adolescents who have been successfully treated for anxiety disorder begin to relax with regard to their schoolwork. At that point, he says, they look around and say, "Listen, I am not afraid of failure anymore. I want to work really hard and do stuff, but I don't want to be crazy, either. I like how I feel. My body's comfortable again. I can sleep at night." Then, something odd can occur. "Parents may notice a slump from all As to four As and two Bs. And they'll say, 'What the hell is happening with my kid? He was all As before.'" To that Walkup responds, "He's beginning to smell the roses."[19]

While anxiety might be described by a layperson as an excess of emotion, in truth the experience of anxiety can act as a block on every emotion *other than* anxiety. Journalist David Adam, who explored his experiences with obsessive-compulsive disorder in his memoir, *The Man Who Couldn't Stop,* says, "I always said that OCD kind of took away emotions, in a way. Anything that happened to me that would normally cause an emotion, like, to make me sad or anxious or angry—didn't seem to hit me as it did other people, because I was already preoccupied. Equally, maybe I didn't take as much pleasure from some stuff as some people would. Ironically, everybody throughout my whole life has always said that I am incredibly laid-back, very relaxed about things. They didn't know, of course, that I was hugely anxious. I think there is a degree to which when you are that concerned about something which is so important to you, everything else seems trivial."[20]

David Adam does not describe himself as having been an anxious child, and when his OCD kicked in it was as if a switch had been flipped in his brain. While in college, an offhand remark from a friend—that he might have contracted HIV from a sexual encounter—settled into Adam's mind and became an unshakeable fear. No number of negative blood tests could reassure him, and he continued to irrationally worry about contamination with HIV, despite the fact that he was a highly educated science writer who knew that his fears weren't based in any kind of fact. The fear overwhelmed his ability to reason with himself, and it became all-encompassing. Despite this, he managed to hide his obsession for nearly twenty years. It wasn't until his compulsions began to impact his daughter's life that he finally sought treatment for his OCD. In his case, an antidepressant has proven effective.

His story raises a fascinating aspect of the experience of anxiety, which is that while people with anxiety are hyperaware and hypervigilant, they can also be highly obsessive. And any obsession, by definition, has a way of taking over one's focus. When taken to an extreme, anxiety and obsessiveness can cause one's vision and one's world to tighten and grow smaller. The anxiety and obsessions dominate and shove aside all other emotions. Nothing else compares to the urgency of the anxiety and one's desire to alleviate it. Prior to seeking out treatment, the only route for the anxious person wishing to mitigate their fears is to avoid altogether what causes them to feel frightened in the first place.

DEVELOPING WORK-AROUNDS

In 2004, ABC news anchor Dan Harris experienced a widely viewed public panic attack on live television during an episode of *Good Morning America*.[21] He'd reported from dangerous war zones, but never before had he experienced the overwhelming loss of control that he endured in that moment. The incident inspired him to completely reevaluate his life. In the immediate aftermath, he sought professional help for understanding the cause of the attack and preventing further attacks (he would eventually have another). To his credit, he was open with his doctor about his recreational drug use, a weekend cocaine habit he'd picked up since returning home from multiple war-torn postings. His doctor informed him that the effect of the drugs on his already anxious brain was to elevate the levels of adrenaline in his body, thereby resulting in an overwhelming fight-or-flight response.

Harris came from a family in which "worry was venerated, you know? My dad has this expression, 'The price of security is insecurity.' I later

learned that that actually wasn't so much his personal motto, it was actually something he invented to make me, his worrying son, feel better about
all the worrying that I was doing." But Harris wasn't the only worrier in
the family; his father was a "pacer and a wringer of hands." By the time
Harris was nine years old, he became "freaked out by the prospect of
nuclear war." His fears were so acute that his parents allowed him to participate in a landmark study conducted by William Beardslee at Harvard,
which looked into the emotional impact of the threat of nuclear war on
children.

However, despite the ways in which Harris's greater-than-average
levels of anxiety have caused him both shame and pain over the years,
ultimately he feels that his hypervigilance gives him "an edge. I believe
that a certain amount of stress and striving and plotting and planning is
inherent in success. Whether you're talking about your career or parenting or grandparenting or volunteer work or art—any human endeavor—a
certain amount of worrying, really, is important." Harris couldn't have
come to that conclusion, however, if he hadn't been able to manage and
work around the challenges of his anxiety. For him, the practice of meditation has made all the difference. "We tend to make our suffering worse—
worse than it needs to be—and what mindfulness helps you do is draw
the line between what I call 'constructive anguish' and 'useless rumination.' And so, you are getting the good, strategic worry and less of the
useless worry that constricts the mind, makes you tighten up, become less
creative, less open, less kind—and harder to live with."

In addition to meditation, Harris follows his doctor's advice to take
excellent care of himself. He eats well, sleeps well, and exercises regularly,
all of which has given him deep reserves for coping when under pressure.
"The other thing I do is to prepare very well. The days I do the best are
when I really have learned as much as possible about all the stories that
we are doing—even if I'm not going to use that information, I just . . .
feel more confident." Thanks to all that preparation, when he is performing in the moment, he's not preoccupied with worry, rather he can be

truly present. "I can be aware of what's actually happening, and reacting to things as they happen, instead of [fearing or being distracted by] things I'm imagining might happen."

Still, Harris stresses, there must be an endpoint to the preparation—there must come a moment at which you believe that you can perform under pressure. He credits his meditation teacher, Joseph Goldstein, with providing his most helpful mantra. "The seventeenth time that you're worrying about all of the awful consequences of, say, missing a flight—maybe ask yourself, 'Is this useful?' It's a great corrective to those of us who venerate anxiety and worry. Yes, the first sixteen times you were worrying about making a plan B and C for what's going to happen if you miss the flight, those were useful—but, by the seventeenth time, maybe it's better to think about something else."

High school student Sidney has found that having greater control over her own time eases her feelings of anxiety tremendously. Her mother has been allowing her more unstructured time with her friends and has eased her curfew, which makes Sidney feel less constrained. In addition, she makes sure that she gets to do things that she genuinely enjoys. While this doesn't serve to make her schedule less full, it does give her great pleasure. At one point, she was tempted to quit her job at the museum, since she was so anxious about having time for her schoolwork. However, "honestly, it's something that makes me excessively happy. So, it was worth it, and I find the happier I am, the better things become, even if they're stressful."

Sidney went through a dark period of anxiety during her first few years of high school, but at a certain point she experienced a shift in attitude. "I became considerably more self-aware. I understood that if I wanted to be happy, I had to strive toward the person I would like to be, rather than making excuses or just procrastinating. And then I realized that I can't hang out with people who are going to make me make bad decisions, or who really influence or impact me poorly."

Sidney's mother, Lisa, has helped Sidney cope with her anxiety.[22] She has done so actively sometimes, and at other times by knowing when to hang back and not pressure. When Sidney is growing overanxious or im-patient with an assignment, "sometimes I'll tell her not to work on some-thing for a while. I tell her to walk away, because she gets very frustrated if she can't get something right away." She's also petitioning the College Board to allow Sidney to take the SAT in a separate room. "She gets a lot of anxiety in testing—crazy anxiety. I think it's the comparing" herself to other students' progress on the test that exacerbates her panic. "Are they done yet? Oh my God. They're racing through!"

Lisa is also learning when to push her daughter to communicate and when to leave her alone. Sidney, quite understandably, doesn't like to dis-cuss anxiety-provoking topics at the dinner table. "Sidney said to me, 'I don't want to hear talk about college or school at the dinner table.'" Then she went on to give Lisa a list of stressful topics that she wanted to be off-limits. Lisa said, "Well, what can I talk about? There's nothing left to talk about." While this can be challenging when a parent is trying to connect with her child, nonetheless it's a positive development for Sidney and her mother. As Lisa says, "She knows her triggers."

The only treatment that Sidney is currently receiving for anxiety is acu-puncture and an herbal supplement. Lisa found that the supplements helped her own acute anxiety, and she's noticed an improvement in Sidney as well. "I mean, it's not 100 percent better, but I do see it sort of takes the edge off." Sidney's stomach problems have lessened considerably.

David Sedaris has come to find the right balance between disengaging from his problematic obsessional thinking and productively focusing his obsessive brain. While, as a writer, it can be helpful for him to mull and ponder, "sometimes it's not good for me to be with my thoughts." He of-ten finds himself thinking of long-past events, "wishing that I had behaved differently, wishing that I had said the right thing, or wishing that I had spoken my mind, instead of trying to hide it to make it look like it wasn't really bothering me or it was no big deal." But that kind of obsessional thinking "doesn't do me any good, and it's actually kind of painful." To stave off obsessional thinking, Sedaris likes to entertain himself with podcasts and books on tape. "They can kind of protect you from your obsessive thoughts that you return to over and over and over and over and over and over again. If it's not a very good book on tape, then my obsessional thinking can win, and I am walking along, and I am thinking, Oh, I haven't really listened to this in twenty minutes, because I'm thinking about something that happened, like, twenty-five years ago.' "

Notably, Sedaris's obsessional thinking kicks in hardest when he's bored—"if I am doing housework, or if I am doing the dishes or swimming." Swimming in particular turns on the obsessional thoughts. "There's nothing you can listen to." While swimming, Sedaris would obsessively ponder past relationships, one in particular that involved a lot of breaking up and making up. "I remember thinking other people didn't do [as much obsessing as] I was doing, you know? Like, other people would break up with somebody and then they could go out and they could go to the movies and they could go to dinner with friends, and they weren't thinking about it every second, you know? They didn't think about it from the moment they woke up. That was a certain kind of person who did that, and it was the kind of person who I was—and it was the kind of person you really didn't want to get involved with."

Always, for Sedaris, the work-around is to concentrate his mind on something else. Writing, in particular, is a break from his obsessional rumination. "The world is messy." In his writing, though, he can "control things" and also "put it to order, or make it small enough so you can understand it. Every morning, I sit down and I write in my diary, and that's what I'm kind of doing—is putting my world in order. Nothing quite makes sense to me until I write it down. It puts it in perspective for me."

GIFTS OF THE BRAIN WITH ANXIETY

Although David Sedaris's hypervigilance and obsessional thinking often cause him pain, they also provide him with practically endless fodder for his writing. Sedaris finds it interesting that other people don't recall the minute details of what occupied their thoughts at a particular point in time. When he asks his boyfriend, Hugh, for example, what Hugh was thinking about while painting a picture, "he never has an answer for me. Whereas, I could give very detailed answers if somebody had asked me that same question."

This attention to details that others miss—whether the details of their own thought processes or of the environment around them—is characteristic of people with anxiety. Perhaps one of the most famous examples of obsessive attention to detail put to positive use is Charles Darwin.[23] While diagnosing a historical figure can be risky business, there is ample historical and biographical evidence revealing that Darwin had a predisposition toward anxiety. Others in his family also reportedly suffered from anxiety disorders, and Darwin himself had a blood phobia that caused him to reject the field of medicine (unlike his father and grandfather before him).

Darwin suffered what appears to have been his first panic attack while contemplating embarking on his initial trip on the *Beagle*. Very likely the cause was his acute separation anxiety with regard to leaving his family for such an extended period of time. Darwin had tremendous fears of abandonment, having lost his mother at the age of eight, and having essentially lost his father to grief at the same time. He described feeling panicky and enduring an eruption of rashes and stomach discomfort. He would experience other such attacks of anxiety throughout his life, but especially in the setting of loss. His anxiety also bubbled up when he assumed new responsibilities, such as marriage, the birth of his children, and his moral conflict regarding his development of a theory that would directly confront and contradict most people's religious beliefs.[24]

Darwin's physical complaints were practically textbook psychosomatic in nature—stomach pain, nausea, flatulence, and rashes. It's fascinating to note that one of his areas of research was on the nature of blushing. He noted that only humans blush, women blush more than men, and babies do not blush at all, and posited that there was a genetic component to blushing. One wonders if his fascination with the subject was also personal in nature. In any case, it's clear that the very troubling and even embarrassing physical ailments he described caused him enormous anxiety when leaving home, and eventually caused him not to want to leave home at all. It's poignant to consider that a man who no doubt considered himself riven by physical weakness was exploring the concepts of survival of the fittest in nature. He often pondered why nature would be so cruel.[25]

On the timeline of Darwin's life, however, there is a parallel track of positive attributes and accomplishment. As a child, with an unusual degree of precision, he collected animal shells, birds' eggs, and minerals— behavior that anticipated his obsessive, repetitive, and precise collecting on board the *Beagle*. As an adult, Darwin was a granular observer, noticing change and adaptation that had previously been invisible to others. In addition, he was a prolific reader and he wrote—and aggressively revised his own writing—in an intense, perfectionist manner that would serve him and his revolutionary theory extremely well.

David Sedaris has channeled his perfectionism and desire for control into his own writing. As a child, he felt compelled to lick lightbulbs. As a young man, he had to clean the house on a certain day at a certain time. When he began writing and making art, he put himself on just as compulsive a schedule, much to his benefit. "Everything—everything, everything had its schedule. And so writing had its schedule, or when I was doing visual artwork, that kind of fell into its schedule, too, until it just became— until it just became who I am. I don't have to force myself to sit at my desk anymore, I just get up in the morning and I just go right there and do it. I don't have to force myself to do five hundred sit-ups every morning, I just do it."

Sedaris's diligence and obsessiveness didn't only contribute to the quantity of his output, but also positively affected its quality. He was twenty-seven years old when he returned to finish college and found himself in writing classes with eighteen-year-olds. He'd look around the class and find himself shocked at how relaxed the other students were. Very often, they'd written their stories the night before they were due. "And I remember thinking, You didn't write it seventeen times? What kind of a person are you? I mean, I figured that out pretty early. You just understand from the very beginning that a first draft is just a first draft and you don't want anybody to see it, because it's not worth being seen."

The other ingredient in Sedaris's success was sheer determination. "I really cannot believe that anybody ever wanted it more than me. That's all I ever fantasized about. In junior high school and high school I would walk for hours, or I would ride my bike for hours and hours, and that's all I ever thought about, was being somewhere and having somebody say, 'Wait a minute, aren't you?' Or, you know, having people come up and get their book signed. I've been practicing for that all my life, you know?"

Sedaris acknowledges that a significant element in his drive to succeed is the desire to prove himself to the naysayers—in particular, his own father, who attempted to make Sedaris conform by wearing him down. "I wouldn't trade my father for anyone. I'm so grateful to have the father that I did, because he was just there for me to work against all my life. You know, he would give me a piece of advice and I would just do exactly the opposite. When I was growing up he must have said to me one hundred thousand times—'Do you know what you are? A big, fat zero.' He said it over and over. 'Everything you touch turns to crap.' And I would just think, 'I'll show you.'"

Not long ago, Sedaris was talking to his father about a college fund that his father wanted to establish at a local Greek church. He asked Sedaris to contribute, and by way of explaining why he wanted to set up the scholarship, Sedaris's father said, "You know, when I die, the name dies with me." In response, Sedaris said, "Well, speak for yourself, my name is on ten million books."

It felt good for Sedaris to be able to say that. Even better for Sedaris is the knowledge that he's "celebrated for being exactly who I am. Not for hiding, not for lying, not for molding myself into anyone else's idea. I remember when I started on the radio, my father would say, 'Why do you have to talk about that for?' And nine times out of ten, what he was talking about was—you know, 'Why do you have to say the word "boyfriend"?' Or, you know, he was embarrassed because I had talked about cleaning apartments and he didn't want his friends knowing that that was my job. And I remember thinking, Well, it's working. I am being me. I'm not hiding anything. I am exactly who I am, and people like it."

There is an inherent risk in pointing out the positive elements of any brain difference—namely, that in doing so one minimizes the considerable pain and suffering of the negative symptoms. With anxiety disorders, it can be particularly difficult to see upsides. It's not as if one can look at a brain scan and see exactly where a talent or acuity correlates with the experience of anxiety. Moreover, as with all difficult-to-treat chemical disorders, the unchecked symptoms can wholly take over one's existence. David Adam, who suffered for years due to his irrational fear of contracting HIV, is hard-pressed to see a direct correlation between OCD and any particular strength that he possesses. In fact, he says that prior to that switch being flipped in his brain, he considered himself fairly calm and even-keeled. Even he, however, has found that there has been one benefit, "if you want to call it a benefit—it's that I like doing things that quiet the chatter in my head. And one of them is public speaking. You know, lots of people get very anxious about standing up in public, whereas I really enjoy it, and that's because I have to really concentrate on what I'm doing. And so those intrusive thoughts about HIV tend not to bother me while I'm doing that."

Moreover, Adam says, "I don't look for reasons to be miserable now, because I know that they can be thrust upon you."

HOW PEOPLE WITH
ANXIETY CAN FLOURISH

When the symptoms of anxiety are severe, we don't have the luxury of contemplating what our strengths are. In fact, even those who have experienced moderate and isolated bursts of panic know that no other thought is possible in those moments. The idea that the panic might end, that some rational thought process can be applied to end the anxiety—that simply does not compute. The first step, therefore, in ensuring a better, more fulfilling, more productive life with anxiety is to seek treatment.

According to Barbara Milrod, the average amount of time before the person with anxiety seeks treatment is ten years. This is extraordinary, considering how prevalent anxiety is. However, there is a big difference between saying that one is stressed—which, in fact, we are all expected to be if we are working hard enough—and saying that one's stress is unmanageable. The latter feels like failure. This is unfortunate, not least because anxiety is so treatable.

Contrary to the assumption that drugs are almost always required to alleviate symptoms, in fact, in the majority of cases, cognitive behavioral therapy alone can make all the difference. A meta-analysis of fifty-six effectiveness studies that was published in the *Journal of Consulting and Clinical Psychology* found that the contrast between pre- and post-therapy testing was large and positive.[26] This is why I strongly recommend that patients try at least eight sessions of cognitive behavioral therapy (CBT) prior to seeking a prescription. CBT is a structured therapy whereby the therapist incrementally and repeatedly exposes the patient to the feared situation or object so that the conditioned fear (and its associated response) can be extinguished. Drug treatment of a phobia—for example, a tranquilizer for someone with a fear of flying—simply throws a blanket over the problem, muffling it but not making it go away. However, CBT works with the brain's plasticity to truly sever that connection between the stressor and the individual's emotional response. That said, those who suffer from OCD, which can have a biological component, often do require a combination of medication (typically the class of drugs known as SSRIs) and cognitive behavioral therapy.

Multiple studies suggest that aerobic exercise has real and measurable positive impact on stress levels—both in protecting the body from the harmful effects of stress and in boosting physical and emotional resilience to stress.[27] Other self-help measures such as meditation and getting the proper amount of sleep have been shown to have positive impact. There is also some clinical evidence, though mixed, that acupuncture can have concrete benefits.[28] Indeed, because anxiety spurs the fight-or-flight response, anything that naturally relaxes the body can be beneficial. For those who have difficulty reaching a meditative state (which is not always easy for those who have obsessive thought patterns), muscle relaxation can be beneficial. Simply lie down and tighten, then relax, each muscle group, one by one.

Mentally, there are a few exercises that can help with symptoms. While the person in the throes of an obsessive thought (such as checking that the front door is locked) can feel that the impulse will never pass, in fact most obsessive behaviors don't last. One of the most effective forms of CBT is simply to instruct the patient not to do the thing that they feel compelled to do for just fifteen minutes. With repetition, that can help break the cycle of magical thinking (the thoughts that make the individual believe, If I do this, then disaster won't occur). The student who suffers from test anxiety can similarly break negative patterns by reminding herself at moments of panic that she can never be 100 percent sure that she will pass the test. This kind of self-talk is about learning to tolerate the anxiety, rather than convincing oneself that there is some predetermined amount of studying that will take all the risk away.

Sidney's mother, Lisa, has learned that her daughter reacts much more positively when she doesn't try to fix her problems, but rather simply listens to them. (This is good advice for any parent, or spouse, for that matter.) Sidney will say to her mother, " 'I just want to tell you about this. I don't want your advice.' And I'm like, 'All right. Okay. It's hard. But okay.' " From a clinical perspective, Sidney and her mother are on to something. John Walkup points out that many young adults who have been highly protected by their parents are smacked with their first experience of serious anxiety when they head off to college. Certainly being off on one's own for the first time is stressful for anyone, but some kids react to it better than others, and often the difference is in how emotionally prepared they are to cope with anxious feelings. We learn by doing—and if every anxious moment is eased away or medicated, adolescents never have the opportunity to develop those habits of resilience.

There is a right amount of anxiety that can spur us to action, that can keep us financially solvent, that can even keep us going to the doctor for annual checkups. A blithe belief that everything will turn out all right might be pleasant, but it's not realistic—not for us, and not for our children. As Barbara Milrod pointed out, wouldn't you rather have the child with a healthy degree of anxiety behind the wheel of the car, rather than the unworried risk-taker? The trick is in finding the right notch on the dial for us, the level that keeps us on our toes and doesn't freeze us in our tracks.

Dan Harris says, "it's like titration, and I'm constantly tweaking it, because, you know, I screw up." He had an experience recently that brought this home to him. After a gunman attacked the Canadian Parliament in 2014, he was sent to Toronto to cover the story. "Normally, when breaking news happens, I go into this high alert." This time, though, he didn't. "And I was kind of patting myself on the back for being pretty calm. I was really kind of telling myself a story—you know, I'm so evolved now. And I got there, and I did my story. Afterward, I got a note from my boss, Ben Sherwood, who is featured prominently in my book as somebody who likes to kick my ass—and he's like, 'Ya know what? You were pretty flat tonight. Your manner did not capture the urgency of the story.' And he was totally right. And so, the next day, I got it right. I mean, I wasn't out of my mind the way I used to be." He was examining all the angles, ensuring that his competitors didn't have anything that ABC News (his employer) didn't, but only "to the extent that I thought that it was useful. And you know, we got a lot of great elements, we had the appropriate urgency, and we did it right. And I wasn't a jerk to anybody, and I didn't make myself more miserable than I really needed to be. So, I am not here to tell you that I am perfect. I am constantly learning and failing."

In his highly regarded book *My Age of Anxiety,* longtime journalist and magazine editor Scott Stossel writes:

> Even if I can't fully recover from my anxiety, I've come to believe there may be some redeeming value in it. . . . My anxiety can be intolerable. It often makes me miserable. But it is also, maybe, a gift—or at least the other side of a coin I ought to think twice about before trading in. Perhaps my anxiety is linked to whatever limited moral sense I can claim. What's more, the same anxious imagination that sometimes drives me mad with worry also enables me to plan effectively for unforeseen circumstances or unintended consequences that other, less vigilant temperaments might not. The quick social judging that is allied to my performance anxiety is also useful in helping me to size up situations quickly and to manage people and defuse conflict.[29]

Stossel's assessment of his gifts speaks directly to the anxious individual's ongoing quest for a sweet spot between misery and complacency. We can all occasionally fear that if we lose even a bit of our—or our child's—perfectionism, then mediocrity is sure to follow. Similarly, we can fear that grappling with anxiety means that we simply can't hack it, that like one of Charles Darwin's inadaptable creatures, we're not cut out for surviving this world. In truth, the very opposite is true: these qualities of worry and hypervigilance and perfectionism can be the source of our greatest contributions.

4.

MELANCHOLY

COMMON DIAGNOSES
_____

DEPRESSION, DYSTHYMIA, AND DYSPHORIA

"If you banish the dragons, you banish the heroes."

—ANDREW SOLOMON

When Peter Lanza, father of Sandy Hook Elementary School shooter Adam Lanza, was finally ready to tell his story, he reached out to just one person whom he believed he could trust: Andrew Solomon.[1] Solomon is an enormously well-respected author and journalist, but there are many other journalists who could also have reported Lanza's story. Certainly major television networks would have paid big money for the exclusive interview. Yet, repeatedly in his work—especially in his National Book Critics Circle Award–winning book *Far from the Tree*—Solomon has displayed a remarkable skill for gaining the confidence of his interviewees. Solomon himself posits that the extraordinary psychological pain that he has experienced in his own life has given him unique compassion for others who suffer.

Today Andrew Solomon is happily married with children, and he has a highly successful career as a writer. However, he feels a constant awareness that he could lose everything. Throughout his life, Solomon suffered from depression. He continues to worry that he could fall into one of his deep clinical depressions and thus become incapable of working or maintaining his important relationships; or that he could die at a young age, like his mother and her father did. For Solomon, the clock is always ticking.

His first experience of major depression occurred when he was twenty-seven, and coincided with his mother's death. Now he can recall episodes as far back as adolescence that were indicators of depression. "I wasn't so symptomatic that I was unable to function. But it was not so great. So, it goes back a long way." He has written, and has wanted to be a writer, for at least as long a time. Except when he is in the most acute phases of depression, "I write even when I'm depressed. It's sort of a way through for me. It makes me feel like I'm still at least alive. So, there's a kind of redemptive function to writing when I'm depressed, and there's a kind of celebratory function to writing when I'm well."

Instead of allowing his sense of potential doom to paralyze him, he uses it as a well of creativity. In fact, he has felt the need to be in a dark place in order to accurately write about despair. "If you banish the dragons, you banish the heroes. I sometimes feel as though the experience of depression has given me a grand struggle to be involved in. And that grand struggle has defined a lot of my writing. It's made it possible for me to empathize with and respond to people who are going through similar struggles and difficulties. It's been central to my life narrative, and I use my own life enormously in everything that I write. I feel like the perception that there's some creativity attached to [my depression] helps me to get through those difficult periods."

Solomon freely embraces the idea that the pain he has experienced in his life has been integral to his work as a writer and a journalist. "There's been a generative aspect, I think, to real depression. There's been a generative aspect, I think, to my experience as a gay person, and all of the difficulty it exposed me to when I was a kid. And I feel like all of those experiences have allowed me to empathize with the suffering of the people I've written about. The reason that people open up and talk to me, I think, is that they feel I can understand. My work is at its best when it describes both the extreme darkness and the redemption that can be found in [suffering in life]. And I think my own life has to run through that cycle of darkness, redemption, and darkness and redemption, all the time."

WHAT IT MEANS TO HAVE MELANCHOLY

Some of us are more melancholic than others. The melancholic view the world in a darker way; they are more likely to see the downsides of a scenario or to predict the negative result of an action than more blithe individuals. Sometimes this is a matter of temperament; sometimes it's a result of upbringing and environment. Perhaps most often, it's a combination of factors. When the tendency toward melancholy deepens into profound and recurrent sadness that interferes with quality of life, we call it clinical depression. Under the umbrella of clinical depression fall a variety of experiences. These can range from severe, suicidal depression; to a condition known as dysthymia, which is a more moderate form of chronic depression; to dysphoria, which, rather than a diagnosis, is actually a set of symptoms that are best described as extreme and agitated unease, and which can accompany both clinical depression and bipolar disorder.

Those who suffer from dysthymia experience cycles of low and even despairing mood, but tend not to be utterly incapacitated by it. They are more likely to power through while experiencing a decrease in productivity or quality of life, yet they manage to stop short of the type of utter shutdown that can be a result of the severest forms of clinical depression. This type of shutdown is perhaps the stereotype of depression—the person who is truly incapable of getting out of bed, who pulls the shades and can't get dressed. However, depression isn't always so obvious. In fact, in men it can often present as anger and extreme irritability.[2] Major depression disorder (MDD) affects 6.7 percent of all adults in the U.S. per year and 10.7 percent of twelve-to-seventeen-year-olds. It is actually the leading cause of disability in the fifteen-to-forty-four-year-old age group.[3] The median age of onset is just over thirty-two years old, but depression can and does occur at almost any age.[4] Standard treatment ranges from various types of psychotherapies to medications to several types of electrical stimulation of the brain.

A stereotype of depression is that it's synonymous with pessimism, or a pathological tendency to expect the worst. This is construed as a kind of irrational negativity. However, the converse has been shown to be true. In a study published in the *Journal of Behavioral Therapy and Experimental Psychiatry,* researchers found that individuals with milder depression and dysphoria were actually more accurate in assessing their abilities than were those without depression.[5] Therefore, it's not that the moderately depressed suffer from an irrational lack of confidence, but rather that the nondepressed can suffer from irrational overconfidence.

The now-classic example of what has come to be known as "depressive realism" was described by Joshua Wolf Shenk in his book *Lincoln's Melancholy.*[6] Shenk put forward the theory that it was Lincoln's tendency to expect the worst outcome that enabled him to guide the country through the Civil War. The same theory has been applied to Winston Churchill, who all his life contended with what he called the "black dog" of depression, and who saw the Nazi threat far more clearly than many of his more optimistic contemporaries. Marie Curie, who suffered from depression all her life, not only threw herself into her work as a way of escaping her sadness, she also ferreted out strands of scientific study that other scientists had dismissed as fruitless.[7] She was extraordinarily self-effacing—she dressed drably, she didn't pursue reward, and she no doubt put herself in harm's way during her pioneering work with X-ray radiation—but she also achieved greatness and saved innumerable lives. Lincoln, Churchill, and Curie form a fascinating profile of the enormous benefits that all of us have derived from individuals who struggled with a sense of despair that might have leveled others.

A review of clinical studies into depression reveals a recurrent pattern:

low to moderate forms of depression, particularly when accompanied by above-average IQ, are associated with gifts of empathy, insight, and even creativity. For himself, Andrew Solomon notes, "the depression is part of what allows me to empathize with people and to understand the depth of other people's pain, which is very valuable. I've talked to a lot of people who've been depressed and haven't been able to make anything of value out of it. And I feel lucky that I actually have that capacity, and was able to build something meaningful from that experience." Solomon points out an important distinction, which is that the existence of any benefit to depression must go hand in hand with the individual's ability to use it as creative or emotional fodder. Depression alone doesn't make Solomon a writer; his depression is accompanied by exceptional intellectual gifts and the ability to use his depression productively.

Solomon also notes that he can't produce when he is in the very depths of despair, and his experience is borne out in clinical studies. Once depression reaches extreme levels, the individual is rendered less able to view him or herself realistically, or to function well, much less to produce or create. The good news is that once properly diagnosed, depression can be extremely responsive to treatment. In addition, proper treatment can prevent depression from returning to a severe degree. Nassir Ghaemi, author of *A First-Rate Madness* and director of the Mood Disorders Program at Tufts Medical Center, notes that there is a "kinetic effect where the more you have depressions, the more you'll have depressions, the more you'll keep working that road until it's a superhighway. This is why it's important for current as well as future reasons to treat a depression that is growing."[8]

It should be emphasized that even milder forms of depression can cause considerable suffering. Anyone who has had to force herself out of bed to take care of her family and go to work can attest to the considerable pain of having to wade through feelings of despair. However, studies suggest that this suffering can be character building. A 2015 study published in the *Journal of Psychology* found that high levels of empathy are more strongly associated with depression.[9] A 2014 study published in *NeuroImage: Clinical* found that people with depression, and even those who have a resolved depression in their past, get more activation in an area of the brain called the septal/subgenual cortex (sgACC).[10] This is the region of the brain concerned with guilt and altruistic behavior, and these findings suggest that people with depression are more likely than the nondepressed to act altruistically.

Perhaps even more surprising than the greater empathy among those with depression is the finding that those with chronic low-level depression might also receive a neurological boost in the area of creativity. A 2007 study published in the *Journal of Affective Disorders* found greater than average cognitive flexibility among people with dysthymia.[11] Nassir Ghaemi believes that even unipolar depression (that is, depression that is not paired with the upward swings seen in bipolar disorder) is cyclical in nature, and this is what allows the person with depression to be creative. The depression offers empathy, insight, and realism. Meanwhile, the more elevated mood that those without depression might simply identify as normalcy marks the times when depressed individuals are most able to produce. And it makes sense that those with greater talent and intelligence will be better able to take advantage of those periods of elevation and to produce better work.

Ghaemi posits that there may also be nonbiological factors involved in determining how a person with depression handles their symptoms. "Maybe there were other experiences in their lives that made them more resilient. As we know in the PTSD [post-traumatic stress disorder] literature, there are various things, for instance the experience of limited trauma early in life, that seem to make some more resilient to trauma later in life." That is, the child learns their own capacity to overcome challenges. As Ghaemi points out, Lincoln faced numerous difficult experiences early in his life. "It's not trauma in isolation, it's trauma interacting with the whole person and the personality and maybe even other social factors," such as "more social support versus less social support." In other words, while depression is not solely responsible for works of genius or selflessness—no more than ADD is solely responsible for originality—there is considerable evidence that when combined with sharp intelligence and the right support network, it can create just the right environment for such work to flourish in extraordinary ways.

THE EXPERIENCE OF MELANCHOLY

There is no degree to which any of us would choose to feel despair. There is a reason that we call certain kinds of wisdom "hard won." The insight and perspective derived from depression are gained at a terrible cost. We wouldn't wish that cost on ourselves, and we certainly wouldn't wish it on our children. While we recognize that our children learn from challenges and heartbreak, we would all choose to spare them if we could. Any exploration of the gifts of melancholy therefore must include a serious and thorough acknowledgment of the enormous and sometimes debilitating effects of depression.

THE CHALLENGES OF LIVING WITH MELANCHOLY

Journalist and author Evan Wright experienced a great deal of anger as a child, largely in response to his chaotic family life.[12] This anger often appeared to adults as self-destructiveness. In Wright's mind at the time—and to the degree that he was conscious of the cause of his anger—he viewed the adults around him as variously crazy, unreliable, and deceitful, so his response was to rebel. "I think that, looking back, certain behaviors were personally self-destructive. But being a kid I thought I was indestructible. I didn't see it as, I'm going to hurt myself. It was more like, I'm going to prove that you guys are stupid by having a belief that I'll follow your rules, and therefore I'll do things that are self-destructive. But that wasn't the intent."

As a child, Wright recalls, "I wanted to smash things and fight and be destructive. I knew this. But I knew it was wrong. And so I had to put on this patina of 'Well, I'm actually a revolutionary.'" Wright has carried this angry, contrarian urge into his career as a journalist. "I still have a lot of these tendencies that don't fit properly, like anger and aggression and a desire to transgress." But whereas in childhood Wright was unable to express his anger in constructive ways, as an adult he's been able to channel that rage into journalism that takes him into dangerous, aggressive situations, and has driven him to depict the experiences of individuals who feel as powerless as he did as a child.

Wright's depression first hit at the age of eleven or twelve. "It was this sense as if the colors just seemed to drain out of things. I would walk outside and everything looked metallic to me. Like gray lead. I couldn't function. I couldn't do my schoolwork." While this sounds now like textbook, easily diagnosable depression, this is not how Wright presented outwardly. One of the difficulties in diagnosing depression in men and boys is that they often don't come across as stereotypically sad and despairing. To the contrary, they can seem, as Wright did, agitated and aggressive. "I loved shooting guns and blowing things up as a kid, but that wasn't an impulse control problem. When I got kicked out of school, what was really going on is I was unable to read or do anything for about six months, I was so depressed. And I have often wondered if I covered it up with this other stuff. I used to bring the books home and try to sit and open them. And I couldn't."

Wright's mother also suffered from depression, so there was a certain amount of genetic loading that made him predisposed to the condition. This is not uncommon. The average person (without any relatives with diagnosed depression) is at an approximate 10 percent risk of developing depression. Those with a genetic predisposition are at closer to a 20 to 30 percent risk. We don't yet know whether genetics and environment always work together to result in a diagnosis of depression, or whether in some cases depression is a result strictly of genetics or environment. In Wright's case, a violent and traumatic event in his childhood nudged his family into chaos. When he was seven years old, his mother's closest friend, who had been his babysitter and to whom he was very close, was brutally murdered by her own son. It was a "centerpiece of my family life. I think that I was very terrified, because of the details. First of all, [the murderer] disposed of the weapon near our house, and the police theory was that he was coming to kill us. I don't know if that was true or not, but that's what we were told. So I started to think a lot about the murder, and I would visualize it, and it was so terrifying." This frightened fascination with that incident would later contribute to his interest in crime reporting and "man's inhumanity, because it terrified me and I wanted to have control of it."

At the age of thirteen, Wright's behavior had become increasingly defiant, and he was sent away to a program that featured extreme behavior modification. There were no mental health professionals in charge of the program. "It was completely insane. I actually went there willingly, because I thought it was going to help. And so I was very dismayed when the doors locked and I saw what it was. And that again [fueled my interest in] the idea of powerless people within powerful systems. I knew that I was bad and I had problems, but I also knew that these people were insane. So later on, as a reporter, that made me highly suspicious of the presentation of organizations and their motives. If they say they're doing this for the good of the people, I am very suspicious."

There were some bright spots in Wright's teen years. An English teacher in high school named Martha Kay Brown was a particularly strong influence. When his class was studying *To Kill a Mockingbird,* she gave him a visual image that has stayed with him ever since. "She went up to the chalkboard one day, and she drew a circle. And she drew a line down the center of the circle, and she wrote 'good' and 'bad' on each side of this line. And she said, 'This is basically what a person is. They're divided right down the center. And maybe in some people, it's a little more in one direction, or a little bit in another.' What she did that one day in the classroom probably influenced my entire life." The labels *good* and *bad* were ongoing themes in Wright's life. More often than not, he felt that adults viewed him as a problem rather than a child who was suffering. When Wright was at his angriest and least able to focus because of the severity of his depression, the adults in his life were frustrated with him and unaware of his deep despair. "I was displaying all this rebellion and this 'I don't care' kind of attitude, but there was never an adult figure, even among the good ones, who ever said, 'Hmm, you seem really troubled, what's going on?' I always had the sense in my interactions that they were saying, 'You're a really bad kid. Why won't you do your homework?'" Wright in turn believed that he was a bad kid. Not depressed: bad.

Wright's father left home when he was quite young, but became more involved in Wright's life when he was a teenager. This, combined with going away to college and finding studies that he could be passionate about, gave Wright the self-esteem and drive that would help him through exceptionally dark periods later in his life. "I studied medieval history in college. A useless degree. And [my father] completely supported that. Without somebody influencing me, I don't think I would have succeeded." His college history professors were also a positive influence. "History was a means of understanding civilization and its discontents. And history gave me a sense of neutrality. It's a way of studying how horrible humans are, but without a sense of shame and self-recrimination. It made me understand, okay, my mother is an alcoholic and my family is crazy. But society, you know, it doesn't have a great track record, either." Essentially, Wright's history studies reinforced a quality he already had in spades: depressive realism.

Evan Wright has gone on to enormous success in his career, both despite and in some respects because of the challenges he experienced in his childhood. Of course, he has exceptional intelligence and talent in his favor; children who lack his capabilities and positive influences don't fare as well. Children who suffer from depression often grow into adults with less education and lower incomes. According to Centers for Disease Control and Prevention statistics, people who don't have a high school diploma are two and a half times as likely to experience depression than those with at least some college. High school graduates who don't go on to college are one and a half times as likely to experience depression.[13] People with depression are also more likely to be subsequently unemployed, resulting in a loss of family income.[14] And thus the cycle of depression and decreased achievement and financial stability continues into another generation.

Depression is the number-one cause of medical disability among people aged fourteen to forty-four.[15] In addition to depression's devastating impact on individual lives, the financial burden to the country in terms of lost productive hours and benefits is massive. According to an article published in the *Journal of the American Medical Association,* workers with depression reported losing five or more hours of productive work time each week.[16] The study extrapolates that this costs employers an estimated forty-four billion dollars per year.

Given how few people with depression seek out or receive treatment—estimates are that only a third of all those suffering from depression seek help—it's not surprising that there is such a high percentage of drug abuse and alcoholism among depressives. People with depression are five times more likely to abuse drugs and 30 percent more likely to commit suicide.[17]

As a child, Evan Wright's way of coping with his depression was to react with anger to any perceived injustice and to refuse to go along with authority. As an adult, alcohol gave shape and form to his depression. He found comfort in the cycle of drinking to the point of blacking out and the accompanying fear that he had done something terrible—which was then followed by elation that he'd gotten away with near self-destruction. Wright partially credits his ego for his ability to pull himself out of depression and alcoholism. During his bottoming out with alcoholism, "I would come out of a blackout and I would realize I had fallen over and had cut my face, and there was a feeling of humiliation and despair, and then a motivation to prove that I was not defined by that. I'm going to either prove that I'm going to succeed at something publicly so people will know, or I am going to prove that they can't break me like all of the forces of the universe. So I think ego is a huge part of it."

It was only once he quit drinking with the help of Alcoholics Anonymous that Wright was able to focus his anger and aggressiveness on his work. Of course, many people are unable to do this. As with the other brain differences explored in the book, often the dividing line between those who can and can't use their differences to positive effect is a combination of qualities that include flexibility and grit—qualities that can be in short supply when one is in the depths of despair.

DEVELOPING WORK-AROUNDS

Dom, a teenager in the New York City public schools who has struggled with ADD and dyslexia, has also experienced significant bouts of depression.[18] When Dom is depressed, the feeling can go on for days or weeks, and he describes the sensation as being "deeply in thought. I don't want to talk to anybody."

In a way that is similar to Evan Wright's embrace of his history studies, Dom's central work-around is his passion for music. An exceptionally talented drummer, he spent a summer at the Berklee College of Music, where he was free to play the drums whenever he wanted. During this time he felt no anger or depression. In fact, he uses his music to get out of feeling depressed. Music alters his mood in powerful and positive ways, and the synesthesia he experiences when he is most intensely affected contributes to his euphoria.

Remarkably, Dom has been able to derive a positive benefit from his depressed periods—what he describes as a kind of peace, or an "emptiness that's full." Essentially, this is a meditative state in which he is able to rest his mind. However, when he's angry or irritable, feelings that often accompany his periods of depression, he can't reach that contemplative place. He describes this calm place as being a kind of space between the lines, or a balance beam. "It's like if you go too north, you're going to fall off; that's why you have to stay directly in the middle."

This sense of emotional precariousness pervades the lives of those with depression, and there can be considerable fear and dread of falling into a deep depression at any time. The work-arounds that those with depression develop (in conjunction with proper treatment by a professional) tend to be a combination of staving off deep, unworkable despair while also working through more moderate depression, and utilizing the insights gained from both.

One powerful and well-researched method for coping with depression is exercise. A Harvard Medical School Special Health Report outlined the overwhelming evidence gleaned from more than thirty years of studies on the power of exercise to alleviate depression.[19] The conclusion of these studies is that exercise stimulates the body's production of endorphins as well as the neurotransmitter norepinephrine—both of which are strongly associated with mood regulation. Moreover, the practical impact of exercise on physical health can yield a better quality of life and higher self-esteem, both of which certainly influence mood. What is perhaps most fascinating is that not only can exercise be as effective as antidepressant medication, but its effects are longer lasting. One study, published in the *Archives of Internal Medicine* in 1999, divided men and women into three groups. One-third of the participants were given an aerobic exercise regimen, one-third were treated with Zoloft, and another third were given both. While those who took Zoloft experienced positive results more quickly, after sixteen weeks, in each of the groups, approximately two-thirds no longer exhibited symptoms of major depression. In addition, when researchers followed up with participants six months later, those who continued to exercise were less likely to experience another depressive episode—whether or not they took Zoloft.[20] Since starting an exercise regimen is daunting for anyone, much less for someone who struggles with depression, it's encouraging to note that the effect of even moderate amounts of exercise is significant.[21] One study suggests that simply walking fast for an hour three times per week, or for a half hour five times per week, can stave off symptoms of mild to moderate depression.[22]

Given the physically strenuous nature of drumming, it's possible that Dom's lack of depressive episodes when he was able to play the drums every day might not have been due solely to the music itself, but might in fact have had a physiological cause as well. Evan Wright has found palpable relief via exercise. When he's depressed, he feels "the bleakest despair. I know some people can't get out of bed. I get out of bed and do things, but it's pretty black. When I'm depressed I can't sleep and start to hate being in bed, so I will get up exhausted. I try to do physical things." During a recent episode of depression related to having finished two big writing projects, he felt "a really profound meaninglessness. So I got up and forced myself to climb a steep mountain outside of LA." One of the symptoms of his depression was a nonspecific anger so strong that "I was actually afraid that if I interacted with people I would get in a fistfight." Instead, "I drove pretty far out and went up this mountain even though I hadn't slept." Once he'd exhausted himself physically, he knew that he would be able to sleep.

Novelist Anne Rice has written through depression her entire life. It's not surprising that she would choose that method of coping with and working through her feelings of despair, since she says, "I grew up in a family of natural storytellers, influenced by the stories of my grandmother and mother from an early age. My mother saw the world in terms of stories, stories about the houses we passed, people she had known, things that happened to her, and she frequently recounted the plots of great old movies she'd seen, or stories of the great writers' novels."[23]

Like Andrew Solomon, Rice knew from a very early age that she wanted to be a writer. "I tried writing a story at the age of five. I had to ask for the spelling of every word. It was 'Lily is sitting in her chambers.' That was my story." When her father returned from World War II, he wrote a novel for children and read Anne and her siblings chapters in the evenings. She was eleven or twelve when she discovered a trove of her father's stories and poems, including a poem he'd written to a friend who'd died in the war. Thus she had many early examples of translating deep personal emotion into written words.

As a child, Rice lost her mother, and her father struggled with alcoholism. The trauma of losing her mother at such a young age and having an alcoholic father "has had a pervasive influence on everything I've written, but I don't analyze or think about this when I write. I know it's there, but it would block me to think of it. But my writing is filled with darkness, grief, and tragedy. My writing is also filled with a great rebellion against helplessness and paralysis since I felt so helpless as a child in an unhappy but interesting and loving family, as things slowly disintegrated due to my mother's illness."

The greatest tragedy of Rice's life occurred when she lost her daughter to leukemia in 1973. The powerful grief that followed fueled her first novel, *Interview with the Vampire*. "I pitched myself into writing and made up a story about vampires. I didn't know it at the time but it was all about my daughter, the loss of her and the need to go on living when faith is shattered. But the lights do come back on, no matter how dark it seems, and I'm sensitive now, more than ever, to the beauty of the world—and more resigned to living with cosmic uncertainty."[24]

Rice has found that she can write "whether I am happy or depressed, and really nobody much can tell which novels were written in which state." In fact, the process of writing itself is calming to her. "I love the obsessive focus I fall into when writing, as it alleviates anxiety by providing a productive focus for mental energy. The content of my writings certainly reflects my fears and anxiety, fear of death, insecurity, awareness always of cosmic angst, etc. I deliberately write about particular fears in my writing, and the writing is cathartic."[25]

Andrew Solomon also turns to his writing even when he is depressed. "I write a lot more when I'm feeling well than when I'm feeling depressed. I feel I am functioning for more hours a day. I write more easily and more fluidly. But, I kind of cling to writing as a—you know, it goes through however I'm feeling. To some extent, I write from the mood that I'm in. And there are parts of every one of my books that are extremely dark. And parts of every one of my books that are extremely joyful. In a way, I subscribe to the psychoanalytic idea that the best way to gain control of your circumstances is not by denying them, but by punching yourself deep into them and trying to understand them."

GIFTS OF THE BRAIN WITH MELANCHOLY

While obsessiveness and persistence are not traits that are stereotypically associated with depression, these qualities run through the life stories of many high-functioning people with depression. These feelings of obsessiveness, fear of failure, and perfectionism can be deeply unpleasant, but they can also yield spectacular work.

When Evan Wright was reporting on a group of neo-Nazis, he was highly aware that he was alone and vulnerable in a group of dangerous people. "I felt that one slip-up, if I say the wrong thing, they're going to beat me up." It is "very similar to the experience that I had when I was in that program as a kid." At that program, he was essentially "held prisoner by this group of people that were bigger and older and wouldn't let me sleep and yelled at me and would put me in a boxing ring and beat me up every few days. I went through that, and so as a reporter, it gave me this sense of 'I can do this.' Because I've been through this gauntlet in the past and I know I survived. "

This persistence bordering on obsession is also a major part of his writing process. Wright says, "Some of my best work is because I researched the hell out of things, because I'm afraid to start writing. And it's worked to my advantage, because my stories tend to be much better researched. And I'll just spend infinite time with them. It's not that I'm a patient person. It's that I'm afraid to start writing. I'm afraid that once I start, the writing will reveal that it's not going to be as great as I thought it was." Wright's standard for doing the best job possible is, "Did I exhaust myself and go beyond the limit of what I can do? It's not so much the outcome. I'm very much interested in the process. I want to lose myself in the work."

Andrew Solomon says that accomplishing the monumental task of writing *Far from the Tree* required "a lot of obsessionality. I would do nothing but write for fourteen or fifteen hours a day. And I felt, in some of those periods when I was doing that, I felt crazy. And I thought, in a way, I have to work myself into a state that is at least related to my depression, if it's not identical to my depression, in order to generate all of this complicated material."

Evan Wright combines his qualities of persistence and depressive realism while also drawing on the reserves of anger that are still a feature of his depression. In his view, he couldn't have written his book *Generation Kill,* about a battalion of marines in the Iraq War, if this anger weren't an ongoing part of him. "I also like being an outsider. I came to reporting via *Hustler* magazine. I didn't have the background of a *New York Times* reporter, so I had a chip on my shoulder."

James Kocsis, professor of psychiatry at Weill Cornell Medical College and director of the Affective Disorders Research Program at the Payne Whitney Psychiatric Clinic, says "certain reporters benefit from the fact that they have skeptical, negative points of view about everything. That causes them to dig deeper or to not accept unrealistic or positive statements from others."[26]

Wright's contrarian nature, and his ability to see through to underlying truths, are qualities gained from difficult experience, having grown up in a chaotic, sometimes violent home. "When you're in a combat zone, there's a weird familiarity with that. There's a reassuring sense of Oh, this is how the world really is. When you go into a city and everybody starts shooting at each other, it's sort of like, in a cynical way, Okay, the masks are off, this is people as they really are. I'm mature enough as an adult to know that's not exactly how people are. But there is a certain clarity to that that's almost reassuring."

Andrew Solomon's version of depressive realism is the knowledge that nothing is forever. "I've always had a sense when I'm not depressed of being so relieved not to be depressed that I throw myself into life. It's my sense, which I think came out of the episodes with depression, that life is short. And if I've got a good period right now, I should really try to do everything I possibly can. And I also think the fact that my mother died at fifty-eight, and her father died at fifty-seven, has left me with the sense that life may be finite—a sense which has only escalated as I've gotten older. So I don't expect to die at fifty-seven, but I know it's possible. And I feel like there's a lot to do before it happens. I don't [think], Oh, I feel great, and I can just do anything, and I can do anything for the whole rest of my life." Instead, he thinks, "I feel great, and I'm going to do everything I can, because maybe I'm not going to get depressed again for a long time, and maybe I'm going to get depressed again on Tuesday. And I want to get as much done as I possibly can before [depression] strikes again."

Both Solomon and Wright have experienced for themselves what researchers have found—namely that tremendous insight can be derived from the experience of depression. Wright notes that one of his greatest strengths as a reporter is his empathy. "Empathy for the bad guy as well as the victims. Trying to see things from all sides." Wright's tremendous empathy for the powerless in particular has strongly influenced his writing. "As a journalist there's an anti-authoritarianism [in me] for sure, but there's also a sense of trying to empower people. In my book *Generation Kill* I was able to let lower-ranking enlisted Marines say things that they couldn't say in their normal lives within the command structure. At the root of depression is this sense of meaninglessness in life. So to do a good murder story or a good military story, there's a sense of wanting to do something that's important, something meaningful, and give voice to people who don't have voices."

Psychiatrist James Kocsis notes, "Having gone through a serious depression and having come out the other side of it, people have a more nuanced view of life and a more nuanced view of other people, and maybe more empathy particularly for the foibles and sufferings of others. It's character building to have gone through major depression and to come out the other side of it."

Like Wright, Andrew Solomon views his empathy not only as a gift but also as an essential part of his process. "I think I have to allow myself truly to empathize. Which is to say, to descend to the level of the pain of the people I'm writing about. I have to do it twice. I have to do it when I interview them, and I have to do it again when I write about them. So in some sense, it's almost as though I make an effort to slip into a controlled depression, so that I can express the agony of the people I'm writing about. And then I try to pull myself out from it before it plunges to such a deep, clinical level that I'm completely disabled by it. A lot of what I've been praised for in my work has been [my] honesty about complex emotional states. And I'm able to achieve honesty about those states in other people through my struggle to achieve it in my own life."

HOW PEOPLE WITH
MELANCHOLY CAN FLOURISH

The goal in exploring the positive benefits of various forms of brain difference is not to wallpaper over the tremendous suffering that can also occur. Andrew Solomon notes the risk of viewing his own history of pain through a soft lens. "When I'm in my undepressed state, I'm prone to constructing it as, 'Good things have come of it, and therefore it's all wonderful.' And it isn't all wonderful. And I feel like it takes a little depression for me to remember, 'Actually, that was pretty bad. And I have a major mental illness that I have to manage.' And it takes all that medication and a lot of work to keep it in check. And it would be nicer to have a life in which I didn't have to deal with all of that. The fact that I've worked some stuff out since then does not mean that these bad things were so great. They weren't so great. They were bad."

Solomon lives with the constant specter of another major depressive episode, and he is rigorous in his attention to his mental health via both talk therapy and medication. Psychoanalytic treatment "has helped me to

feel that I understand what's happening better than I would have understood it otherwise. And I think understanding it allows me to have some
feeling of control over it. Limited control, but it's definitely a help." Regarding the debate over whether to take medication, he says, "There are a
lot of people who say, 'But I don't want to go on antidepressants, because I
think it might kill my creativity.' I feel like I learned a lot from [depres-
sion], but it was not essentially a creative state, and being undepressed is,
essentially, a creative state. If I'd never had treatment, who knows what my
life would be like. My suspicion is that I would be a lot less creative, and I
would spend a lot more time in bed with the covers pulled over my head."

That said, Andrew Solomon is unequivocal in his belief that he would
not have become a writer without his depression. Nor would he have given
it up for an easier life. "I would never trade away the depression that's in my
past. I think it's made me who I am, and I feel pretty happy with who I am,
which shows I'm not depressed today. And I think it's been incredibly valuable, and I think I've learned from it. If I could trade away the depression
that's in my future, I would have to give that some serious consideration. I
mean, I feel like I've grown from it, but I've learned enough, thank you.
I don't need to go through any more of that and grow anymore."

Certainly the first step in helping those with depression and depressive
episodes is to recognize the problem for what it is, and to take it seriously.
Evan Wright's experiences as a young boy with terrible despair that was
invisible to the adults in his life—even to the well-meaning ones—should
be a cautionary tale to all of us in the importance of digging deeper when
we see troubled behavior in children and adolescents. We too easily fall
prey to labeling children and young adults as good or bad, obstreperous or
well behaved. Just as good behavior can hide the suffering of the child with
a learning difference, so-called bad behavior can camouflage the suffering
of a child or young adult with depression.

Because depression affects one's judgment, it can be hard even for the
depressed adult to recognize they are in fact depressed. That is why it is so
important for loved ones to know the red flags and help the person with

depression to seek evaluation and treatment. Since people with depression tend to pull away socially and to isolate themselves, which more often than not serves to make their depression worse, it is all the more important for those around the individual to take charge of making plans and scheduling time to engage.

Another way to help people with depression is to help them identify their own strengths and to provide a more objective, external eye for the person who might have difficulty seeing him or herself in anything other than the most negative terms. It can also be helpful to remind the person with depression of the things that previously brought them pleasure and to encourage them to pursue those activities (perhaps by joining them). Expressing distressing feelings via creative outlets (writing, art, music) is often therapeutic. The creative expression of these feeling states often resonates with others. Evan Wright was drawn to experiencing and writing about dark things, which has very much tapped into his dark internal world. His writing in turn spoke to others who connected with that dark place, and also led to considerable professional success.

For the individual, treatment is essential—therapy at minimum, and in some cases in combination with drug treatment. Self-care is key as well: examining and understanding one's triggers for depression and what helps to stave off such episodes (such as exercise) can in some cases eliminate the need for drug therapy altogether.

Recasting the experience of depression as an opportunity for connection—rather than as a lonely affliction—is also a powerful step. Andrew Solomon says, "I feel like having been depressed puts me in touch with the suffering that's at the heart of so much human experience. And in that sense, it makes me less alone. I mean, almost ironically. Because one thinks of depression as very isolating. And if I'm in bed and can't move, it's pretty isolating. But having been depressed is the opposite of isolating. It's the basis for whatever intimacy I have with humanity."

5.

CYCLING MOOD

COMMON DIAGNOSIS

BIPOLAR DISORDER

"I don't see an idea, I see the whole thing: the beginning and the end, all at the same time. I can't explain it, but it's all there."

—CHUCK NICE

While we tend to associate anthropology with the study of far-flung cultures, the idea for cultural anthropologist Emily Martin's first book came to her from a nearby and arguably familiar experience: childbirth in America.[1] In her provocative and critically lauded book *The Woman in the Body,* Martin examined popular and scientific theories about childbirth and turned our long-held cultural assumptions up in the air, approaching them from new and original perspectives. Martin says that the idea for the book came to her in a flash, as many of her ideas do. It's as if "something's being said and it's very common, it's common sense, you keep hearing it and hearing it and hearing it—and then, all of a sudden, you hear it in a different way. You realize the implication of talking that way or thinking that way. One of my friends said I'm like a set of iron filings when [I] go into the field. The field is magnetic, and [I] just go boing."

That image of going "boing" is a powerful one and perfectly describes the creative rush of fully realized ideas that many people with bipolar disorder—with which Emily Martin was diagnosed in her early forties—experience during their upswings in mood.

Prior to being diagnosed with bipolar disorder, Emily Martin had a number of depressive episodes, and it was one of those that first caused her to seek help from an expert at the age of twenty-five. "I thought, this isn't right, something's really wrong. I reminded myself of my mother, who was, I think, chronically depressed." Although Martin doesn't recall ever having been depressed as a child, she does remember being "terrified of going to sleep" between the ages of six and twelve. During that time, she was repeatedly sexually abused by her father. "I had horrific nightmares." She also sleepwalked. No one sought to get to the bottom of her terror, however. "They just thought, Well, kids have nightmares. It was a different time." Finally, when she turned thirteen, her mother intervened and sent Martin away to boarding school, where she thrived. "The nightmare was over."[2]

Martin's first manic episode (an upswing in mood associated with bipolar disorder) occurred in the mid-1990s, when she was hard at work on a book. Martin says she felt a presence, "a cold gray gargoyle perched tenaciously on my shoulder," and she realized that what she was experiencing was quite different from the prior depressive episodes she'd endured. The doctor whose help she sought diagnosed her with bipolar disorder and surmised that the antidepressant she'd been taking had nudged her into mania, thereby revealing her underlying bipolar disorder.[3] Martin thinks her father, an entrepreneur, might also have received the diagnosis of bipolar disorder "if he'd been born decades later. I can remember him being just crazily active in going around and doing things, and starting companies and all this stuff, and then just being in bed. I remember this cyclical flow of energy, of activity."[4]

Brain differences do not operate in a vacuum—they're influenced by environmental factors just as personality and physical health are. In

Martin's case, a combination of her bipolar disorder and the abuse she lived through as a child caused her to become comfortable with the concept of "two realities [that] coexist." Her fluidity—both of mood and perception—translates into her anthropological fieldwork, "where you are required to immerse yourself in another reality and then move in and out of it and to make sense of the differences, to handle the differences cognitively. And that's what I do very well. It's a real skill." In addition, her experience of sadness, grief, and depression "certainly plays a part in the writing that I do about other people's lives. Because [the people I study] are not all at one level. They have all kinds of heights and valleys." And heights and valleys in life—from euphoria to the darkest misery—are feeling states with which the person with bipolar disorder can deeply empathize.

The hypomanic stages of bipolar disorder—when most people feel tireless and confident as well as creatively productive—can be enormously pleasurable. However, the pleasant euphoria doesn't last. After a period of having lots of ideas, Martin describes feeling that "you burn out, like a lightbulb that's burned out."[5] Martin credits her excellent doctors with keeping her from swinging high and low—and from burning out—while maintaining her ability to remain creative.[6]

In addition, she's grateful to have found work that she loves and that suits her brain's extraordinary gifts. She even turned her anthropological eye to bipolar disorder in her award-winning book *Bipolar Expeditions,* which examined our culture's treatment of individuals with the disorder. "As soon as I discovered [cultural anthropology] existed, I went for it. It was empirical. You did research, but it wasn't mathematical, it was based on somehow taking the measure of a form or life, ours or someone else's. And it involved immersive experience. So I felt there's a lot of luck that I happened to find it early on, early enough to go to graduate school" and to make enormous contributions in her chosen field. "Why is it, I ask myself, that I'm almost seventy years old and I'm in the middle of a new project? You could say, 'Well, it's my bipolar mania.' Or you could say, 'There's something about fieldwork.' I feel I can't do without it. It's totally my sustenance. It's the challenge of entering something really foreign. And coming back out of it, and finding a perspective."

WHAT IT MEANS TO HAVE BIPOLAR DISORDER

Bipolar disorder—the term refers to the shifting between two poles, depression and mania—is a diagnosis that can be applied to people who present in vastly different ways. There are those with bipolar disorder who tend more toward depression and those who tend more toward mania. There are those who alternate. Someone is diagnosed as manic when they experience a period of notably elevated, expansive, and irritable mood for at least one week, and also present with three or more of the following symptoms: inflated self-esteem (also referred to as "grandiosity"); dramatically decreased need for sleep; unusual gregariousness; racing thoughts, or what are called "flights of ideas"; distractibility; dramatic increase in some goal-oriented activity (this can range from work to sex drive); heightened risk-taking and pleasure seeking (ranging from excessive spending to sexual activity). If not successfully treated, the mood disturbances of mania ultimately impair those who experience it to a degree that hospitalization is necessary and symptoms of psychosis can emerge. Unlike mania, hypomania can last as few as four days, it does not cause marked impairment, and there is no psychosis.[7] Typically, what the layperson thinks of as "mania" is actually hypomania. Hypomania results in the kind of sleeplessness, heightened productivity, extreme confidence, and magnetic charisma that we often associate with bipolar disorder, but without many of the more damaging side effects. It can feel wonderful to the person experiencing it, and can be attractive to those in his or her orbit— and that is why so many people with bipolar disorder resist seeking treatment. While the depressions are terrible, the highs can feel extraordinary.

If all of us could settle in at the exhilaratingly energized state of hypomania—the slight upswing during which most acts of creativity occur—we might certainly choose to do so. Who wouldn't want that extra dose of energy (in Emily Martin's words, "Sleep? Who needs sleep?"), verbal fluency, and sex drive? If only it could be bottled. However, there is no settling into pleasant hypomania; the nature of bipolar disorder is its fluidity. In some, hypomania inevitably leads to mania—a psychotic state marked by highly irrational thinking. In all of those with bipolar disorder, hypomania and mania end with a deep crash into seemingly bottomless depression. There are also those who suffer from what is called a mixed state, which features elements of both mania and depression and brings enormous risk of suicide. This is because the individual experiences the distressing, negative thoughts of depression, while at the same time they have the energy and agitation of mania, which makes taking action on those negative thoughts more likely. There is also rapid-cycling bipolar disorder in which the individual's mood state might alter radically from day to day. The more the individual with bipolar disorder cycles without getting treatment, the more they will cycle, as a result of what is called the "kinetic effect." (The same holds true for those who suffer from clinical depression—the more untreated depressions one experiences, the more likely one is to experience another, and at increasing frequency.) This is why bipolar disorder must be treated—there can be no white-knuckling of symptoms, which will only worsen and become more dangerous and devastating over time.

Although the treatment and understanding of bipolar disorder has evolved in the last few decades, we haven't made revolutionary strides. The same drug—lithium—that would have been prescribed to the patient with bipolar disorder in 1966 is still prescribed in 2016, although typically in lesser dosages to mitigate the serious side effects of long-term use. Despite some advances in treatment, and while other brain differences are taken in stride (mention ADD in an educational setting and you're often met with a shrug), the words *bipolar disorder* still have the power to shock.

It's terribly frightening, particularly to the newly diagnosed, to feel at the mercy of brain chemistry that isn't even entirely understood.

Under the umbrella diagnosis of bipolar disorder there are two forms of the disorder—bipolar 1 and bipolar 2. Bipolar 1 features manic episodes that can become psychotic in nature. Bipolar 2 features only hypomanic episodes. In both types, the manic or hypomanic periods alternate with periods of major depression. Hypomania itself, while associated with creativity—in fact, even those who don't ordinarily write can experience hypergraphia, which is the overwhelming urge to write in great volume—can also be terribly damaging in individual lives. Behavior becomes inappropriate in social and work settings. Speech speeds up. Sexual behavior becomes extreme and even risky. Risks of all kinds are taken—including excessive spending. It's not difficult to imagine how this could destroy relationships and careers. For all these reasons, the goal of this chapter is not to romanticize bipolar disorder as a magical creativity disease. However, when we stigmatize bipolar disorder, when we misunderstand what the diagnosis means, and when we don't acknowledge its cognitive benefits, we're doing a disservice to individuals with the disorder and ignoring vast quantities of clinical evidence.

If you removed all the people with mental disorder from the history books, there would be no history left. Arguably, if you removed all of those with bipolar disorder from the arts and creative fields, there would be vastly less creativity in the world. We would have no Hemingway. No Anne Sexton. No Virginia Woolf. Very possibly no Beethoven, either.

In multiple studies, bipolar disorder has been scientifically, clinically proven to correlate with creativity and the artistic temperament. In a longitudinal study of seven hundred thousand Swedish teenagers, researchers found that the highest-performing children tested were four times more likely to be diagnosed with bipolar disorder within ten years.[8] The biochemistry of the brain with bipolar disorder is so strongly linked to various forms of creativity that studies have shown that those with bipolar 1 disorder are more likely to write when swinging upward, and those with bipolar 2 are more likely to draw.[9] A study conducted at Oregon State University found that even in ordinary, noncreative industries, those with bipolar disorder sought out positions that required greater than average creative thinking.[10] In my clinical practice, I have often heard those with bipolar disorder describe in engagingly positive terms the confidence, high energy, and prolific output that accompany the initial onset of mania. Emotions are intense and word associations become electrically fast and uninhibited.

Perhaps the most tantalizing question posed by the mounting research is why brain differences such as bipolar disorder persist in the human gene pool. Researchers at Yale University School of Medicine studied twins— in each set, one twin had been diagnosed with bipolar disorder and the other had not. They found that the nonaffected twins *also* exhibited enhanced creativity and cognitive functioning. In other words, there was some set of genetic factors that contributed both to bipolar disorder and to greater acuity in those areas. The study's senior author, Tyrone Cannon, told *Psychiatric News,* "If people at genetic risk for bipolar disorder have higher levels of these traits than the general population, then this pattern would support the theory that some of the bipolar promoting mutations are expressed in the form of positive temperament and intellectual features that, in turn, lead to greater fertility—and hence, greater likelihood of persistence of those genes."[11]

In a paper published in the *Journal of Frontiers in Psychology,* two researchers at the University of Kansas examined the various research into the question of creativity and bipolar disorder, attempting to ferret out the anecdotal from the scientifically supportable.[12] Specifically, they asked, what is the neurological process whereby hypomania—that slightly elevated, energetic, prolific state—yields creative work? Not surprisingly, the answer is flow and balance between disinhibition and inhibition. When the prefrontal cortex, the area that is more focused on rule-bound information, is somewhat impaired (which is called hypofrontality), this allows the more emotional and sensory-sensitive subcortical regions to have greater input on thought processes. These subcortical areas are where we generate novel ideas, and the more freely they operate, the greater quantity of creative ideas are generated. In addition, there is a greater likelihood these will be out-of-the-box ideas, or ideas that are atypical. The increase in originality plus the quantity of ideas generated result in a greater likelihood that some of those ideas will also be of superior quality. However, left to their own devices, the subcortical regions can't be relied upon to edit, evaluate, or discern which ideas are best to pursue. This is when the prefrontal cortex—the rule-based structure—needs to kick in again. This balance between the subcortical and prefrontal is what makes all the difference between those who generate a profusion of wonderful but impossible ideas, and those who are able to, for example, conceive and then write a novel. This balance only occurs during the hypomanic stage—as soon as the brain veers toward mania, the prefrontal cortex is overwhelmed and ignored.[13]

Dean Keith Simonton, professor of psychology at the University of California, Davis, and an authority on genius and creativity, says that when hypomania yields the best work, there is a "profusion of ideas, and then you move into complete focus. And so that suggests that you have this kind of megacognitive control that's associated with general intelligence where you all of a sudden say, 'It's time to stop. I've got enough material to work with, and I'm going to have to weed a lot of it out, and a lot of it's worthless.' When they look at [Beethoven's] notebooks and sketchbooks, it's a nightmare. He has all these ideas, and most of them he ends up never using."[14] That is, Beethoven combined the ability to produce vast quantities with discernment and self-control. "Highly creative people tend to go back and forth between cognitive disinhibition and cognitive inhibition. So they allow their minds to wander and come up with all these bizarre thoughts, and all of a sudden [are taken] by something really good. And then they focus on it and develop it, and don't allow themselves to be distracted. You can get these bizarre thoughts, and then you can channel them into more useful areas. And even reject them, if you have to."

Not all of the linkage between creativity and mania is due to this balance between disinhibition and inhibition. There is some indication that specific traits of bipolar disorder that are not necessarily directly related to creativity—such as grandiosity, risk-taking, and ambition—are also major contributing factors. A 2014 study published in the *Journal of Affective Disorders* found a strong correlation between motivation and bipolar disorder.[15] This may be related to the typically strong desire for recognition and respect from others that people with bipolar disorder often exhibit. While we can associate an excessive concern with the opinion of others with insecurity, it nonetheless drives a desire for accomplishment. Combined with talent, intellect, and productivity, this is a potent brew. Nassir Ghaemi, of Tufts Medical Center, says, "If you have a manic-depressive illness [Ghaemi's preferred term for bipolar disorder], you have the opportunity to become a very creative, charismatic person—and create—and that doesn't mean you will be. But if you don't have a manic-depressive illness, it's much, much less likely you'll be a very creative, charismatic person."[16] His research even indicates that what he calls the "hyperthymic temperament" may be psychologically protective. One study after 9/11 in which Ghaemi was involved "found that the bipolar patients had fewer PTSD symptoms than other groups. The kinds of symptoms and traits that [are described] as being protective for PTSD are the kinds of traits you see in mania: being future oriented, having a great sense of humor, being very sociable and extroverted, so you have a large social support network, etc."

Like the split nature of the disorder itself, the irrefutable benefits of bipolar disorder are just as extreme as the unavoidable downsides.

THE EXPERIENCE OF BIPOLAR DISORDER

In her book *Touched with Fire: Manic-Depressive Illness and the Artistic Temperament,* Kay Redfield Jamison describes bipolar disorder as "a disease of perturbed gaieties, melancholy, and tumultuous temperaments."[17] These extremes of temperament have contributed to some of the greatest writing and artistic output of any century. When considered through the lens of the great minds who have experienced those highs and lows—and what those minds have accomplished—the disorder can seem, to the innocent bystander, like something well worth having and even celebrating. However, the pain and suffering that go with the spark and excitement of the disorder come both from within and from an often-uncomprehending world.

CHALLENGES OF LIVING WITH BIPOLAR DISORDER

With proper diagnosis and treatment, the impact of bipolar disorder on individual lives needn't be as crippling as it was to writers and poets such as Ernest Hemingway and Anne Sexton—both of whom ended their own lives after producing tremendous work while also suffering the worst effects of cycling mood. But what cannot be addressed by treatment is the stigmatizing of mental illness by the world at large.

Bill Lichtenstein is an award-winning print and broadcast journalist who was first hospitalized with symptoms of bipolar disorder (among them the paranoid belief that he was being surveilled by the FBI) in 1986, but wasn't correctly diagnosed until 1987.[18] "I was working at ABC News as a producer and then producing Jimmy Breslin's show for ABC in 1986, and over a three-week period, I just sort of came unwound. [I] ended up at St. Luke's–Roosevelt Hospital for three weeks. Now they would have seen [that I had bipolar] as I walked through the door, but in those days I was there for three weeks and they kept giving me medication and upping the dosage and I left without a diagnosis, even though it was clearly mania and hypomania." The following year, the doctor who diagnosed him said, "I've got bad news and I've got good news. The bad news is you have something called manic depression. And the good news, if you take this drug, lithium, you'll likely be okay."

After suffering through the misery of not knowing what exactly was wrong with him, Lichtenstein felt some relief upon hearing that there was a concrete explanation. "I called people thinking, Oh, this is good news. Like, Hey, you know, I know what's been going on, I was diagnosed with manic depression. And then was stunned the phone didn't ring. People didn't call me back—people I had been through war zones with. And it became clear this was not something you wanted to have."

Fearing that owning his diagnosis would alienate not only friends but also potential employers, "I sort of dodged it for a couple of years and then ended up back in the hospital twice before I finally decided, I have to take this very seriously." Still, he felt alone and isolated. "I never outside of the hospital met anybody who had manic depression, [or] heard it in any context—I knew nothing of it. It was like I had this kind of obscure ill-ness that on top of it was stigmatizing, and I didn't want to tell people about it."

This extra measure of caution wasn't paranoia on his part. After one of his hospital stays, "I was offered a job at a local station, producing for an investigative reporter." Once he'd already been told he had the job, the reporter "confronted me and said, 'You know, I heard you had an episode while you were working with Jimmy Breslin.' I had never had to explain it before, but I said, well, I was just exhausted and I ended up in the hospital for a couple of weeks, but I'm fine now. And the job went away. That was a real wake-up call."

One night in 1990, Lichtenstein was up late distracting himself and "for some reason I used to read phone books. At midnight I looked under 'manic depression' in the phone book and was stunned to find this thing called 'Manic Depressive Support Group.'" When he called the number, he heard in a recorded message that Kay Jamison would be speaking on bipolar disorder and creativity. "And I was shocked that there were actu-ally other people who had the illness."

Eventually, he and some others formed another group that "became the Uptown Mood Disorder Support Group of New York. And I think sitting in a room with people who all have the same experience and are dealing with the same issues—like, if you are dating, do you tell people? And where do you put your medications if you don't want people to see it?—that, to me, was the first realization that gave me back my life. I feel like I got my life back at that point. "

The experience of having a brain difference has heavily influenced Lichtenstein's work in terms of subject matter. In 1990, he produced a Peabody Award–winning documentary radio series titled *Voices of an Illness,* which shone a light on people living with and recovering from serious mental illnesses. Perhaps more profoundly, his illness and experience with stigmatization made him "more interested in what people have gone through, and expanded my work because of it. I [have] much more empathy for people who are struggling."

DEVELOPING WORK-AROUNDS

A recurrent theme among high-performing people with bipolar disorder is the extreme importance of finding a way to express their creativity via their work. As Kay Jamison wrote, "creative work can act not only as a means of escape from pain, but also as a way of structuring chaotic emotions and thoughts, numbing pain through abstraction and the rigors of disciplined thought, and creating a distance from the source of despair."

Comedian and radio and TV personality Chuck Nice was twenty-two when he was first diagnosed with bipolar disorder, which is a typical age at which symptoms become more apparent—at least half of all cases emerge before the age of twenty-five.[19] Nice exhibited the typical signs of mania, including sleeplessness, as well as one of the more beneficial aspects: prolific creative output. It is the latter that feeds his natural drive and ambition to succeed. But while Nice's work is his passion, for the sake of his mental health he has learned to keep his manic tendencies in check. He doesn't feel the need to push himself to the limits doing stand-up comedy every night—which to him would be a sure path to burnout. "I do it enough where I'm good and I love it. When I start not loving it, then I'm like, all right, time to write some new material. I've got to do something so I can stay in love with this thing. I've got to maintain the love." Nice sees that as a big difference between him and some of the comedians who've been drawn into a downward spiral.

Nice came to comedy and performing as a second career. Earlier in his life, he was drawn to business and owning companies, and was interested in being an entrepreneur. Throughout his childhood, though, the only positive feedback he received from close family members was for being funny. He was often asked to perform at family gatherings. "They would call me in the room and they would say, 'Do that thing you did the other day.' What I realized is that from a chemical standpoint" performing and receiving adulation for it "was releasing a certain feel-good chemical in my brain that was in my reward system that said, 'Hey man, this is a good thing, you should do that.' And then many, many years later when I first stepped onstage and I got that same reaction, I was hooked."

Nice's choice of occupation is a true work-around for him. He chose to move out of an area (entrepreneurship and business ownership) that involved constant financial risk—a dangerous milieu for someone in a manic state, since being in a manic state is so often associated with grandiosity and overspending. Then he intentionally chose to pursue comedy, an uplifting field that uses humor to deal with hardship. His creative work stimulates his fast-moving brain in a healthy way. For Nice, performing and creating comedy are akin to creatively exorcising his demons. "I do television because I like it, I like being on—I love the camera. But I do stand-up because it's cathartic. Comedy forces you to look in the mirror first and deal with your insecurities. So what you find is that it doesn't remedy insecurity. But it acknowledges, and that acknowledgment I think allows you to say, 'Okay, that's like the bogeyman in the corner. But you know what? He can't hurt me.' Because once he comes out into the light, he disappears. In the shadows, he looms large. But when he steps into the light, he's destroyed, and that's how it feels." He further acknowledges that his painful childhood has contributed to his comedic perspective. "No co-median is going to tell you that they had a great childhood that was filled with support, love, understanding, and encouragement. You cannot be a comedian if that was your life."

Anthropologist Emily Martin also cites the importance of finding "the right profession" for her mental health. "I think if I were [in a job without] a lot of creativity, I wouldn't be thriving. So there's a terrific fit between what I do and what I have to do." She's also found work that matches her energy level. "Because there's a seasonal periodicity to academics—and I think a lot of people feel this—you don't have to be equally active all the time, the way you might in a corporate position. So it allows for you to be on, full-steam sometimes, and relatively off at other times. And that's how I tend to be."

Bill Lichtenstein has learned how to rein himself in at times when he might otherwise lose himself in flights of ideas. For him, "ideas are a dime a dozen. And the first step that I took to impose order on this was [what] I called 'the no game show rule.'" According to his own self-imposed rule, any idea that woke him up between midnight and eight in the morning—for example, a concept for a new game show, or a book series, or a documentary—was immediately put aside. Instead of getting up and hurl-ing himself into planning, he goes back to sleep. "Because people with bipolar can get very caught up in these kinds of ideas and then they become imperatives, and then they are suddenly chartering a jet to go talk to somebody."

With the help of his doctors, Lichtenstein is at the forefront of using cognitive behavioral therapy (CBT) to control his mania in the same way that CBT has been successfully used to treat depression. Via a combination of intensive individual and group CBT and dialectical behavioral ther-apy, he has been able to remain on an even keel minus medication for more than a decade. He began to wean himself from medication under the close observation of his doctors in the nineties. "I had a conversation with my doctor, [because] I felt blunted, I just could feel it. And I had been stable for years. And so, we started sort of tapering it down, and eventually, I just took the plunge, I was fine and have been fine for a long time." Lichtenstein believes—and his doctors agree—that in his case behavioral therapy is as effective as drug therapy, and, in fact, is serving to rewire his brain. This involves hard and devoted work as well as constant vigilance. "I have weekly one-hour therapy sessions where a lot of it is mindfulness and exercises and really talking about dealing with moods, and then an hour and a half weekly CBT group. And then every couple of months, I meet with a psychiatrist."

This path might not be right for everyone, but it's nonetheless fascinating to consider that there could be safe, nonpharmaceutical ways of mitigating the downsides of bipolar disorder. And as Lichtenstein stresses, "It's not like I've walked away from this. I'm working really hard."

GIFTS OF THE BRAIN WITH BIPOLAR DISORDER

In her book *Touched with Fire,* Kay Jamison identified a pattern of bipolar disorder among deceased poets and writers. In a focused study of thirty living writers at the Iowa Writers' Workshop, she found that "fully 80 percent of the study sample met formal diagnostic criteria for a mood disorder." In contrast, 30 percent of the control sample (individuals whose professional work fell outside the arts but who were matched for age, education, and sex) met the same criteria. As Jamison aptly notes, "Many of the changes in mood, thinking, and perception that characterize the mildly manic states—restlessness, ebullience, expansiveness, irritability, grandiosity, quickened and more finely tuned senses, intensity of emotional experiences, diversity of thought, and rapidity of associational processes—are highly characteristic of creative thought as well."[20]

Indeed, Chuck Nice recalls that when he was first diagnosed with bipolar disorder, "I loved it. I was like, no, I feel great, man. You can't sleep. But the fact is I felt really creative and really just literally flashes would come to me, whole concepts of very involved things. I'll get on a rush and

I'll write a half hour of material and I'll perform it and it works." This is comparable to the "boing" Emily Martin feels when she enters the field. Nice notes that when creative ideas come to him, they are very often fully formed, and he's not even conscious of how the idea arrived. Prior to becoming a performer, when he was working for a large toy manufacturer, "we were coming up with a marketing campaign, and I'm sitting in the meeting, and I think I slept like two hours the night before. And I came up with the entire campaign right in the meeting. [The idea] was just so complete, because that's how I see things when I'm in that state. I don't see an idea, I see the whole thing. All the beginning and the end, all at the same time. I can't explain it, but it's all there."

He became a comedian while he was national sales manager for a company that was bought out by Tyco Toys. Encouraged by a coworker to go to an open mike night at a comedy club, he said, "I'll do it if you invite the whole office. If one person doesn't show up, I'm not going on." Everyone came. "I had written five minutes of material. I went up and I killed it. People were flabbergasted."

Nice not only comes up with fully formed ideas, he has the heightened linguistic ability—a trait also strongly associated with bipolar disorder— to express them. He was aware of his skill with words from a very young age. Sexually abused by an adult member of his extended family throughout his childhood, Nice also endured bullying and physical abuse at school. It was as if "other kids sensed that I was a victim." Nice felt he couldn't fight back physically, so he used words. "That's where [my sharp tongue] came from. With teachers, I always had a witty comeback. With bullies, I always smashed them with my tongue. They hit me anyway, but I might as well get the satisfaction of telling you what an idiot you are first. You can beat me up, and that black eye, in a week it's gone. No one will ever know that I've been beaten up. But what I'm going to say to you, I will change your life. Your life is now changed. [This is why I try not to] talk to the audience when I do stand-up comedy, because if it goes wrong, I know that somebody's leaving very upset. My wife said, 'You go, you don't have any in between.'"

Emily Martin describes her particular talent as making "unusual juxtapositions." This, combined with increased output, is the seed of her remarkable creativity. "I can recall one time that my mood state was very elevated. I wasn't doing anything bothersome to anybody. I wasn't acting crazy. I just remember thinking, Oh my God. Just one idea after another was occurring to me."

Like Emily Martin, Bill Lichtenstein has noticed in himself and others with bipolar disorder a very particular type of creativity. "You can look at a box on the side of the road and say, 'That would make a great lamp.' That kind of ability to take two disparate things and make a connection between them that other people don't see is heightened, especially when people are hypomanic. I think [people with bipolar disorder] often look at the world as more of a three-dimensional chessboard. They can see where they want to get to, they can see all the things that would have to happen for that to happen. They can see the things that you would do along the way to make that happen. So they're really looking at systems in much more sophisticated ways [compared to those with neurotypical brains]. Part of it is that with bipolar you get ideas that are fully formed. It's not just, Oh, I want to start a restaurant, but the whole thing comes out of nowhere and you get a whole big picture. I think it's also the ability to hold that much information and strategic thinking in your head at one time."

This was Lichtenstein's experience when he came up with the idea for an hourlong documentary on bipolar disorder. He wrote to an executive at NPR saying, "I'd like to do an hour documentary on manic depression," and received a note back saying, "That sounds really depressing." Undeterred, "I literally woke up one morning and thought, you could do an hour show and it would have all these people talking about what happened to them, and how they got better, and then you could have all these experts explaining and putting it into context, and Patty Duke would narrate it. Now, she didn't know me from a hole in the wall, but I sat down and wrote a letter and said, 'I'm doing this documentary, and I want you to narrate it.' I sent it to William Morris and they called back and said, 'Yes, she'll do it.' So that's the kind of thing where, you know, it's a hair-thin [line] away from crazy. So I guess I'm proposing the line between quixotic craziness and brilliance."

It could be argued that Ernest Hemingway spent much of his creative life balancing on that hair-thin line.[21] He referred to his elevated, energized, grandiose state as "the juice," and it was the juice that enabled him to generate tremendous quantities of genius-level original writing, and with seemingly endless energy. While many people who struggle with bipolar disorder think their creative output is brilliant while they are hypomanic or manic, in Hemingway's case it really was. Unfortunately, Hemingway's illness went largely untreated, and his hypomania veered into the kind of self-destructive behavior that makes a manic episode all the more likely. And in just the way that Emily Martin described a lightbulb burning out, Hemingway would crash into deep depressions that he described with words such as "gigantic" and "bloody."[22]

When he was most productive, it was in that sweet spot between depression and full-on mania. During these hypomanic periods, he was not only extraordinarily prolific; the quality and creativity of his work were also exceptionally high. His agitation was such that he was compelled to write standing up, and his compressed writing style, which is so prized by admirers of his work, is also reflective of his rapid, hypomanic thought process. Moreover, his tendencies toward risk-taking and grandiosity fueled both his choice of subject matter (wars, bullfighting) and his relentless ambition and desire to impress the world.

Bill Lichtenstein's experience with delayed diagnosis and stigmatization occurred in the late 1980s and early 1990s, so we can imagine the lack of understanding of bipolar disorder that existed during Hemingway's lifetime. There was also shame. Hemingway was highly resistant to seeking help and wrote to friends that he didn't want anyone to think that he was losing his mind. In fact, he expressed anger with the writer F. Scott Fitzgerald after Fitzgerald wrote of his own struggles with mental illness. The kinetic effect of repeated episodes of mania and major depression, in addition to Hemingway's attempts to medicate his pain with alcohol—which only exacerbates mood swings—contributed to Hemingway's lightbulb dimming even before it burned out. But when it was lit, none shone more brightly.

HOW THE BRAIN WITH BIPOLAR DISORDER CAN FLOURISH

There are several keys to living well with bipolar disorder, and central to all of them is vigilance. Yet this can run counter to the natural inclinations of the person with bipolar disorder. Bill Lichtenstein says, "This whole idea of being in the moment and working through things—you know, it's almost like I feel like I've lived my life [doing] whatever the opposite of that is, which is to just not get caught up in any of the minutiae of the moment, but just sort of look at the big picture and move through things, focusing on, you know, what the big goal is." While this big-picture thinking is excellent for coming up with creative ideas fully formed, it can run counter to the kind of day-to-day self-care to which the person with bipolar disorder must devote herself—such as paying close attention to internal rhythms and the ways in which diet, exercise, stress, workload, and sleep all influence those rhythms.

Of all of these elements of self-care, perhaps the most important is sleep. There is a vicious circle in hypomania in which energy levels are so high that there is no desire for sleep—and yet without sleep the person who is elevating into hypomania is driven even higher into mania. In addition to the dangers of mania itself, there is the inevitable suffering of the depression that follows. Emily Martin compares this to "running too hot." This is both a physical and a mental wearing out, "and then, you don't have any more." Because hypomania feels so good, and can come on grad-ually, it can be difficult for the person with bipolar disorder to willingly recognize when it's occurring. This is why it's so important to have people in one's life who can identify the red flags as that process is starting. In essence, these people act as the frontal lobe for individuals with bipolar disorder—a tempering influence to balance out the disinhibition. Ideally, this is someone who either lives with or regularly communicates with the person with bipolar disorder. Bill Lichtenstein's weekly individual and group therapy serves multiple purposes in that regard.

While Lichtenstein has been able to manage his symptoms with inten-sive, rigorous therapy, the gold standard for treatment of bipolar disorder involves both therapy and pharmaceuticals. Yet it can be difficult for people with bipolar disorder to take medication. Lichtenstein felt "blunted" by lithium, and others worry that medication will rob them of the extraordi-narily quick thoughts that fuel their creativity. Nassir Ghaemi, who treats many bright students in their teens and twenties, addresses that concern this way: "What I talk about with them is that there's two ways to approach this. One is to take drugs that really have no cognitive effects. There are a few, [such as] Lamictal, [that] won't impair their creativity. And the other is to take drugs that might affect them cognitively, like lithium, but you can always use low doses and that seems to have less of a problem."

More to the point, Ghaemi says, is that people with bipolar disorder can benefit from taking a broad view of their own creativity. When patients resist medication, "the real issue they're having is that they think about creativity as just one thing, as this kind of flash of inspiration that happens when you're manic. And that is part of creativity, but there's another kind of creativity." He cites the work of psychoanalyst Elliott Jaques, who wrote about what he called "sculpted creativity." This is not "a flash of inspira-tion, but it's insights that over time you put together, like a sculptor. And it's not something that happens all of a sudden." This durable sort of creativity depends on maintaining equilibrium over the long haul—that is, not burning out like a lightbulb or losing time to severe manic and depressive episodes. "So what I tell my patients is, instead of having a lot of creativity really briefly and then being depressed and fallow for a long time, you're better off having less creativity more regularly, more consistently. It actually adds up more that way."

For Emily Martin, the benefits of the right medication have meant that she does not sink into major depression. "I certainly don't have as many super high states as I did before I went on lithium and all the other things I take. But my psychiatrist says, 'If you can recall a time when you were like that, were your ideas really good ones, or were they just pouring out helter-skelter, and kind of all over the place?' She would like me to say they were pouring out helter-skelter and all over the place, [but] I don't necessarily agree. I do agree that I will trade the high highs for not having the low lows any day. That seems to be the bargain."

Most important, she is still doing creative work while medicated—and launching into new fieldwork at the age of seventy. Her experience mirrors the "sculpted creativity" that Ghaemi points to as a benefit of long-term treatment. Martin says of herself, "Even though the top and the bottom are lopped off, mood-wise, there's this other engine, and many other engines—who knows what it all is? Curiosity, risk-taking, pushback, rebelliousness. Ambition's another one. I believe in the effects of the medicine, but they coexist with all this other stuff, which is huge. I've learned by now that if I just do the work, the research, at a certain point, stuff will start to connect for me."

Perhaps the first and most important step is the shedding of shame. Stigma and shame are what prevent individuals from seeking the treatment that would enable them to stay vital and productive and to live up to their full potential. Bill Lichtenstein poignantly recalls when he first realized that he was not alone. It was a "magic moment, to go to a support group and suddenly, people are saying what you are thinking. I've always said, it's therapy, medication, and support groups. They are equally important."

6

DIVERGENT THINKING

COMMON DIAGNOSES

SCHIZOID PERSONALITY DISORDER, SCHIZOPHRENIA,
AND SCHIZOAFFECTIVE DISORDER

*"For me, work is the last thing to go. Even if I start getting
very, very symptomatic, I can work through it for a long
time before I fall apart."*

—ELYN SAKS

Elyn Saks experienced her first symptom of schizophrenia when she was sixteen years old.[1] She was walking home from school and felt certain that threatening messages were being transmitted directly into her brain. A brilliant student born into a stable home with loving parents, she didn't appear troubled to anyone else. But as a child she had experienced night terrors, phobias, and strong obsessions, and later, while an undergraduate at Vanderbilt University, she suffered from several bouts of detachment from reality similar to what she'd experienced as a sixteen-year-old. Still, she graduated first in her class and went on to study philosophy at Oxford.

While in England, her symptoms became far more severe, perhaps heightened by her distance from home and her cultural disorientation. She made a few friends, but at a time when she desperately needed support, she found it impossible to communicate. Of her attempts to maintain a connection with one particular friend, she wrote in her memoir, *The Center Cannot Hold,* "Literally, the words in my head would not come out of my mouth. Our dinner conversations grew increasingly one-sided and I was reduced almost totally to nodding in agreement, feigning a full mouth and trying to express whatever I was thinking with my face. The friendship trickled away." Coupled with the sudden inability to articulate her thoughts, she was seized by self-loathing. "Nothing I had to say was worth hearing, or so said my mind. It's wrong to talk. Talking means you have something to say. I have nothing to say. I am nobody, a nothing. Talking takes up space and time. You don't deserve to talk. Keep quiet."

Saks's description of the onset of her symptoms is both poetic and devastating. "Schizophrenia rolls in like a slow fog, becoming imperceptibly thicker as time goes on. At first, the day is bright enough, the sky is clear, the sunlight warms your shoulders. But soon, you notice a haze beginning to gather around you, and the air feels not quite so warm. After a while, the sun is a dim light bulb behind a heavy cloth. The horizon has vanished into a grey mist and you feel a thick dampness in your lungs as you stand, cold and wet, in the afternoon dark . . ."[2]

It's no wonder that her symptoms began to interfere with her work.

"What was real, what was not? I couldn't decipher the difference and it was exhausting. . . . I could not understand what I was reading, nor was I able to follow the lectures. And I certainly couldn't write anything intelligible."[3] After she felt that she'd embarrassed herself by delivering an incoherent paper at her weekly seminar, she experienced suicidal thoughts—and planned out the details of particular methods she could use to kill herself. She thought about dousing herself with gasoline and setting herself ablaze, since she felt she deserved a painful death. Only the prospect of bringing pain to those she loved prevented her from going through with it. When she saw a doctor and confessed the nature of her thoughts, he made an appointment for her at Warneford Hospital, the site of the psychiatric division of Oxford's medical school. Thus began Saks's journey toward a diagnosis of schizophrenia.

Today, Saks is a professor at the University of Southern California Gould School of Law. She writes extensively in the areas of law and mental health, and has published five books and more than fifty articles. Her research topics have included the ethical dimensions of psychiatric research and forced treatment of people with mental illness. After winning a MacArthur fellowship, she founded the Saks Institute for Mental Health Law, Policy, and Ethics, which works toward the improved treatment of people with mental illness. Despite the seriousness of her diagnosis, until the publication of her memoir in 2007, very few people knew that Saks herself suffered from mental illness. In addition to her considerable professional accomplishments, she is happily married and sustains rich friendships.

It's tempting to look at the outlines of her story and find nothing but silver lining, but Saks is clear and unflinching when discussing the negative impacts of her illness. She chose not to have children, fearing that the stresses of parenting might be too much for her. She has experienced some notable cognitive deterioration over time, which is not uncommon among people with schizophrenia. In her thirties, Saks suffered an unrelated subarachnoid hemorrhage, and she now tests in the range of borderline impaired for working memory measures and spatial skills. This is most likely due to a combination of factors, including the hemorrhage as well as her mental illness and the medication she takes to treat it. In the more than twenty years since the hemorrhage, her memory has continued to decline. In particular, she can lose the thread of conversations.

As part of her ongoing work to destigmatize mental illness, Saks has spoken to many people with schizophrenia, and she says, "That magic pill question—if you could take a pill to make it go away, would you? I haven't had one person say no. Some bipolar people would say no, that they miss the highs and that kind of thing." But the symptoms of schizophrenia are not euphoric, they're often terrifying and debilitating. "Typically, I feel like

I kill hundreds of thousands of people with my thoughts or nuclear explosions going on in my brain or people in the sky are controlling my actions. I have had occasional visual hallucinations at night, which is not supposed to be diagnostically significant, but for me correlates with being worse off. Typically, it would be a person standing at the foot of my bed, and I would wake up, open my eyes, and say, 'Oh, shit, I hope that's a hallucination.'"

Saks is gifted with a brilliant mind, but perhaps what has saved her most of all is her own tenacity. "I can work through symptoms unless they're really, really severe, and in fact, work is one of my best defenses against symptoms. So, [while] focusing on an argument or constructing a counterargument, that crazy stuff recedes to the sidelines. For me, work is the last thing to go. So, even if I start getting very, very symptomatic, I can work through it for a long time before I fall apart."

Something else Saks has at her disposal—a rare skill among people suffering from schizophrenia—is what she calls social insight. "I've always known, even if I think what I believe is true, that other people will think it's crazy, and I don't want to appear crazy, so I don't say it out loud. Or, if I feel like I can't *not* say it out loud, I stay at home. So I maintain a professional demeanor because I have . . . social insight."

The drug Clozapine has been the pharmaceutical key to the ongoing control of Saks's symptoms. "When I was in England and not on meds for the first three or five years of my illness, I would say 80 percent of my waking thoughts were psychotic. . . . When I was on and off medication and not [on] one of the [effective] ones, I would say 30 percent of my waking thoughts were psychotic, and now, it's down to like 4 percent. So, it's a very small part of my life now." That said, Saks's threshold for divergent, even disturbing thinking is much higher than someone else's might be. "Oh, I have transient unusual thoughts all the time, but I just dismiss them."

For Elyn Saks, schizophrenia is not something either to celebrate or stigmatize, it's something to manage, understand, and treat. "I spent years trying to get off meds, but once I decided to stay on them, my life got better." The quality of Saks's life—and the contributions that she has made to society—are powerful proof that it's society's shame and loss if we dismiss and mistreat those with mental illness.

WHAT IT MEANS TO HAVE DIVERGENT THOUGHTS

The phrase *divergent thinking* refers specifically to thoughts that are atypical and out of the box—even odd. Schizotypal thinking contains elements of divergent thinking, but also might involve magical and even paranoid thinking that is disconnected from a concrete reality. This is not the same thing as schizophrenia—many people without mental illness diagnoses, when tested for schizotypal thinking, will exhibit these thought processes to some degree. Schizophrenia (from the Greek "split mind") is characterized by an inability to determine what is real, which is called psychotic thinking. In the *DSM-5,* schizotypal thinking is not categorized under the schizophrenia spectrum. However, for the purposes of this chapter, schizotypal or divergent thinking will be considered as existing at the mildest end of the schizophrenia spectrum because of the commonality of behavior and thought processes. Divergent thinking is not nearly as rare as many people might think. In fact, studies by Dutch researchers suggest that as much as 4 percent of the healthy population experience auditory hallucinations in the form of hearing voices.[4] These researchers theorized that the phenomenon can be brought on by stress—for example, the individual who hears a beloved's voice in her head after that person has died—and they also suggest that healthy individuals, particularly those who are optimistic by nature, tend not to be troubled by these hallucinations, and therefore don't feel the need to consult with a doctor. In addition, according to Thomas Sedlak, director of the Schizophrenia Center at Johns Hopkins, "it's [a] little-known fact that about 20 percent of first psychotic episodes are the only one someone will have."[5] We still do not understand the mechanism whereby someone would have a singular episode—

whether it might be brought on by extreme stress or some other set of factors. In any case, these are individuals who are either never diagnosed because they never experience another symptom, or are initially diagnosed as schizophrenic, but never again have need of psychiatric treatment.

The National Institute of Mental Health estimates that approximately 1 percent of the United States population suffers from schizophrenia.[6] That figure is ten times as high for a first-degree relative (parent, child, or sibling) of someone with schizophrenia. And identical twins are 40 to 60 percent more likely to be diagnosed with schizophrenia if their twin sibling is also diagnosed.[7] This clearly suggests genetic linkage, although the less than 100 percent correlation among identical twins suggests that there are other elements also at work. We simply don't know yet what interaction of genes and environment might be at play.

There is a debate among clinicians and researchers as to whether schizoid personality disorder, schizophrenia, and schizoaffective disorder exist on a spectrum at all, or whether they are separate and unrelated disorders. Nonetheless, there are clear overlaps between the three in the realms of divergent thinking as well as behavior. The differences between the three disorders primarily concern the treatability and severity of symptoms. Generally speaking, a person with schizoid personality disorder might be viewed as eccentric, difficult to get along with, and even withdrawn. They might experience the symptoms of schizotypal thinking (for example, hearing voices), without revealing this fact to anyone—even to a doctor. The person with schizophrenia who presents with more dramatic symptoms of divergent thinking would have a much more difficult time hiding in plain sight. Someone in this category would exhibit symptoms such as paranoid delusions—the belief that government agencies might be listening in on their thoughts, for example. Elyn Saks tried to continue as if there weren't something very seriously wrong until she simply couldn't carry on without others taking notice. Those with schizoaffective disorder not only experience the more severe symptoms of schizophrenia, but also present with elements of mood disorders, such as the highs and lows of bipolar disorder. Of the three, schizoaffective disorder is the most difficult to treat and those who suffer from it are at the highest risk for suicide, due to the combination of cycling mood and psychosis.

Individuals who suffer from any of these three disorders can become socially isolated, outwardly withdrawn, and seemingly lacking in emotion and affect. Inwardly, individuals with all three disorders can experience recurrent loss of touch with reality. Symptoms of this disconnect fall into two clinical categories: "positive" and "negative." Positive symptoms include hallucinations, delusions, and disorganized thinking—all of which Elyn Saks experienced to one degree or another—and are among the more treatable by antipsychotic medications. Hallucinations are most commonly auditory, although sometimes they are visual and quite vivid. Auditory hallucinations can be just as convincingly real. Elyn Saks experienced both auditory hallucinations (voices telling her that she was worthless) and visual ones (a figure appearing at the end of her bed). In addition, she experienced delusions—for example, she believed she could cause nuclear holocaust with her mind. Among those with paranoid schizophrenia—which is a subtype of schizophrenia that Saks does not have—the delusions are typically the unshakeable belief that someone or something is out to get them, or that thoughts are being extracted from or implanted in one's brain. Saks did experience disorganized thinking, the third category of positive symptoms—to the point that she was unable either to understand her course work or to articulate what she knew. Many people with schizophrenia will use nonsense words (referred to as neologism) while attempting to communicate, and engage in what clinicians call "word salad," which are collections of verbiage that make no coherent sense.

While these "positive" symptoms of psychosis can be frightening to the loved ones of people with schizophrenia, they are in fact less intractable and more susceptible to treatment than what are called the "negative" symptoms of schizophrenia. Positive symptoms can be cyclical or episodic—in that there are some people with these symptoms of schizophrenia who go through periods of being better integrated, i.e., experiencing fewer intrusive effects. Negative symptoms of schizophrenia are much more difficult to treat and can appear similar to depression—one of the first negative symptoms to emerge is often an inability to find joy or comfort in everyday things that used to bring the person pleasure. Eventually individuals with schizophrenia may exhibit an entirely flat affect, which reflects this devastating loss of enjoyment—their faces don't move, their voices become monotonous. This apathy can extend to a lack of interest in personal hygiene—getting up to brush teeth and take a shower can seem like a pointless effort. Other negative symptoms include cognitive disabilities such as deficits in working memory and loss of the ability to pay attention, to understand information, and to make use of it.

With age, many people find that some of the symptoms of schizophrenia burn out, particularly when they are well and consistently treated. When left untreated, however, symptoms of schizophrenia can worsen due to the brain's kinetic effect. That is, the more psychotic episodes the individual has, the more the rate of those episodes will increase. It's therefore not at all surprising that there is such a high incidence of untreated schizophrenia among the homeless population. However, it's also worthwhile noting that Elyn Saks has experienced a number of the "negative" symptoms of schizophrenia over the years, including a marked inability to enjoy her daily life (this was especially the case prior to being diagnosed and treated) as well as loss of working memory (a condition that appears to be ongoing despite treatment). And yet her case also provides evidence that people with schizophrenia can not only function but can also achieve great things. In fact, she translated her experience of traumatic hospitalization into her work as a lawyer representing the interests of patients.

The fact that many people with schizoid personality disorder never seek treatment adds to the difficulty of accurately assessing the incidence rate of schizophrenia spectrum disorders. Therefore our understanding of how much of the population experiences occasionally divergent thinking—and to what degree it affects their lives—is unknown. In the coming decades, largely as a result of the National Institutes of Health's Human

Connectome Project, which will scan thousands of human brains, we will have a much better understanding of the diversity of the human brain and its inner workings. Until then, we're forced to theorize the exact link between schizotypal thinking and creativity. That said, clinical research into the possible overlap dates back decades, and newer research drawing on advances in MRI technology is raising fascinating questions as to the impact of schizotypal thinking on creative output.

Nobel Prize–winning mathematician John Nash, subject of the book *A Beautiful Mind,* by Sylvia Nasar, and the movie of the same name, is a celebrated and oft-cited example of a person with schizophrenia who exhibited remarkable creativity and made a substantive contribution to his field.[8] However, he published the bulk of his most revolutionary work prior to the age of thirty, before his symptoms became debilitating, which leads some researchers and clinicians to question whether there is a positive link between his exceptional creativity and his schizophrenia. Like Elyn Saks, even as a child and young man his behavior could be eccentric and often off-putting. He walked off in the middle of sentences, whistled at inappropriate times, and could come across as arrogant, even rude. This suggests that his greatest creative output occurred while he was in what is called the "prodromal" stage of schizophrenia—when early symptoms of hallucination, delusion, and disorganized thinking have emerged, but the individual still has some control over thought processes. That is, his work may have benefited from divergent thinking prior to being overwhelmed by the severity of his symptoms.

A study conducted by researchers at the Orygen research center and the Department of Psychology of the University of Melbourne and published in the *Schizophrenia Bulletin* examined the thought processes of one hundred artists (forty-three men and fifty-seven women) across a range of disciplines. Each participant filled out an "Experience of Creativity Questionnaire."[9] Compared to data from nonartist respondents, the artists were found to be "elevated on 'positive' schizotypy, unipolar affective disturbance, thin boundaries, and the personality dimensions of Openness to Experience and Neuroticism." Moreover, "schizotypy was found to be the strongest predictor of a range of creative experience scales . . . suggesting a strong overlap of schizotypal and creative experience." A particularly fascinating result of the study is the correlation researchers found between elevated levels of schizotypal thinking and creative flow. First coined and popularized by psychologist Mihaly Csikszentmihalyi, *flow* was defined by these researchers as "deep absorption, focus on present experience, and sense of pleasure." It is the state of mind that an artist enters when fully immersed—distractions fall away and the individual typically experiences losing track of time. These researchers theorize that the neurologically based latent inhibition found in schizotypal individuals may facilitate "greater absorption in present experience, thus leading to flow-type states."

In their article "Creativity and Schizophrenia Spectrum Disorders Across the Arts and Sciences," published in the November 2014 issue of *Frontiers in Psychology,* researchers Scott Barry Kaufman and Elliot S. Paul encapsulate why schizotypal thinking might contribute to creativity—and also why it must work in tandem with other gifts and skills: "One aspect of creativity is obviously novelty or originality. So, by its very nature, schizophrenia disposes one toward satisfying one requirement for creative thought: namely originality. Originality is not sufficient for creativity, however. For a product to be creative it must not only be new but also useful, effective, or valuable in some way. These two features—novelty and utility—respectively depend on two cognitive functions: the generation of ideas popping up in conscious thought, and the selection of ideas to be explored, developed, and ultimately expressed or realized in the form of an observable product."[10] This is essentially what Elyn Saks described when she said that she knew when her thoughts might be perceived as crazy, so she kept them to herself. And this is why such a balance between originality and self-control is most likely to be seen in either the prodromal state of schizophrenia, or the milder forms of schizotypal thinking in which many creative people engage even without calling it such.

In an article titled "The Mad-Genius Paradox" and published in *Perspectives on Psychological Science,* Dean Keith Simonton of the University of California, Davis, also addressed the question of whether "creativity and psychopathology are positively or negatively correlated."[11] For the purposes of his study, creativity was defined as "the production of one or more creative products that contribute to an established domain of achievement." He then found statistical evidence of two seemingly contradictory facts: first, among all creative individuals, the more creative are at higher risk for mental illness than are the less creative; second, among all people, creative individuals exhibit better mental health than do noncreative individuals. Simonton ultimately concluded that these two facts were not at all contradictory. When he looked at the number of actual creative achievements each individual had accomplished, and he measured the psychiatric symptoms and diagnoses of these individuals, he found marked differences in rates of mental illness among those who had accomplished significantly more. In this way, he found that the most creative people were more likely than the average person to have psychopathology, but also that moderately creative people tended to be more mentally healthy than the average population. Until we have more physical data, we can't know what neurological function both contributes to creativity and also makes one more vulnerable to mental illness—nonetheless, the correlation is clearly present.

One intriguing potential source of this correlation was put forward in a study published in the *British Journal of Psychiatry* in 1976.[12] Researchers at the Royal College of Psychiatry found that when three groups of adults were measured for attention—people with nonparanoid schizophrenia, highly creative people, and people of equal intelligence but low creativity— both the highly creative and schizophrenic individuals "habitually sample a wider range of available environmental input than do less creative individuals." We all screen out some environmental input in order to decipher meaning in what is happening around us—that is, we couldn't perceive coherence in the world around us if we indiscriminately took in all of the stimulation we encountered. But in terms of degree, less creative individuals screen out more environmental input—sights, sounds, etc.—because it feels less relevant to them. Those with schizophrenia and those who are highly creative are actually screening out fewer stimuli. The creative person might then also make productive (as opposed to psychotic) meaning out of these extra stimuli they take in. One example of a test used in the study is the "Lovibond Object Sorting Test," in which subjects are asked to sort common objects into categories. The instructions "permit divergent thinking in the form of unusual and idiosyncratic sortings." These sortings are then "graded on a four-point scale denoting the degree of conventionality." The people with schizophrenia and the more creative individuals tended "to return a high score by employing more unusual sortings." In the case of the person with schizophrenia, "this involuntary widening of attention tends to have a deleterious effect on performance, while in contrast, the highly creative individual is more able to successfully process the greater input without this incurring a performance deficit." This, in a nutshell, is an example of the potentially harmful and advantageous upsides of a neurological predisposition toward divergent thinking.

In 2013, a group of neuroscientists led by Andreas Fink at the University of Graz in Austria recruited study participants who exhibited both high and low rates of schizotypy.[13] They then scanned the brains of these participants while they completed a task in which they were asked to come up with original uses for everyday objects. They found marked similarities between the most creative thinkers and those who measured high for schizotypal thinking. The part of the brain that showed low activation—the right precuneus—strongly points to what the Royal College of Psychiatry researchers could only theorize back in 1976, namely that the creative and the schizotypal engage in less filtering of the information they take in from the world around them.

In 2014, Annukka K. Lindell at the School for Psychological Science at

La Trobe University in Melbourne published an article in *Frontiers in Psychology* analyzing the growing body of research indicating that atypical brain lateralization may have an impact on individual levels of creativity.[14] Atypical brain lateralization simply means "differences in the typical side of the brain where [the average person has] their structures and functions." One example of this is that a larger than average percentage of both highly creative people and people exhibiting higher than average levels of schizotypy or divergent thinking are both left-hand and left-ear dominant. She argues that this particular difference in the structure of the brain "prompts a cognitive processing style that enhances both creativity and schizotypy, suggesting a potential biological foundation for the link between genius and madness."

These studies all contribute to a picture that becomes more complex the more we look at it. Ultimately, creativity can't be pinned to the workings of one particular part of the brain, and as brain science has evolved, we're learning just how little we understand. Increasingly, we realize that our brains' higher cognitive functions must be considered in the context of connectivity among various parts of the brain, and not purely attributed to the internal mechanics of isolated parts. In a 2015 study published in *Neuropsychologia,* researchers at the University of Auckland scanned the brains of healthy subjects while they performed a drawing test.[15] They also had subjects fill out the Oxford-Liverpool Inventory of Feelings and Experiences, or O-LIFE, a questionnaire that measures schizotypal thinking. The scans revealed that "neural activations associated with the creativity task were observed in bilateral inferior temporal gyri, left insula, left parietal lobule, right angular gyrus, as well as regions in the prefrontal cortex." What this means is that multiple parts of the brain are engaged when you complete a creative task. This suggests that "creative production [is] the result of collaboration between these regions." In addition, this same pattern of brain activation is associated with "having unusual mental experiences" and "nonconformity"—both of which are features of schizotypy.

THE EXPERIENCE OF HAVING DIVERGENT THOUGHTS

While milder forms of divergent thoughts can be seen as beneficial to creativity, on the more severe end of the schizophrenia spectrum, clinicians and researchers are understandably hesitant to ascribe any clear upsides to having the disease. As Elyn Saks noted, she has never encountered anyone with schizophrenia who wouldn't opt for a cure. It's a devastating diagnosis to receive—both for individuals and their families—and there should be no sugarcoating of the experience. Anyone suffering from recurrent breaks with reality or a loss of enjoyment in everyday life should immediately seek help and treatment. Medication is essential to enable people with schizophrenia to lead productive lives. And there are many people with severe forms of schizophrenia who can never hope to achieve the kind of independence and relative peace of mind that most of us take for granted. There is, however, reason for optimism. Researchers such as Deanna Barch at the Human Connectome Project, who helps direct the team that is scanning thousands of brains, will bring us closer to discovering the causes of schizophrenia, and to successfully treating even the most severe cases.[16]

The cloud of fear around mental illness of all kinds is thick, and around schizophrenia it's thicker. There is no other brain difference so strongly associated with negative stereotypes—when we think of the hallucinations and delusions that are the symptoms of schizophrenia, we use words such as *crazy, psycho,* and *bonkers.* We might know not to use words with negative connotations about people with developmental disorders or brain differences such as depression, but when we are describing the homeless person walking down the street talking to himself and gesticulating, we tend not to think first of untreated illness. Rather, we think he's "nuts" and perhaps also dangerous. In actuality, just like the rest of us, people with schizophrenia are much more likely to be the victims of crimes than the perpetrators.

The stigmatizing of schizophrenia spectrum disorders hurts all of us, and it's not clinically justified. In fact, Thomas Sedlak, director of the schizophrenia clinic at Johns Hopkins, says, "I've had patients with milder cases of what I think is schizophrenia spectrum who are more functional than some cases of depression. There's a spectrum of schizophrenia, which I think is less well appreciated—there are some milder cases and there are some terrible cases. The term 'schizophrenia' or 'psychotic disorder' can lead to this terrible stigma in the [families'] eyes. Or the patient's eyes as well—such that they refuse to even accept the diagnosis."

And with a lack of acceptance of the diagnosis comes a lack of acceptance of the necessary treatment. Elyn Saks delineates the enormous difference that Clozapine has made in her life—helping her go from 80 percent psychotic thinking to increasingly rare occurrences of such thoughts. In addition to benefitting from pharmaceuticals, she's worked hard to understand her symptoms for what they are—signs of disease and not voices of doom. Remarkably, she's actually been able to find humor in some of her symptoms. "A friend of mine, when I was a junior scholar, totally trashed a paper I wrote, and I woke up in the middle of the night, and at the foot of my bed, I saw a little devil stationed nearby." Saks immediately recognized that envisioning a devil by her bedside was an excellent metaphor for a writer's attitude toward criticism. "I thought that was kind of funny."

She now finds enjoyment in channeling her feelings into her work. "When I was in college and in law school, I was really stressed around writing and took the minimum number of writing courses. But once I became an academic, a switch was opened up, and I just have so many things that I want to write about." In her book *Interpreting Interpretation,* she addressed various theories of hermeneutic psychoanalysis, one of which is that the analyst's interpretations are "just stories that make sense of your life and don't have to necessarily correspond with reality." Saks took strong exception to this. "I think patients, if they understood that, would and should reject interpretations because who wants to know a story? You want to know the truth." Saks came to recognize that her position grew from a very personal place—namely her own need for clarity and solidity. "A former professor of mine wrote a paper about my book, and pointed out that maybe I was so preoccupied with . . . getting at the truth of the matter because [my thoughts and those of other patients with diagnosed mental illness] are so often in the dark or confused."

That place of darkness and confusion is terrifying for those with diagnosed mental illness. The experience is made vastly more difficult when it's combined with societal stigmatization. Those with mental illness can help themselves via treatment and vigilance to their own emotional and physical well-being. The rest of us have an equally important task: to educate ourselves about the contributions made by people with mental illness and not further isolate those who are in need of our compassion and understanding.

GIFTS OF THE BRAIN WITH DIVERGENT THOUGHTS

For every study that illustrates a strong correlation between divergent or schizotypal thinking and creativity, there is a researcher or clinician warning against painting too rosy a picture. Just as there are far fewer geniuses than there are people of average or below-average intelligence, there are far fewer success stories such as Elyn Saks than there are devastating stories about individuals whose symptoms are impossible to overcome. But when we talk about schizotypal thinking as it relates to both creativity and schizophrenia spectrum disorders, the fact that there is a scientifically supportable linkage is astoundingly meaningful. People with schizophrenia spectrum disorders are not only entitled—as we all are—to excellent medical treatment, they should also be looked to—as we all should be—for the contributions they can make to society.

In the case of Elyn Saks and other high-functioning individuals with schizophrenia spectrum disorders, divergent thinking is only one piece of the creativity puzzle. Intelligence is another. Thomas Sedlak also underlines the importance of tenacity and risk-taking, both of which can run strong in people with schizophrenia spectrum disorders. "When people are talking about creative geniuses or great innovations, often there's an important strain of persistence and tenacity. Persevering in the face of adversity. A creative idea is one [that] is somewhat novel and nonmainstream. Often the initial acceptance of that is slow to come on [and] is not faced with a ringing endorsement from the get-go. And it takes persistence and tenacity to endure. And also I think another thing that's not always [appreciated in this context is] risk-taking. You know, as a psychiatrist, you've certainly seen risk-taking in individuals with mental illness. [That is] an important part of creativity."

Elyn Saks draws inspiration from her brain difference in multiple ways. As a mental health advocate, she brings both empathy and passion to her work to advance the rights of the mentally ill. In addition, she brings her unique creativity, her way of thinking, and her desire to question the more "typical" approaches. "I think in a quirky kind of way, a little bit outside the box, with the writing that I do, which is kind of theoretical. It's helpful not to be bound by conventional ways of thinking. As an example, early in my career, I studied multiple personality disorder and criminal law. And I said, you know, how we think of criminal law depends on how we conceptualize altered personalities. Are they people, by the best criteria of personal identity? Or are they parts of a complicated person? Now, most people would not buy the idea that someone with multiple personality disorder could have different people in him or her. But, if you look at philosophers talking about psychological and bodily theories of personal identity, it's not that far-fetched. And I think you have to be pretty open to different things to actually contemplate that. I think it's very interesting that a lot of things that philosophers play around with are things that people with mental health disorders live. As an example, we all know from Locke and Hume and other people that you can't prove the existence of an external world. No philosopher lives as if there's no external world, but some patients do."

Human innovation of all kinds—artistic, scientific, entrepreneurial—is driven by people who aren't thinking the same way everyone before them has thought. Discovery results from the coexistence of both originality and openness—a novel way of thinking, combined with sensitivity to stimuli and environmental input that others ignore. These are the precise gifts of the person with schizotypal thoughts.

HOW THE BRAIN WITH DIVERGENT THOUGHTS CAN FLOURISH

As with the other brain differences discussed in this book, schizophrenia symptoms exist on a continuum from mild to severe and debilitating. Much evidence exists that it is schizotypal thinking itself—as opposed to the broader diagnosis of schizophrenia—that most contributes to creative output. It's inadvisable and simply inaccurate to suggest that all people with the more serious forms of schizophrenia have above-average creative potential. Many people with schizotypal thoughts are simply too debilitated by their symptoms to be prolific in creative fields. However, while we don't want to whitewash the tremendous challenges that a diagnosis of schizophrenia presents, we also shouldn't dismiss the estimated 3.5 million Americans diagnosed with this disease as being incapable of making a contribution to our world. Unfortunately, we as a society are guilty of dismissing them on a daily basis. As a result, many people with schizophrenia spectrum disorders are understandably afraid to share their diagnoses even with close friends. It took Elyn Saks decades to publicly reveal her own diagnosis. This hesitation is understandable. It is often the case that once a diagnosis is known, all of the patient's thoughts, feelings, and actions are viewed through that lens. And no one wants the fullness of their lives and emotions reduced to a diagnosis.

Perhaps the first step in changing our views toward people with mental illnesses is to change our words. Just as we've wrung the word *retarded* out of our lexicon, we need to banish words such as *crazy* and *nuts*. Using derogatory language such as this infiltrates our thinking about the mentally ill in general, discounts the whole person, and enables us to dismiss them and their roles and rights in the community. Instead, we need to educate ourselves about brain differences and mental illness and use what is called "people first" language. That is, Elyn Saks is not a schizophrenic. She is a person—a brilliant lawyer and a funny, compassionate, and productive person—with schizophrenia. John Nash was a Nobel Prize–winning mathematician, husband, and father with schizophrenia. These individuals are not their diseases.

In addition, we need to keep researching better ways to treat people with schizophrenia. Thomas Sedlak says that treatment of schizophrenia is "an area in which psychiatry needs to do a better job. The easy part is suppressing psychotic symptoms. You don't need to be too bright to look up an antipsychotic and just increase the dose. But the hard part is finding the balance in which you can control symptoms and allow someone to thrive. Because if you're in a quasi-comatose state or sleeping fourteen to sixteen hours a day, it's hard to realize your potential. Everybody's a little bit different and [it's important to find] where they want to draw that line—that fulcrum of where's the right place on the seesaw of balance that they want." It should be noted that over the decades, tremendous pharmaceutical advances have been made, resulting in far fewer and less severe side effects.

While most people with milder schizoid symptoms don't seek treatment—whether because of fear, denial, or aversion to treatment—talk therapy and cognitive behavioral therapy can be helpful on multiple fronts. Therapy can help people on all parts of the spectrum to organize their thoughts and better socially relate, particularly while they are experiencing symptoms. It's essential for anyone with a diagnosed mental illness to have a support network—which is why it's tragic that the stigmatization of mental illness itself causes so much suffering in isolation. People with schizophrenia spectrum disorders need professional help, and they also need the emotional support of family and friends who can step in at the onset of symptoms, make sure medication is being taken, and offer assistance as needed.

Individuals with mental health diagnoses also do best when they are taking care of themselves physically. Avoiding mind-altering substances is extremely important, as is regular exercise and good nutrition. Simple routines such as sleeping at night and engaging in activity during the day can help tremendously in tethering individuals to a positive reality— even while they allow their brains to view the world in their own unique way. A differently thinking brain is much likelier to be productive in a healthy body.

People with schizophrenia spectrum disorders can flourish and contribute, but they can't do so alone. None of us can. Elyn Saks continues to work and achieve thanks to a combination of factors that include a remarkable commitment to her work on behalf of people with mental illnesses as well as to the love and support of her husband, Will Vinet. John Nash would not have been productive right up until his final days if it weren't for the steadfast support of his wife, Alicia Nash. We all need people—to diagnose and prescribe, to turn to, and to help create opportunities for us to offer our gifts to the world.

7.

RELATEDNESS

AUTISM SPECTRUM DISORDERS

"We have to think, why do these traits get passed on? Why have they survived in evolution? It's that the very thing that makes our brain incredibly fragile and easy to damage in terms of neurodevelopmental disorders is what makes us very, very smart, and human, and adaptable. Otherwise we'd be like sharks, and everything would be programmed in. And you don't have a shark with autism."

—*KEVIN PELPHREY, DIRECTOR OF THE CHILD NEUROSCIENCE LABORATORY AT THE YALE SCHOOL OF MEDICINE*

At the age of two, pianist and composer Matt Savage was an intellectually precocious (he read at eighteen months), likable toddler who loved music. By the age of three, he had become hyperactive and unable to socialize or to tolerate most sounds—even music.[1] As Savage recalls, this acute sensitivity to sound was one of his most painful symptoms as a young child.[2] "I just wanted everything to be quiet." In addition to these symptoms, Matt became increasingly consumed by and facile with numbers.

At the age of three, Savage was diagnosed with autism. Soon after, he began auditory integration therapy (AIT), which is aimed at overcoming the child's acute sensitivity to sound by gradually introducing auditory stimulation (in the form of music) in a controlled environment. Matt's mother, Diane, also played piano for him as a way of attempting to further desensitize him. According to her, within a day of starting AIT, Savage was drawn to play an old eight-key toy Fisher-Price piano. Seeing his strong affinity, his mother immediately steered him toward a real piano. Looking back on what the secret was to drawing out her son, she says, "I would follow him. Whatever interested him, I would join with him on. And after a while I would try to use that to connect with him."[3] Prior to his discovery of music, she applied the same approach to the way he played. He was obsessed with building blocks, for example. Initially she would watch very closely how he played with them. Eventually, she would join in and begin placing blocks herself, following his example. While this made him uncomfortable at first, when he saw that she wasn't disrupting his way of playing, he was able to adapt to her participation. In this way she was teaching him a degree of flexibility.

A year after first discovering piano, Matt began studying classical piano. After another year, his parents played him Miles Davis's album *Kind of Blue,* and he moved on to jazz. "I liked [*Kind of Blue*] because the songs were long, they just went on forever. I love big numbers, I was obsessed with math, probably more so than music at that age." While he didn't love to practice, he did love repetition. "I played the same jazz line, the same jazz melodies over and over again when I was improvising."

Within just a few years of first touching a piano key, Savage could hold his own alongside adult musicians. When he was eight years old Diane regularly dropped him off at the Acton Jazz Café in Massachusetts, about an hour from where Savage and his family lived. She picked it because it was small, and she thought it wouldn't overwhelm Matt but would give him the opportunity to play with other musicians. She asked a few of the adult musicians there about lessons for Matt. They said, "He doesn't need lessons, he needs practice. And practice means gigs." Diane recalls, "So

I would help find gigs for him and these other two guys, and they were a little group." The gigs were modest initially—one was for the fundraiser thrown by a local synagogue—and she took her cues from Matt's enthusiasm. As soon as he finished one gig, he'd ask when his next one was.

Playing with other musicians—and having to perfect pieces for performance—was another opportunity for Matt to challenge his comfort levels. Because of his obsessiveness, it was hard for him not to play a song from beginning to end without stopping. But learning and practicing a piece involves repeating small sections over and over. So Diane set up a reward system—if Matt wanted to learn a piece well enough to perform it, then he was going to have to approach that process in a way that might make him initially uncomfortable. Over time, this built up Matt's frustration tolerance. For Matt's part, he was entirely calm while playing with other musicians. "I wasn't really thinking in terms of passion or obsession or anything. It's just my mind was here [playing music] at one particular moment."

Playing music also connected him to people—not that he was consciously aware of this at the time. His first experiences interacting with adults outside of his family and school were the evenings he jammed with musicians who were otherwise strangers to him—he was a small child among unfamiliar grown-ups, and yet they all spoke the same musical language. In time, Savage's remarkable talent gained him a reputation and a record deal with two fellow Acton Jazz Café musicians, bassist John Funkhouser and drummer Steve Silverstein.

Savage played his first concerts and also started touring when he was nine years old. By this point, he was enjoying more than just the performing— he became more highly aware that he was advancing his career. However, it was never easy for him socially. While no nine-year-old could be expected to handle himself with complete ease among adults, there was a clear disparity between Savage's savant musical ability and his inability to read social cues. For any child or adult with autism, the way the nonautistic brain works is a mystery. For example, it's enormously confusing to people with autism that others don't always mean what they say. The kind of social niceties that neurotypical people engage in naturally, without effort—subtle social manipulations, such as knowing when to keep one's opinion to oneself—can be entirely unnatural to people with autism. It can therefore be enormously difficult and stressful work for the person with autism to socially engage. In Savage's case, he presented as being a brilliant and gifted artist, so the adults who spoke to him expected him to be socially precocious as well, despite his youth. "Some of my interviews back then were really weird, because I was so young and sometimes didn't answer questions properly." Emotionally, "there were a lot of ups and downs associated with it, too. When somebody told me I had a special talent, I would take it literally, I would feel like I'm the most talented person in the room, egotistically. It helped my music a lot, and sometimes it helped me socially—giving me confidence." But he didn't always know how to take into account other people's feelings and egos. "I would throw a tantrum, and my mom would say, 'You're being very rude,' and I would feel like I'm a rude person, a bad person."

Savage's extraordinary musical ability and ambition were certainly motivating factors in encouraging him to confront challenging social situations. He's also intelligent and tenacious. But perhaps more than anything else, what drives Savage to overcome the social hurdles of being a person with autism spectrum disorder is his strong desire to be independent. "I had no choice. Even if I had never become a musician, I would still have gone through that just because it's necessary. I have to be in uncomfortable situations sometimes if I'm going to make a living outside of just staying around at home and being with my family." At age sixteen, after having been homeschooled for high school and passing his GED, Savage decided that it was important for him to leave home for college. He entered the Berklee College of Music in Boston, and after that he attended graduate school at Manhattan School of Music. In choosing Manhattan, he was consciously forcing himself into a chaotic environment. "New York is a very uncertain place, you never know what's going to happen each day.

It's very hard to plan things in advance here because there's always so much going on. I've definitely gained a lot of flexibility through urban life both at Berklee and at MSM. I was also in public school for a couple years as a kid, and those experiences all made me more flexible."

Today, at age twenty-four, Savage has no memory of a life without music. From the start, one of the strong appeals of music to him has been "the way everything works out together. That the act of touching the key corresponds with the act of hearing the note, which also corresponds with music theory." It's impossible to delineate what—and to what degree—brain differences have contributed to Savage's phenomenal success at so young an age. Certainly he has savant musical ability—and people with autism are disproportionately represented among savants.[4] He also has numerous qualities that might fall under the umbrella of grit: an abundance of ambition, insatiable curiosity, a strong work ethic. In addition, as a young child with autism, he took extraordinary joy in repetition—which is required of anyone wishing to develop mastery in any discipline.

Still, for Savage, having autism is a mixed bag. Despite his enormous strides and accomplishments, he wishes he were more flexible. But he can't imagine what his life would be like without autism, nor can he separate his autism from his creativity. And if given the opportunity to rid himself of his autism, he wouldn't take it. "I've never known any other life besides this one. Any other lifestyle besides being a musician with autism. It's my life, it's what's gotten me here."

WHAT IT MEANS TO HAVE AUTISM SPECTRUM DISORDER

Autism spectrum disorder is an umbrella classification that covers an enormous amount of individual variation. People with ASD can be cognitively and linguistically impaired. They can also exhibit tremendous difficulty with social interactions. Perseveration—repetitive behavior that can be physical or verbal in nature—is also a hallmark of ASD. This trait often goes hand in hand with exceptionally rigid behavior that can result in extreme distress when the individual is asked to deviate from routine. Children and adults with autism can also exhibit impulsive and even self-endangering behaviors. However, not all people with autism present with all of those traits. On the extreme end of the diagnosis, there are children who are so severely cognitively impaired (either lacking behavioral self-control, or having profound intellectual disabilities, or both) that they will never be able to lead independent lives. On the other end, there are re-markably high-performing people such as Matt Savage. When discussing the complex nature of autism—its challenges and its gifts—it's important to acknowledge these extremes.

In the past, individuals with ASD were diagnosed with one of four separate disorders: autistic disorder, Asperger's disorder, childhood disin-tegrative disorder, or the awkwardly named "pervasive developmental disorder not otherwise specified." The most recent edition of the *DSM-5,* published in 2013, removed those designations and created a single diag-nosis of autism spectrum disorder, meant to be applied to the full range of people with ASD, from the lowest to the highest functioning. This stirred controversy, especially among individuals with Asperger's and their parents. Asperger's was usually diagnosed among people on the high-performing end of the autism spectrum. The disorder was named after Austrian pe-diatrician Hans Asperger, who noticed among his patients a particular kind of child who experienced extreme social discomfort as well as obses-sive interest in subjects that particularly entranced them. He dubbed these children "little professors."[5] While no longer an official diagnosis, the term Asperger's is still used widely, and it has entered popular speech as a way to describe someone who is bright but socially awkward and uncomfortable—someone who doesn't like to be touched, for example, or someone who is occasionally blunt to the point of rudeness, or who has difficulty looking people in the eyes when they speak. The term Asperger's is now bandied about so freely that many undiagnosed people use it to describe themselves and their perceived quirks.

According to the Centers for Disease Control, currently one in sixty-eight children is identified with ASD.[6] This is an increase from the previously reported statistic of one in eighty-eight, and that jump (which took place over the course of four years), was shocking and concerning to many. It's unclear whether this higher rate is due to increased occurrence or diagnosis—or some combination of the two. Along with this worrisome statistic is another figure that casts ASD in a much different light. Prior to 2014, only one in three people with ASD was thought to be of average to above-average intelligence. However, current CDC statistics suggest that nearly half of all people with ASD have average to above-average intelligence.[7] The causes for this increase are also poorly understood—but there may be a connection. That is, the children least likely to be diagnosed in the past were the most high functioning. However, as awareness of milder forms of autism and the importance of early intervention have increased, more parents of high-functioning children with autism now seek diagnoses. Therefore, it could be that the percentage of children with ASD with above-average intelligence has increased in conjunction with the incidence rates.

There is another autism statistic that currently stumps researchers: five times more boys than girls are diagnosed with ASD.[8] This statistic has remained constant for years, even while others have changed. This means that while one in 189 girls is currently diagnosed with ASD, one in forty-two boys is diagnosed. The reason for this enormous disparity is a lingering question—and the answer may shed light on the disorder's neurological causes.

Researchers can't explain exactly why it is that people with autism are just as likely to be gifted at math as they are linguistics, and why it is so rare that they are gifted at both. That is, an aptitude in one area tends to come at the cost of another. This teetering balance—a lack in one area corresponding with an aptitude in another—is potentially at the heart of why people with autism have such a hard time with faces, both looking at them and differentiating them. A study published in *Biological Psychiatry* by researchers at Stanford University compared children with autism and children with neurotypical brains—and with the same IQ—and found that the children with ASD displayed greater mathematical problem-solving ability.[9] Moreover, the researchers found that while the children with autism were working on math problems, the ventral-temporal-occipital cortex of their brains was more highly activated than in the neuro-typical children. This is, perhaps not coincidentally, the area of the brain normally devoted to face processing.

Despite the vastly different ways that autism can present, there are two particular hallmarks of the disorder that can be found across the spectrum, and which seem to be connected. On the one hand, people with autism have much greater than average difficulty in individuating faces. On the other, people with autism tend to exhibit "hypersystemizing." An exam-ple of the latter is the child with autism who becomes fascinated by a par-ticular subject and then inhales every detail about it to a degree far beyond what a neurotypical child could consume. One intriguing study published in *Neuropsychologia* found that a boy with autism who had an exhaustive knowledge of Digimon cartoon characters could individuate those char-acters even faster than he could familiar faces and objects.[10] Moreover, he individuated familiar faces and objects at about the same rate as each other—that is, he showed no preference for faces over objects. In contrast, a typically developing boy—even one with a strong interest in similar sorts of cartoon characters—would be equally fast at individuating familiar human faces and those characters. In addition, unlike the child with autism, the neurotypical child would be faster at individuating familiar faces and cartoon characters than at individuating objects. The reason for this disparity is neurological and observable. In autism, there is abnormal activation in the amygdala and the fusiform gyrus, the areas of the brain associated with face recognition and social interaction. In the case of the boy with autism and an obsessive interest in Digimon, those areas of the brain lit up for Digimon characters, but not for familiar or unfamiliar faces.

To be clear, this is not due to any kind of deficit in visual acuity. In fact, a study published in *Biological Psychiatry* revealed that those with autism spectrum conditions actually have *heightened* visual acuity.[11] They could detect at twenty feet what those with average vision could see from seven feet away. This is comparable to birds of prey, which have visual acuity twice that found in humans. A study by researchers at the University of Montreal found that people with ASD exhibit "enhanced perceptual abilities when engaged in visual search, visual discrimination, and embedded figure detection."[12] Moreover, the areas of their brains devoted to those tasks were visibly more activated than in nonautistics. Meanwhile, the people with ASD once again showed less activation in the frontal cortex, the area of the brain responsible for face processing.

Researchers at King's College London who reviewed the various studies performed to date concluded that the autistic brain's heightened powers of classification or hypersystemizing—which seem to come at the expense of face recognition—are quite possibly related to the higher incidence of savant ability found among people with autism.[13] "Strong systemizing requires excellent attention to detail, and in our view the latter is in the service of the former. Talent in autism comes in many forms, but a common characteristic is that the individual becomes an expert in recognizing repeating patterns in stimuli. We call this systemizing, defined as the drive to analyze or construct systems. What defines a system is that it follows rules, and when we systemize we are trying to identify the rules that govern the system, in order to predict how that system will behave."

Heightened attention to detail was also identified by another group of researchers at King's College, who found that people with autism process information differently than those without.[14] They gathered data on 6,426 eight-year-old twins in England and Wales and found that the children with autism took in groupings of information with greater preference and attention given toward each individual detail, independently of its relationship to the others. They did this to a far greater degree than those children without autism. For example, in children with autism who have perfect pitch and maintain that ability into adulthood, the researchers theorized that this ability stemmed from their repetitive focus on individual notes within a larger melody. By solely rehearsing each note—albeit sometimes at the sacrifice of processing the meaning that might be revealed via the relationship between the notes—they could maintain perfect pitch. This attention to detail was also found in the areas of lightning multiplication, identification of prime numbers, calendar calculation, perfect-perspective drawing, and factual memory.

In other words, the person with autism, who can be rigidly devoted to routine, is also acutely sensitive to patterns and highly capable of making sense of—and remembering—those patterns. The King's College researchers who studied hypersystemization also point out that its requirements are at odds with flexibility and are quite conducive to rigidity. "Strong systemizing is a way of explaining the non-social features of autism: narrow interests; repetitive behavior; and resistance to change/need for sameness. This is because when one systemizes, it is best to keep everything constant, and to only vary one thing at a time. That way, one can see what might be causing what, and with repetition one can verify that one gets the very same pattern or sequence."[15] That is, the same qualities that can contribute to mastery of a particular skill set or body of knowledge—repetition and acute attention to detail—occur quite naturally in the brain with autism.

THE EXPERIENCE OF HAVING AUTISM SPECTRUM DISORDER

As described in the introduction, the abilities associated with particular brain differences exist on an inverted U-shaped curve. That is, the special strengths of a particular difference exist more strongly in those with more mild to moderate symptoms, and to a lesser degree for those with no brain difference or for those who are severely ill. On the U-shaped curve of those with ASD, there is a particularly wide range of ability and disability. It would be insensitive and incorrect to suggest that there is a positive flipside to every symptom of autism—there is no question that some individuals with autism spectrum disorder suffer nothing but ill effects, including profound cognitive disability. As with brain differences such as bipolar disorder and clinical depression, intelligence has an enormous impact on personal outcomes—as do the severity of symptoms and any number of intangible qualities that might be described as grit. Matt Savage, whose rigidity and sensitivity to sound were so pronounced as a child, and who still describes himself as struggling with social connection, also benefitted from early intervention and enormous familial encouragement, as well as tremendous musical and intellectual gifts.

Greg Wallace, assistant professor at George Washington University and expert on ASD in children, says, "It used to be thought that autism necessarily meant that you had a low IQ, which would make learning difficult. But now we understand that is not true. You can be impaired by your autism in that you can't look at people's faces, you have difficulty reading people, perseverative behavior, repetitive physical movements, flapping hands—but that doesn't mean that you don't have a high IQ."[16] In addition, even among those with below-average IQ, "it is a measure of one thing, [but] it's not the whole ball of wax by any stretch."

Matt Savage is an extraordinary individual, of course. However, believing that people with autism can lead fulfilling lives and achieve great things is entirely realistic—and advisable. With new statistics suggesting that nearly half of all people with ASD are of average to above-average intelligence, and with the percentage of the population with ASD on the rise, there is every reason to encourage people with ASD to fully participate in all aspects of life—academic, work, and social. It can be a challenging and confusing road for people with autism, but the journey benefits all of us.

CHALLENGES OF LIVING WITH AUTISM SPECTRUM DISORDER

As it is for children with dyslexia and ADD, one of the challenges of being a child with ASD in school is the expectation that we should all perform equally well at everything. However, children with ASD often exhibit very uneven performance. According to Kevin Pelphrey, director of the Child Neuroscience Laboratory at the Yale School of Medicine, "Whereas a child with intellectual disability without autism, in general, will be intellectually disabled across the board, kids with autism will often show an unusual split," for example, "between verbal and spatial functioning. No one really knows exactly why. It's part and parcel of autism spectrum."[17] Greg Wallace describes this phenomenon as "scatter." In a child with ASD there might be "islands of excellence and then [others of] big-time impairment."

Moreover, it can't be assumed, as it once was, that children with autism will lean more heavily toward the mathematical or spatial versus the verbal. Pelphrey notes that "about as many will have higher verbal than spatial [abilities]" as will have "higher spatial versus verbal. When you break it down in an IQ test, it's more that they're simply spread to the extremes and lack the middle. But they're equally spread in each domain." The children with ASD who exhibit stronger verbal skills are often those who would have been diagnosed as having Asperger's. "They would have very high verbal abilities, but not in a social sense. They would kind of talk at you and talk about things that interest them with incredible vocabularies, but not seem to be sensitive at all to whether or not their audience is interested. So they have that profound social disability, but they kind of mask it by having a very high verbal IQ."

Traditional intelligence testing is therefore an unreliable indicator of ability in people with ASD. It's nonetheless important to evaluate each child's cognitive abilities in a way that takes into account these wide variations in ability. Pelphrey considers cognitive assessments helpful in describing to parents what the child's aptitudes are. "For example, we often find that kids with autism will have extremely good memory skills. [This] allows us to say, 'Your child has this set of strengths and you should lever-age those in intervention.' So it's okay to focus on weaknesses, and try to improve weaknesses, but don't forget about the strengths. A successful life is about finding the right fit for your strengths, and finding your way through."

There are of course variations in what we mean by leading a successful life. For some individuals with autism, success is achieving a measure of independence. For the 10 percent of people with autism who have savant ability—such as Matt Savage—success might mean far more.[18] The inci-dence of savant ability—that is, ability far above what would otherwise be considered average or normal based on age or training—is vastly higher among people with autism than any other population (10 percent of people with ASD versus 1 percent of the population overall). We don't know why this is, but it may be that people with ASD have an edge. According to Pelphrey, "'Savant' implies that you have a very isolated ability. [Savants] have a high IQ, but what separates [them] is extraordinarily focused inter-est and willingness to practice." In other words: perseveration. There's a theory that people with ASD "have more plasticity, actually, in their brains. And the ability to form those loops, that's what underlies the tendency toward perseveration. Autism in so many ways is an elongation of the [normal] developmental process. So it's not unreasonable that that could be seen as an advantage. It's a perfectly reasonable hypothesis that kids with autism have an unusual amount of plasticity for a longer period, which leads to a failure to specialize, and that probably helps make us the adaptive humans we are. It's just run amok a little more in kids with this disorder."

It's worth noting that while the brain with autism possesses this ten-dency toward perseveration and repetitive behaviors, the individual is also experiencing pleasure. Many adults who witness the repetitive behavior of a child with ASD (such as assembling complex arrangements of toy train track over and over again, or playing the same string of notes seemingly endlessly) negatively associate it with disordered thinking, but the child with ASD is often soothed and entranced by the repetition. This feeling of pleasure and comfort makes the development of savant ability even more likely. Pelphrey notes, "[Brain] plasticity is best engaged when there's motivation and dopamine pouring over all of those neurons and resonating in reward centers. That's the key. That's forgotten by a lot of people who talk about putting in ten thousand hours to become an expert. You can do something for ten thousand hours that you don't enjoy and you will be better at it. But you'll never become an expert, I would argue. In these kids, dopamine actually lubricates the ability of those synapses to form and solidify. You're dreaming about it, you're thinking about it, you're doing it. It's even more than ten thousand hours when you put all that into it, because you like it."

To encourage and facilitate mastery in children with ASD, and for them to succeed in a mainstream school setting, they need to be allowed to immerse themselves in what they love. Unfortunately, some school settings seem to aim toward the least of the child's abilities, rather than to the greatest. For this reason, there are bright children in special education settings that don't offer them the intellectual stimulation that might spark a latent talent that will see them into a highly successful adulthood. Parents of high-functioning children with ASD are in a difficult quandary. On the one hand, their children might have profound social difficulties and experience grave anxiety when asked to deviate from routine. On the other, these parents want to encourage their children to challenge their limits so as to overcome them. There is no one right answer, and in fact no single answer. The right school situation might change over time. Matt Savage attended both private and public schools before being homeschooled from fifth grade through high school. After he passed his GED, he decided for himself that he wanted to attend college.

It can be a tremendous strain on parents to find the right academic setting for their children with ASD. It can seem that every choice requires a sacrifice of something else important. A specialized setting might feel too academically constricting or stigmatizing, while a mainstream setting can feel overwhelming and demanding of conformity. Parents of children with brain differences of all kinds can feel that their full-time job is advocating for their children. And this job never ends. It requires constant vigilance. Because intervention can work so well particularly in high-functioning children with ASD, the right school setting will and should change over time. In the case of children with ASD, the goal should be to offer them the flexibility that their own inflexibility requires.

FOR CHILDREN AND ADULTS WITH AUTISM, the world can be a confusing place. Because individuals with ASD are in the minority, they are expected to conform to nonautistic standards of politeness and social conduct, and not the other way around. Even people with ASD who have high IQs can have a difficult time in school and in the workplace, because the intricacies of human interaction can be so mysterious.

Matt Savage offers moving insight on what it feels like to be a child with ASD. "When I was a kid, I would throw temper tantrums, just when I couldn't deal with something. I would be positive and bouncy one [moment], and then just getting angry— like not feeling disappointed, or frustrated, or even sad, just angry. Nothing in between. I didn't know how to feel some other kind of emotion. That was true of everything, whether I was feeling happy [or some other emotion], it would just be like, this is an eternity, this is wonderful, that was all I knew. [The idea that a mind or mood could change], that it's flexible and people can be subtle and not literal, that was the hardest part [of social interaction] for me."

At age twenty-four, Matt Savage has spent his entire life learning how to get along with people who aren't autistic. He's also been required to engage with large numbers of people on a daily basis—both in academic settings and in the bustling city he's chosen to live in. He's proud of his ability to challenge himself in social settings, but it continues to be hard work, and it exacts a toll. "I get physically tired a lot." At times like this, he needs to give himself a break. "I'll want to look at something else other than the person [who is talking to me]. It happens a lot. I'll just want to look outside the window. I won't have any specific attraction to social skills or a person when I'm tired."

He's also found himself embarrassed by his difficulty recognizing faces and spoken names (he has much less difficulty with written names). He's learned to admit to his difficulty rather than to feel so mortified. "This happened [a lot] at the beginning of [attending] Berklee and Manhattan School of Music. I'll confuse people so much. I would say hi to one of my friends thinking it was another person. There were a couple of moments where I had to clarify that kind of thing. It was terrible. They would have a different haircut, or I'd just been spending a lot more time with another person than with this person. [Now] I don't feel like I need to explain. I just say I'm terrible with faces. "

It's common for people with ASD to experience some social anxiety— imagine a world in which you're constantly afraid of missing social cues. This heightened vigilance has been both a positive and a negative for Savage. He's a perfectionist, and he's inflexible, so this means that scheduling is particularly stressful for him. While juggling school, his job as a music teacher at a school for children with ASD, as well as his concert and studio work, "I'm constantly worried about making sure that everything I need to get done gets done so that I can completely relax." His inflexibility actually feeds his perfectionism and makes it very difficult for him to multitask, something that we're all increasingly expected to do. "I'll be so focused on doing one thing, and I'll do another thing [too] but not as meticulously as I would have liked. It's hard for me to let things go. Because I feel like that's a sign of weakness from either me or the other person."

He continues to have a hard time with human unpredictability. He's frustrated when invitations are extended but not confirmed, and he struggles with the fact that people don't always mean what they say. "That was a huge point of confusion, especially during the first couple of years of college, because so many people, you can never tell what they mean to say. The first day of college at dinner, there were these guys talking about sex and it took me a long time to realize that people aren't literal a lot of the time with social things, not just relationships and dating and sex and all of that, but just with planning their lives, like planning their jobs. It's hard to tell what people mean."

To a degree that's both poignant and impressive, Savage continues to hone his emotional response to the world, both in professional and social settings. He's learning to embrace flexibility, while also seeking out people he can trust. "A lot of the musicians that I knew [as a younger musician] were still finding themselves, and it was kind of hard to plan things. You have to find people who are reliable who want to work with you." Perhaps most promising of all, Savage has a strong awareness that there is more to life than work and music. "I've been playing music since as long as I can remember. So many of the kids I know are spectacular musicians, but they didn't even start till high school, and they knew a life without music. I never knew that. In many ways, I want to get away from music a lot of the time and not have a specifically musical mind. I just want to hang out with friends and see the city. "

DEVELOPING WORK-AROUNDS

Matt Savage is an inspiring example of what early intervention can accomplish in the life of an intelligent and gifted person with ASD. There is no one therapy that is known to be most beneficial for children with autism. In his case, auditory integration therapy had the most profoundly positive impact. Perhaps the most obvious and dramatic effect has been on his professional life, but even more impressive than his musical achievements are his personal ones. He exhibits a remarkable self-awareness for a man in his early twenties, much less for someone with his particular constellation of brain differences.

One of the challenges that parents and loved ones of people with ASD face is the question of how much to push limits. Given the rigidity and extreme social discomfort of the person with ASD, is it helpful or damaging to urge flexibility and engagement? Parenting any child involves a delicate balance between involvement and release, offering supervision and allowing independence. Parenting a child with ASD makes the balance even more challenging—there is the desire to protect our children and respect their differences, but also the responsibility to adequately prepare them for the larger world. Diane Savage challenged Matt, but did so within a comfortable framework. So, as noted, she observed Matt closely and learned how Matt liked to play with blocks prior to attempting to engage with him. When she was looking for a place for him to play with other musicians, she chose a smaller, less intimidating environment to start with. She used the same kind of careful pressure when Matt's strong desire was to play a piece straight through, rather than do the hard work of learning it bit by bit. She says now that she wasn't aware that her methods of careful pressure were methods at all—she thought this was simply good parenting. She was parenting the particular child she had in the best way she knew how.

While Diane was in fact gradually testing Matt's limits, it's worth noting that he does not emphasize feeling any particular pressure from his parents to engage. He was homeschooled from the age of ten, and at the age of sixteen it was he who decided to go away to college. A planner by nature, he arrived at Berklee College of Music in Boston never having had to organize his own life or schedule appointments for himself before. He knew that he would function best with a system, so he started using a calendar program on his computer, and he still uses it. After college graduation, he decided to challenge himself even further by going to graduate school in New York City. And he continues to challenge himself on a daily basis—while being careful of his needs for quiet and rest.

According to Greg Wallace, it's important to remember that it's not that the high-functioning person with autism can't interact socially; it's that "they may struggle and it may be really effortful. So, for example, I've interacted quite a bit with an extremely bright patient with ASD and we'll talk and talk and it'll be great and this person is so articulate, so smart, oh my God, so much smarter than me, that's for sure." Later this same patient told him that after one of their long talks in which the patient had been utterly involved, "I'll go home and I won't talk to anybody for the rest of the night. I just need my space, my quiet." As Wallace notes, because this patient has worked so hard, and is so intelligent and such a fluent speaker, the patient "seems so smooth and easygoing. [But] it's extremely effortful, and it's just not as comfortable" as it might be for someone else.

When Matt Savage finds himself disappointed that a social plan has been canceled, exercise helps him cope with the frustration. "I don't even like exercise, but it makes me stronger. It doesn't diminish my stress, it distracts it away and makes me more prepared for it." He's also protective of his sleep and his private space. And while he tries to be flexible, there's only so far he can or will bend. It's become easier than it used to be for him to say, "I need things to be this way." Savage also displays a remarkable acceptance of himself and what is required of him to move forward, and to have the kind of life he wants to have. An important piano teacher in his life, Charlie Banacos, with whom Savage studied between the ages of eleven and seventeen, "really taught me life lessons like how to remain grounded, and how to not get carried away." Memorably, he gave Savage a collection of Aesop's fables. Savage's favorite was "The Fox and the Grapes." "The moral was it is easy to despise what you cannot get, and I totally did not understand that at the time, but it's so true. You can't just do everything, you've got to work at it and deal with all the hardships." Now his advice for parents of children with autism is to "think in the long term. Some things might be very difficult for a kid at a young age, but it might be necessary in order to live as an adult in society."

While pursuing his graduate studies, Savage teaches music to children with autism at the McCarten School in Manhattan. These children are less high functioning than Matt was at the same age, but one commonality he sees in them is the way in which learning music can appeal to their tendency toward rigidity and desire to do things in a particular order, over and over. This is an excellent example of fostering perseveration around things that actually work for the person with ASD.

Kevin Pelphrey says, "I think [many people believe that] you've only got so much brain capacity and if it's all filled up with train schedules and computer algorithms and playing chess or drawing, then you're not going to have anything left over. And that's just not true. There's no neuroscience that supports that. There's no limit to the number of [areas of expertise] that humans can have that we know of. So I would say to parents, 'Celebrate those strengths and find opportunities for the child to develop them and don't worry about it taking over brain real estate.'"

Many parents worry that the sort of perseveration that their children engage in—such as video games or repetitive movie viewing—can hinder or replace their social interactions. However, in some cases perseveration can be a pathway to connection. At first, Matt Savage found the repetition of jazz lines fascinating, and he loved that the repetition could go on seemingly infinitely. In time, his mastery of music also became his means of reaching out to a world of people who spoke the same musical language. From there, he's reaching out to a world beyond music. Of course Savage is a remarkable example, but the same can hold true for children with more severe forms of ASD. Author and journalist Ron Suskind wrote a memoir, *Life, Animated,* about reaching his nonverbal, autistic son, Owen, via Disney movies and the characters with whom Owen bonded.[19] When Owen was six years old, Suskind used a hand puppet of Iago, a character from *Aladdin,* in order to instigate their first conversation in four years. In the voice of the cartoon character, Suskind asked Owen, "How does it feel to be you?" Owen answered, "I'm not happy. I don't have friends. I can't understand what people say." This first conversation marked a dramatic shift in their family and in Owen's life. Over time, Suskind and his wife

found that when Owen took on the voices of his beloved cartoon characters, he was able to express emotions that he couldn't otherwise. Suskind
calls their work with the Disney characters "affinity therapy."

Many children with autism are more drawn to cartoon faces than to
human faces. And particularly for children with language difficulty, the
clarity of a Disney movie can be the first gateway to understanding speech.
Walt Disney originally instructed his animators to make the films understandable even without sound. And now that movies can be replayed
over and over, even frame by frame, children like Owen Suskind can
perseverate—to positive result—over their favorite scenes while parsing
meaning and internalizing the emotions.

Kevin Pelphrey says that for the child who is drawn to animation,
"those movies help her navigate the social world. She relates things to the
movies she's seen. And that's fine and that's her strategy. And I help her
play out that strategy and do what she's already doing, but do it a little
better and a little more adaptively." He might help her learn, for example,
"how to not necessarily talk about Disney movies with everyone she runs
into. But if she finds out that they like them, then go for it, you know?
There's no better opportunity. And then I'll use it as a learning opportunity to help her see social cues. Like, did you notice the person looking at
their watch? Or they're saying they really have to get on to the next appointment? You need to stop talking about the different movies at that
point, and tell them goodbye."

Pelphrey says that parents can overemphasize working on weaknesses.
"Brute force—'You're going to look at me, you're going to do social
things'—doesn't work. It doesn't engage that system. But if you can engage
that system and hijack it for teaching social things, then you've got a
chance." He doesn't discount the importance of working on social skills,
but he compares it to exercise. "If you spend 80 percent of your waking
time physically training, you're going to get hurt. And it's going to stop being effective. I think for these kids, 20 percent of waking hours focusing

on their [perceived] weaknesses and 80 percent helping them utilize their strengths would be a good balance. I don't want to be a Pollyanna about this. Sometimes it just can't be worked with. But we have to think, why do these traits get passed on? Why have they survived in evolution? It's that the very thing that makes our brain incredibly fragile and easy to damage in terms of neurodevelopmental disorders is what makes us very, very smart, and human, and adaptable. Otherwise we'd be like sharks, and everything would be programmed in. And you don't have a shark with autism."

GIFTS OF THE BRAIN WITH AUTISM SPECTRUM DISORDER

We know so little about the workings of the brain generally, not to mention the delicate interaction of ability and disability, that it's impossible to make definitive statements as to why people with autism make up such a disproportionate percentage of savants. Greg Wallace acknowledges, "The jury is still out. There's been very limited research in terms of neuroimaging. The most obvious reason is [relative] rarity. Another more concrete reason is it doesn't tend to be something that has been funded because people are more interested in fixing things. They're focused on the problems or the difficulties."

There is less evidence than we would like, but there is enough that we can begin to draw some conclusions. Wallace points out the clear points of connection between autism and savant ability. "People with ASD a lot of times will have restricted interests or circumscribed interests, and there is a brain basis for this." That brain basis, as the research has repeatedly suggested, is inextricably linked to one weakness in particular: face recognition. Individuals whose brains have developed typically are "face experts, because we constantly practice face recognition and face processing every day. We look at each other in the face, look at each other in the eyes, talk to each other." The difficulty with faces that some people with ASD have, paired with the acute pattern recognition that many people with ASD also display, is unlikely to be coincidental. "It seems that this area, the inferior surface of the temporal lobe [which is devoted to face recognition], is adjacent to this area for [developing] expertise." In people with autism, Wallace says, this "might help to explain some encroachment into these areas that would typically [be devoted to] face expertise." Theoretically, this is the reason that while people with autism suffer in the area of face recognition, they shine when it comes to other kinds of pattern recognition. Discerning order within complex patterns is as natural to some people with autism as differentiating faces is to the rest of us. "People with autism are better at seeing the trees for the forest than seeing the forest for the trees. It doesn't mean that they can't see the forest, it's just that they have a bias toward seeing the trees. And that is a building block to the development of certain skills. "

In the past, there has been the tendency to think that savants with ASD were highly skilled, but lacked originality. When Darold Treffert, clinician and expert on savant syndrome and author of *Islands of Genius,* first began studying savants, he believed that as a group they "tended to be rather flat emotionally and were not very creative."[20] Over the years, however, he's seen significant evidence of savant creativity. "What I found by following savants long enough is that there's a sort of transition that takes place. There is this continuum of repetition to improvisation to creation that I've seen now in a number of savants." This transition is evident in Matt Savage's story. In his music career he evolved from being entranced by the repetitiveness of lengthy jazz pieces, to improvising, to composing his own music.

Esther Brokaw, who describes herself as "an untrained artist," is a remarkable example of someone with ASD who has savant-level ability to recognize patterns and uses that ability to express herself creatively.[21] "As a child, I saw [impressionist paintings] at the National Gallery. And I studied the paintings very closely with my hands behind my back so that I could stand very close to them, because I wanted to see how they did it. What I recognized was the detail of the stroke. And each stroke was important. When you looked at it closely, it was as interesting as far away. Everything is a pattern."

Brokaw wasn't diagnosed with ASD until the age of forty-four, in 2004, but her social difficulties were apparent long before. "Socially I was difficult. I laugh loud and I speak loud." She's been told that she has a "flat look. People often would look at me and say, 'Smile.' I didn't think smiling was socially required, you know? I'd smile if I wanted, and I knew I had to smile for work. I have the flat speech [that is often associated with ASD]. I always looked down when I walked. There's a lot of little things that definitely would put me in the category of autism. But I never knew what autism was."

In school she did well. "I got good grades. I never studied. Study was for you guys, not me, that was my joke. Why should I study if I can get As and Bs when I don't study?" She was particularly strong in math, although she had difficulty conforming to expectations. "I got in trouble with math because they didn't like that I wouldn't show my work. My problem is I assume you know what I'm talking about or where I'm going, and I've already jumped ahead two or three steps." She worked a variety of jobs after college, one of which was roofing. "You think about a roof and it's a pattern." That work appealed to her, although it was physically taxing to be on an exposed roof in the hot Dallas sun. She also worked in sales, which isn't a field that one immediately thinks of for someone with social awkwardness. However, Brokaw points out that it's not the social engagement that is the greatest challenge for her in sales, but rather the need to be sincere. "A savant is driven by their passion, their interests, and their love. So if you had me selling something that I didn't believe in, something my heart wasn't in, [that wouldn't work]." As long as she believed in the product she was selling, she was highly effective.

In her thirties, when Brokaw was suffering from ill health, she applied her exceptional math skills to learning swing and day trading. Utterly untrained, she was an immediate success at it. "I am online constantly with traders that I have known for twenty years, and they don't ask me what way the market's going to go, they ask me what time it's going to go there.

[The other traders] want to know how I could predict certain things, and I keep telling them it's the pattern. They're reading indicators, but I'm reading the patterns. If I said to you, ABCDEFG, ABCDEFG, ABCDEFG, ABCDEFG, and then I said A, you're going to say BCDEFG. Well, it's the same thing with me. That's how simple it is to me. But they're not seeing that. It's not as simple to everybody else." Of course Brokaw is wrong about the market sometimes, but when that happens, it's because the pattern breaks. "The market will do the opposite of what it is supposed to be doing. When it does that, everybody's wrong on a short-term basis. Volatility is unpredictable."

Unlike many people with autism, Brokaw is easy to talk to and doesn't seem to tire of engagement. Her work as an equity trader allows her to have strictly verbal and analytical online relationships with other traders with whom she socializes on chat sites. These are people she's never met, but the talking and interacting and comparing of notes with them is something she clearly finds satisfying. And as Diane Savage noted about her son Matthew, this social engagement occurs more easily and comfortably because it revolves around a subject of enormous interest to her.

Although Brokaw was always highly visual, she didn't start painting seriously until after her daughter, Isabel, was born. Her first oil painting was of her baby sleeping, and she used a "five-dollar starter set and a cheap canvas." When she'd finished, she and her husband stood back and looked at it, and both said the same thing: "I don't know anything about art, but I like it." Since that first painting, she has received widespread acclaim and attention for her work.

Brokaw remains fascinated by each brushstroke, and her style is evocative of the impressionists she loved as a child. She photographs and magnifies her paintings by 400 percent and then examines the patterns of each brush stroke. "Because in the strokes there are multiple colors in every stroke, and each stroke is something I want to look at. When I talk about my paintings I'll talk about them as color patterns. So when you look at my paintings you'll see color patterns within the paintings."

The Awakening, by Esther Brokaw

Brokaw's daughter, who was diagnosed with ASD at age four, is visually gifted as well, and she's drawn to animation. "She's learned all the animation programs. She's made her own character called Izzy, and she's hilarious. She's got this great sense of humor. She's brilliant." Brokaw is careful to point out to her daughter when she is copying characters, versus making her own. "When she would draw something that was not her character, I would make her write MGM or Warner Brothers, or whose character it was. When it was her original idea, she could sign her name. And I tried from an early age to congratulate her on her original creations and showed her the difference." In this way, Brokaw is guiding her daughter through the savant stages that expert Darold Treffert delineated—from repetition to improvisation to creation.

It's tempting to focus on savant ability alone when discussing the particular gifts of the brain with ASD, but most people with ASD are not savants. As is the case with all brain differences, at their most extreme, the symptoms of autism would likely overwhelm any inherent strength.

However, for the sake of those more moderately affected but lacking savant-level ability, it's important to remember that the same brain differences that contribute to savant ability exist in everyone with ASD—and the same strengths can also be utilized to varying degrees. In his *New York Times Magazine* piece "The Autism Advantage," journalist Gareth Cook profiled Thorkil Sonne, who left his job as a technical director for Denmark's largest telecommunications company to start a company of his own, called Specialisterne (Danish for "the specialists"), that acts as a kind of placement agency for workers with ASD, particularly in technical fields.[22] He was inspired to do so by his son Lars, who had been diagnosed with ASD. In the article, Cook noted that "to his father, Lars seemed less defined by deficits than by his unusual skills. And those skills, like intense focus and careful execution, were exactly the ones that Sonne . . . often looked for in his own employees." Tasks such as data entry and software testing—both of which require repetition that neurotypical individuals would find challenging to complete with the necessary consistency and accuracy—fall directly into the wheelhouse of many individuals with ASD. Sonne's theory is that "an autistic adult could not just hold down a job but also be the best person for it."

HOW PEOPLE WITH AUTISM SPECTRUM DISORDER CAN FLOURISH

It's possible to diagnose children as young as eighteen months old with autism, and yet the typical age of diagnosis is much later. In some cases this is because clear symptoms don't emerge until the child is older—as was the case for Ron Suskind's son Owen, who became nonverbal after first seeming to have developed normally. In other cases, however, diagnosis is delayed because of wholly understandable resistance. Diagnosing a toddler with autism spectrum disorder can feel like a life sentence. However, the positive impact of early intervention cannot be overstated. Matt Savage is a dramatic case study of the enormous benefit of early intervention for a high-functioning person with ASD. But even—and perhaps especially—among children with more severe symptoms, including cognitive delay, intervention can be powerful. Because of brain plasticity, interactive therapies that work on developing verbal skills and social abilities can help children with autism understand the world around them, and in turn help them make their own needs understood. There is no cure for autism, but there can be vastly different outcomes with the right support and encouragement.

Parents of children with autism can learn from Diane Savage's example and watch their children carefully to determine what activities they're attracted to and what it is about those activities that they enjoy. Maybe it's the stimulation of color, or texture, or movement, or sound. Parents should pay attention to how their children use their toys and other materials. In doing so, parents can find ways to communicate with their children via their interests. This is what Diane did with Matt from a very young age—when he first became interested in manipulating blocks and she studied his methods in order to imitate them. Eventually her close attention to his enthusiasms resulted in her creating the opportunities that would lead him to a career in music.

According to researchers at King's College London, "Teachers, whether of children with autism or adults with Asperger's syndrome, need to take into account that hyper-systemizing will affect not only how people with ASC learn, but also how they should be assessed. IQ test items, essays, and exam questions designed for individuals who are 'neurotypical' may lead to the person with ASC scoring zero when their knowledge is actually greater, deeper and more extensive than that of most people. What can appear as a slow processing style may be because of the massively greater quantity of information that is being processed."[23] It's the responsibility of parents, educators, and employers to create opportunities for people with ASD to gain mastery—to the maximum degree that they are capable, and whether that means playing piano for the president of Singapore, as Matt Savage did, or finding satisfying work testing apps, or being able to live independently or to communicate thoughts and feelings to those around them. Helping our children and adults with ASD to access their strengths and find what they are good at offers them a framework for living—and it benefits all of us as a society.

Savant syndrome expert Darold Treffert believes that within each individual with autism, no matter how profoundly symptomatic, there is "an island of intactness. And our job is to find it and nurture it and encourage it and reinforce it." Indeed, he theorizes that as tablet technology enables even minimally verbal people with autism to communicate, we will uncover a far greater percentage of savant ability. As it stands, we tend to judge intelligence and potential based upon verbal skills, but that linkage is tenuous and unreliable in people with autism. "I think if you begin a search and try to find out where that spark is, and then tend to it and nurture it and reinforce it, then we'll find much more of these exceptional abilities."

This requires stepping over narrowly defined expectations, a task that people with ASD face every day of their lives. Matt Savage has been doing so since he first walked into a jazz club—and probably long before then. The road he has traveled since could seem nothing short of miraculous— except that it isn't. It has required tremendous effort. As a fully engaged adult who doesn't always think the way everyone else does, he's highly aware that there is no one acceptable way to think or feel. "Everybody's thinking so differently. I feel like I think differently, but I've just worked so hard that I'm used to going this way now. Sometimes I don't realize how hard I've worked on it."

Human beings are adaptable creatures, and clinicians and researchers are eagerly standing at the precipice of understanding just what our brains are capable of—and how they can change. When Matt Savage was a child with the same rigid and perseverative tendencies as many children with autism, he was obsessed with roller coasters. He loved reading about them, and he made it his mission to learn about all of them—especially the really big ones. "When I was twelve or so, I finally decided to ride a small coaster, and afterward I just felt so tired and it was so intense." Despite his love for the big "crazy" rides, he thought he simply wasn't capable. It was too much. Recently, however, that changed. On a trip to Florida, he summoned the courage to ride one of those big ones. "This ride, it's called 'The Incredible Hulk.' Instead of going slowly up the hill, it launches you up to the top of the hill, goes upside down at the top, then drops to the ground and goes upside down six more times. It's pretty crazy."

He's no longer afraid of roller coasters. "I've just suddenly gone on a thrill ride spree. And now I'm a huge fan. Part of it is the whole idea of letting go from everything. From the material world, from your fears, from gravity. And part of it is the smoothness of it all. Those new coasters, they're so smooth, even though they go upside down and they're so large, they're a lot smoother than the old wooden ones." It's remarkable to consider that description of what Savage loves about roller coasters: from letting go to smooth control. These are opposite ends of a spectrum; Savage embraces both, and all points between.

8.

THE FUTURE OF THINKING DIFFERENTLY

"It's not so categorical as: this is normal, this is abnormal."

—THOMAS INSEL, FORMER DIRECTOR OF THE NATIONAL
INSTITUTE OF MENTAL HEALTH AND THE HUMAN
CONNECTOME PROJECT

Thomas Insel is a psychiatrist, neuroscientist, and former director of the National Institute of Mental Health, the organization spearheading the Human Connectome Project, President Obama's brain-mapping initiative.[1] The project's researchers are currently scanning the brains of twelve hundred healthy people between the ages of twenty-one and thirty-five, including three hundred pairs of twins, to examine both their structural and functional wiring—as Insel describes it, "how brains look when they're at rest and how they look when they're engaged in a given activity."

One of their most striking findings so far is the wide variation found even among healthy brains. While cells in the heart or kidneys perform set and easily determined functions that don't vary from human to human, the healthy human brain is not nearly so cookie cutter. Not only can we not always successfully ascribe particular functions to particular parts of the brain, we can't even say that brains function the same from person to person. This means that while medicine has been quite naturally focused on illness in the brain—looking for what might be structurally or chemi-cally wrong with the brain with depression or schizophrenia, for example, and how to treat it—we have been operating with little or no sense of how the normal brain operates. This is akin to evaluating heart disease with-out knowing what a healthy heart looks like.

Insel and the group he led while he oversaw the Human Connectome Project are just beginning to understand the delicate and mysterious in-terplay between biology and experience. "What we know is that experi-ence drives connectivity in the brain. And that's what we call plasticity. So that when you learn to play the piano or you learn to play the violin or you learn a new language, it changes brain wiring in a fundamental way, enough that you can see it in a brain scan. What is less clear is whether something about the wiring that you're born with and which we all have also drives you toward certain kinds of experiences."

Insel's son is an excellent example of this interplay. Now an adult, Insel's son was diagnosed with dyslexia as a child. In fact, his dyslexia was so severe that he needed to be in special schools starting at the age of seven. At these schools, educators realized "they could bang away for eight hours in a day the difference between a B and a D, and at the end of the day he still couldn't see it. His brain could not process that. So that was inherent, right? No matter how much experience he was going to get on B versus D, that was never going to happen. It was like putting a blind person in front of a book and telling him to read it. He couldn't see it, and he wasn't wired in a way that allowed that."

At the same time, "there were plenty of things that he could do really easily. In fact, there were things that probably came more easily to him than to anybody else around. He had this amazing auditory memory. We didn't know that he was dyslexic for a long time because he could hear people read something to him and he would remember it, could recite it back, and he'd just fake it. So it wasn't until he had to start reading in class without anybody reading it to him first that we realized he had a problem. So does somebody whose brain doesn't allow them to distinguish a B from a D, do they at the same time have wiring that makes it easier to do something else like memorize a poem that they hear or memorize music?" Since the brain doesn't work like the heart, we can't yet point to an exact cluster of cells or pathway and say, Yes, see, that's it right there, that's the link between letter recognition and auditory sensitivity. But certainly in the case of Insel's son and many of the other individuals who shared their stories for this book, the answer to Insel's question is an arguable yes.

CREATIVITY AND THE U-SHAPED CURVE

If we accept that for some individuals with brain differences, there is a connection between deficit and asset, the next obvious question is why some are able to utilize their gifts and others are not. Studies, empirical evidence, and the examples provided throughout this book show that people suffering at the extreme end of what clinicians and researchers call the inverted U-shaped curve of mental illness are not able to utilize whatever gifts might accompany their brain differences. However, those with brain differences who can function well with treatment—whether talk therapy, CBT, or pharmaceutical intervention—can exhibit extraordinary creativity. These are the people in whom divergent thinking crosses over with creative thinking—with the result being greater qualitative as well as quantitative output. In an article published in *Frontiers in Psychology* in 2015, Rex Jung and a team from the University of Mexico performed a study of 246 people, putting them through a battery of tests for divergent thinking and creative thinking.[2] In this case, Jung and his colleagues defined divergent thinking as the production of many uses or meanings for a common object or single image. They found that a higher number on the divergent thinking scale correlated with creativity. This, they argue, supports the "equal-odds rule," meaning that the more ideas you have— also known as "higher ideational output"—the more likely you are to be creative. On the inverted U-shaped curve, these are individuals whose brain differences allow them to produce many thoughts that aren't just original—they're also usable.

Robert Bilder and Kendra Knudsen at the University of California, Los Angeles, explain the inverted U-shaped curve phenomenon in another article in *Frontiers in Psychology,* in which they observe that the most creative individuals are not the most well or the most ill.[3] The most creative are often mildly ill. These are the individuals who can be diagnosed with all sorts of brain differences—like depression or bipolar disorder—who are simultaneously well treated and flexible enough to move back and forth between convergent and divergent thinking. Examples of this kind of flexibility can be found in a forty-year longitudinal study conducted by Swedish researchers and published in the *Journal of Psychiatric Research.* These researchers found that being an author "was specifically associated with increased likelihood of schizophrenia, bipolar disorder, unipolar depression, anxiety disorders, substance abuse, and suicide."[4] Clearly the authors who suffered from these brain differences were functioning at a level high enough to enable them to produce publishable work. Moreover, these same researchers found much higher representation in scientific and artistic fields among those whose first-degree relatives had diagnosed mental illness.[5] This suggests some genetic linkage between these brain differences and the drive and ability to be creative. That is, the kind of creativity that produces novels, musical scores, entrepreneurial ideas, and scientific theories requires the ability to flip back and forth between organized and messy thinking. In the words of Bilder and Knudsen, the creative brain needs to balance at "the edge of chaos."[6]

This genetic linkage between creativity and brain differences goes to the center of a question that has long baffled us: Despite how devastating mental illness can be, why has it not evolved out of the species, and even more to the point, why does it continue to be so remarkably prevalent? The most recent available NIH statistics estimate that 18.6 percent of all U.S. adults currently have a diagnosable mental illness.[7] Given the stigma associated with mental illness, and therefore the hesitation to seek treatment, the actual statistic is likely much higher. In any case, people with diagnosable brain differences are not outliers, no matter how much we as our society might behave as if they were.

One theory for why brain differences are so common among human beings as a species is described by David Dobbs in his article "The Science of Success" in *The Atlantic*.[8] Dobbs summarizes the work of child psychiatrist Tom Boyce, who coined a "dandelion and orchid" theory of human behavior. Boyce's research suggests that, neurologically speaking, there are two sorts of people—"dandelions," who flourish in any environment, and "orchids," who have much narrower requirements. While orchids are much more difficult to grow, when they thrive, they do so beautifully and with far more extraordinary results. Think of the examples cited in this book—people such as Matt Savage, who, when given the right auditory therapy and exposure to music, was able to become a musical prodigy. Without that early intervention, he might have continued to be unable to tolerate music at all.

Our species can't survive with only dandelions or orchids. In Dobbs's words, "The behavioral diversity provided by these two different types of temperaments . . . supplies precisely what a smart, strong species needs if it is to spread across and dominate a changing world. The many dandelions in a population provide an underlying stability. The less-numerous orchids, meanwhile, may falter in some environments but can excel in those that suit them. And even when they lead troubled early lives, some of the resulting heightened responses to adversity that can be problematic in everyday life—increased novelty-seeking, restlessness of attention, elevated risk-taking, or aggression—can prove advantageous in certain challenging situations: wars, tribal or modern; social strife of many kinds; and migrations to new environments. Together, the steady dandelions and the mercurial orchids offer an adaptive flexibility that neither can provide alone. Together, they open a path to otherwise unreachable individual and collective achievements."

THE FUTURE OF TREATING
BRAIN DIFFERENCES

In their article "Brain Disorders? Precisely," in *Science* magazine, Thomas R. Insel and Bruce N. Cuthbert write, "Mental and substance abuse disorders constitute the leading source of years lost to disability from all medical causes." This cost to productivity is astounding. The cost to human life is tragic. "The World Health Organization estimates over eight hundred thousand suicides each year globally, nearly all of which are a consequence of a mental disorder." [9]

Clearly, we need to do a better job diagnosing and treating mental disorders. Insel's former colleagues at the Human Connectome Project are actively looking for more effective ways to do that—starting with the words they use to talk about mental illness. As Insel and Cuthbert write, "syndromes once considered exclusively as 'mental' are being reconsidered as 'brain' disorders—or, to be more precise, as syndromes of disrupted neural, cognitive, and behavioral systems." In other words, we are moving to a more biological understanding of the brain and behaviors that result from the workings of the brain.

Insel is concerned that the way we currently describe behavior and experience that may result from brain differences is inexact. And he looks forward to that changing. "When someone comes in with a hopelessness and a sense of dread and what we now would label as 'depression,' we'd like to be able to ask what that really means in terms of what's going on in their brain, what's going on biologically, what's going on cognitively for them? There are probably many different ways of having the symptoms. And they may require different treatments, because we know that if you take people who meet the criteria for depression, that some people respond really well to medication and some respond to therapy and some require ECT [electroconvulsive therapy]." Currently, "we can't know who's going to respond to what. So the hope is that [in the future] using other techniques, just like we've done in cardiology, we listen to the symptoms. We take a really careful history. We do a good physical diagnosis. And then we have some sort of laboratory test or something else that tells us what is this person's most likely cause. And that determines the intervention."

The future of treating brain differences, according to Insel and Cuthbert, is about "precision." Once we better understand the workings of the variations among healthy brains, we can then determine the sources of deleterious brain differences in people with brain disorders. These treatments range from what sounds genuinely cutting edge, such as deep brain stimulation, to cognitive behavioral therapy. The learning curve for this will be very steep. We currently understand very little about the natural variation even in healthy brains. But now that we know where we're looking, and resources—financial as well as intellectual—are being applied to the task, we're beginning to progress at a faster clip than ever before.

Harold Koplewicz, founder and director of the Child Mind Institute, is undertaking a study of the functioning of children's brains even larger than the Human Connectome Project's scanning of adult brains.[10] Using MRI and other technology that didn't exist even a decade ago, their ultimate goal is to observe the resting brains of ten thousand children and young adults between the ages of five and twenty-one, while looking for "patterns of connection." One significant difference between the Child Mind Institute's study and the Human Connectome Project is that Koplewicz is looking primarily at children and young adults with diagnosed brain differences. Each study participant receives an EEG and functional MRI as well as psychological testing by licensed clinicians, a stress test, and an evaluation of nutritional status and genetic history. The result will be the largest repository of data on the developing brains of children with mental illness and learning disabilities.

The sheer number of scans being performed by Koplewicz and his team enables them to draw conclusions that weren't possible before now. For example, "we [now] know that as a group, there's a certain pattern of connection in kids with ADHD [attention deficit hyperactivity disorder] versus a group of kids who have ADD [attention deficit disorder without hyperactivity]." Given the largeness of the sample, it's Koplewicz's hope that eventually they will be able to see different patterns of connection among children who present with subtle differences and yet share a diagnosis, or alternatively, who share symptoms but different diagnoses. So, for example, they might be able to see how the child with ADHD who also has social anxiety differs from the child with autism spectrum disorder who is also stressed by engagement with strangers. Already they've determined differences in how the dyslexic brain reads text, even once treated. "When you look at a dyslexic reader they underactivate the left side of their brain. Then when you remediate them with a multisensory approach, they activate both sides of the brain," the way someone would read a second language. "And so they're not reading the way you and I would read. We've taught them to use another part of their brain."

Time will tell what else Koplewicz and his team discover, but for the time being he is a strong believer that there are two factors that distinguish high-performing people with brain differences from those who perform less well: IQ and environment. And of these two, he considers environment the most important. "I love the epigenetics of this, and I think that's the difference between one dyslexic and another. You know, IQ is certainly part of it, but it's the environment that put crayons and pastels in [celebrated artist] Chuck Close's hands even though he [grew up dyslexic and in impoverished circumstances]."

HOW PEOPLE WITH BRAIN
DIFFERENCES CAN FLOURISH

As Tom Insel noted, the most extraordinary finding so far in the Human Connectome Project is that there is a massive amount of variation among human brains—even those considered typical. "We are moving to a more dimensional approach trying to understand certain domains of functioning and thinking about how people are arrayed across these domains in a dimensional way. It's not so categorical as: this is normal, this is abnormal."

Perhaps the very phrase *brain difference* is a redundancy. All of us have differently functioning brains, and therefore, what produces creativity of all stripes may also vary wildly. It's up to us as individuals, clinicians, researchers, educators, parents—and as a society—to find and support the creative spark.

Whether we are considered mentally healthy or we have a diagnosed brain difference, the key to a positive identity is to find a way to feel productive. As important as it is to identify and treat weakness, it's equally important to identify and encourage strength—particularly in the early years when our brains are at their most plastic.

Imagine how different the experience of a child with dyslexia might be if, rather than focusing on their inability to read at the same pace as their peers, we sought out what they might be exceedingly good at? Imagine how much less the stigma of a learning disability might be if a child's identity could be geared toward a particular strength that could be cultivated? In a school setting, the educator might sit down with the child at an early stage and say, "Look, this is difficult for you. We're going to try to help you figure out work-arounds for this. But at the same time you have this incredible strength. And here are ways in which you can pursue that." Instead, too often, parents feel crushed by diagnoses that feel dooming, and children feel broken because they don't fit the mold.

Scott Barry Kaufman, scientific director of the Imagination Institute in the Positive Psychology Center at the University of Pennsylvania, is particularly critical of the cookie-cutter approach to educating children.[11] "I don't think we need these standardized hoops. I don't think we're offering a lot of value. I mean, what do we want to say? Do we just want good students or good learners? Or do we want creators? I think we've really left behind the creators. I'm a big fan of project-based learning. And perhaps if a parent does feel as though their child is being neglected by the school system, [I would suggest they ask,] 'Is it okay if he does a project that incorporates more of what he does love?' And if they say, 'No' to that—then say, 'Is there some way that we can pair him up with a mentor or someone within this field so that he can work on a meaningful project?'" In fact, Kaufman works with an organization called the Future Project that helps match students and mentors in just that way. "To me that would be a great way forward," he says emphatically.

Kaufman envisions a move away from being good at everything—as students in our test-heavy educational environment are currently expected to be—and toward one that focuses on developing expertise. "The more you are solely or obsessively focused on learning a particular domain of knowledge, obviously the expertise is going to be acquired. [That] can be very conducive to creative achievements, because you're constantly thinking about problems. You're very detail oriented and focused. And it's that intense focus that you see in most great creators."

Scott Barry Kaufman's vision, although rooted in brain science, is still only a hopeful future. Our current educational system is focused on having children spend the majority of their time on what doesn't work for them, rather than what does. This is why we drill the child with dyslexia to read with the same fluency as the nondyslexic child. This is why we press children with autism spectrum disorder to engage with subjects and situations that they find distasteful and uninspiring. This isn't to say that we shouldn't want all capable children to function well in the larger world. But that doesn't mean they should all function in the same way. That expectation of sameness is why the school years can be such a torture for so many children with brain differences.

With the help of involved caregivers and understanding educators, our children can make it through the torturous years of lower education and spread their wings when allowed to focus on what they love. For other children and young adults, though—who lack resources at home and perhaps even an accurate diagnosis—success lies on the other side of an impassable brick wall. This is a loss to all of us.

There are alternatives to building that wall.

Intro
- Seek evaluation and diagnosis—early intervention can make all the difference in overcoming and remediating symptoms.
- Lead with strengths—talk to children about their abilities and how they might hone them.
- Avoid drilling weaknesses—use the 80-20 approach: 80 percent of time spent on strengths and 20 percent on weaknesses.
- Encourage and allow more play time and provide more opportunities for children to immerse in their particular passions.
- Enlist the help of educators—speak to teachers about children's strengths and ask for help in allowing children to show and develop them.

For ourselves we can:
- Consider neuropsychological testing to find our particular areas of strength.
- Find and devote ourselves to the right combination of self-care and treatment—from exercise and proper nutrition to talk therapy and prescribed medication.
- Seek out work options that play to our strengths and consult a career counselor to help identify opportunities.

As a society we can:
- Appreciate the enormous potential of those with brain differences. Examples are all around us.
- Stop shaming those who are in the struggle, and banish words such as *crazy* and *nuts* from our speech.
- Talk about brain illnesses openly, as we would any other illness.
- Encourage an emphasis on creativity and expertise versus testing in our schools.

- Foster the pursuit of strengths in hiring and workplaces.
- Apply research dollars to gaining a better understanding of brain illness—commensurate with its prevalence and impact.

Based on my twenty-three years of treating patients, extensive analysis of the geniuses of the last several hundred years, and discussions with my expert colleagues across the fields of medicine and the most cutting-edge neurological sciences, I am convinced that there is something special about the brains of those struggling with mental illness that also yields some of the most astounding and beautiful achievements. I think this is an enormously positive and encouraging message for the nearly 50 percent of Americans who will develop at least one mental illness during their lifetime.[12] As so many of the accomplished people I've interviewed for this book have illustrated, a high-functioning brain is not the same thing as a tidy brain. A great deal of brilliance and creativity is sparked in brains that might be described as a bit messy.

The ability to find the unique strengths in our messy brains is what separates those of us who achieve from those of us who are held back by our differences. Sometimes what's holding us back is the society around us. The stigma of mental illness is deeply damaging and defeating. People with mental illness are often seen strictly through the lens of their deficits and weaknesses rather than their gifts and strengths. In fact, these gifts and strengths are why brain differences have persisted in our genetic makeup: such differences can confer an evolutionary advantage.

As a result of our current wholly negative take on mental health problems, most parents delay taking their children for evaluation and treatment, which serves not only to delay and amplify the weaknesses children experience, but also to hinder identifying their strengths. The same is true for adults. The stigma associated with acknowledging to yourself that you have a mental health issue delays your getting treatment to prevent the associated suffering, and can overshadow the unique abilities that are a byproduct of your brain's wiring.

What does this mean for you, your family, and your children? The people who fare best are those that get early treatment, thereby preventing illness from overtaking their strengths. Educate yourself on the signs and symptoms of mental illness and learning disability. When a problem starts to interfere with your or your child's ability to function well, get an evaluation and follow through on a treatment plan.

As recommended by Kevin Pelphrey, director of the Child Neuroscience Laboratory at the Yale School of Medicine, most of our and our children's time should be spent on discovering, engaging with, and honing our particular strengths.[13] Much less time should be spent on treating our relative weaknesses—he recommends an eighty-twenty split of time. On a case-by-case basis, prior to settling into such a split, psychiatric treatment (medication and/or therapy) might be needed. Once symptoms have been regulated to some extent, occupational therapy, or tutoring in a specific skill set such as executive function, might be recommended. Spend time exposing yourself and your children to opportunities to find what lights their fire and where their strengths arise. Astrophysicist and author Neil DeGrasse Tyson, who has taught children and adults of all abilities and interest levels to love science, told me that one of the most important things his parents did for him as a child was exposing him to a wide range of fields and disciplines such as art, music, dance, and science—everything and anything that could engage his interest and his aptitudes.[14] He didn't always desire to attend every event, but it was this exposure that he found allowed him to stumble on his passion for astronomy and stirred his mind to think creatively. In his opinion, this diverse exposure is important for *all* children. In my opinion, this is especially so for children with brain differences.

Whether you are struggling with illness yourself or your child is, remember that treatment does not diminish your strengths. Treatment allows you to make the best use of those strengths, to employ them unencumbered by the disruptive nature of the symptoms that hamper your functioning. Had Vincent van Gogh been treated, he would still have been a profoundly brilliant painter, but he likely would have lived a longer life with far less suffering. Without the unique wiring of his brain, though, it is unlikely we would ever have seen such a starry, starry night. Anthropologist Emily Martin and legal scholar Elyn Saks could not perform at the exceptional level they do if it weren't for judiciously prescribed medications to treat their bipolar disorder and schizophrenia (respectively). And yet even while medicated they are able to draw on the richness of experience and divergent thinking that their brain differences afford them.

Accepting and embracing our differences is the way forward—for all of us, diagnosed or undiagnosed, parent, clinician, educator, or child. We can choose this way forward, or we can turn away from it. We already know the cost of the path we've been on, both to our families and our communities. The better way is to launch ourselves forward with all the passion, creativity, grit, and determination that so many people with brain differences exhibit so inspiringly in their daily lives.

I have been changed by the stories of adversity and the finding of potential the many people in this book were willing to be vulnerable enough to share with me. What amazes me most is the children who in many ways have more of an ability than adults to seek out their spark and run with it. All of the children I spoke to felt they would never give up their "disability" because intuitively they know it is part and parcel of their spark. They inspired me with their capacity for self-reflection and their striving to make meaning of their struggles and strengths.

I have been struck by the enormous discrepancy between how celebrated the geniuses I've studied and spoken about have been and continue to be and how terribly they have suffered in their actual lives. The suffering came not only from their illnesses, but very much because they felt rejected by others for being different. As a result they were isolated and lonely, often devoid of real and loving relationships and contentment in their lives. They changed our worlds for the better with their art, their music, their scientific discoveries—but their own worlds remained bleak because they were devoid of the warmth and comfort of acceptance by others. Lacking in the kind of understanding we can grasp today, society shunned many of them. And while their spark enabled them to create history-altering innovations, this societal rejection caused them to emotionally wither and experience great misery. The origin of the tortured artist evolves not just from the effects of illness, but from the effects of our reactions to illness and difference.

My hope is that by understanding brain differences and the package of wiring that produces suffering but also unique strengths, we can all appreciate and accept the person who contains that package. Every brain and every life holds potential. Squashing that potential by dismissing those outside some standard mold is not only cruel on an individual level, it is a sad waste on a societal level. Armed with the knowledge of how to treat and manage the differences that cause suffering and knowing how to best mine the potential that accompanies those differences, we can not only increase the genius output of many but also enhance the quality of life for many millions.

My multiyear journey spent researching this book began with questions and observations that sprouted from my personal and professional lives. My fascination with the origins of genius started long ago growing up with a younger brother who endlessly questioned everything and anything. His dogged curiosity and pursuit of answers as a kid made me wonder what was up in that mind of his. Why was he always asking "Why?" And why did he always remain tenacious in his pursuit of the answers to his questions to such an extreme? Why did he break open his toys to see how they worked, even though they would then be broken for good? Why were our minds similar and yet different? It seemed to me that his passion for understanding was clearly always a standard or two of deviation off the curve. It fascinated me, and it still does. When as kids we looked up at the night sky, he wondered how it could be that the light we were viewing from the stars was actually light given off millions of years ago from a star that perhaps no longer even existed. He never gave up looking for answers. In 2011, he received the Nobel Prize in physics at age forty-one, becoming one of the youngest recipients ever, for his discoveries about the accelerating universe and dark energy. I grew up with a genius and then went on to make a career in studying and helping people with brain differences. In my many years of practice I have treated a number of extraordinary people who suffered mightily yet found the power in their differences, and their particular spark of genius. Like my brother, I have been driven by curiosity. So often, I witnessed this coexistence of unique ability side by side with disability. We are just starting to unlock the mysteries of the brain. Only by doggedly asking "why" will we discover our own potential for strength in the face of weakness.

NOTES

INTRODUCTION

[1] Noah, interview by Gail Saltz, October 17, 2014. All quotations credited to Noah are taken from this interview.

[2] Ethan, interview by Gail Saltz, October 14, 2014. All quotations credited to Ethan are taken from this interview.

[3] *Oxford Dictionaries, s.v.* "Genius," accessed September 27, 2015, http://www .oxforddictionaries.com/us/definition/american_english/genius.

[4] Erin Connors, Senior Media Relations Specialist, Corporate Communications and Public Affairs, American Psychiatric Association, interview by Gail Saltz, September 8, 2015.

[5] Allen J. Frances, "DSM 5 Is Guide Not Bible—Ignore Its Ten Worst Changes," *DSM5 in Distress* (blog), December 2, 2012, https://www.psychologytoday.com /blog/dsm5-in-distress/201212/dsm-5-is-guide-not-bible-ignore-its-ten-worst -changes.

[6] Thomas Insel, "Transforming Diagnosis," *NIMH Director's Blog,* April 29, 2013, http://www.nimh.nih.gov/about/director/2013/transforming-diagnosis.shtml.

[7] Matt Shipman, "Study Shows Mentally Ill More Likely to Be Victims, Not Perpetrators, of Violence," *NC State News* (blog), February 25, 2014, https://news.ncsu.edu /2014/02/wms-desmarais-violence2014/.

[8] Taylor Knopf, "CDC: 'Nearly 50% of U.S. Adults Will Develop at Least One Mental Illness,'" CNS News, June 13, 2013, accessed September 27, 2015, http://cnsnews .com/news/article/cdc-nearly-50-us-adults-will-develop-least-one-mental-illness.

[9] Scott Barry Kaufman, "The Real Link Between the Psychopathology Spectrum and the Creativity Spectrum," *Beautiful Minds* (blog), September 15, 2015, http://blogs

.scientificamerican.com/beautiful-minds/the-real-link-between-psychopathology
-and-creativity/.

[10] "Any Anxiety Disorder Among Children," National Institute of Mental Health,
accessed September 27, 2015, http://www.nimh.nih.gov/health/statistics/prevalence
/any-anxiety-disorder-among-children.shtml.

[11] Christopher Lehmann-Haupt, "Books of the Times: Odd Angles on Alcoholism
and American Writers," *The New York Times,* November 7, 1988, accessed
September 28, 2015, http://www.nytimes.com/1988/11/07/books/books-of-the
-times-odd-angles-on-alcoholism-and-american-writers.html.

[12] Dean Keith Simonton, "The Mad-Genius Paradox: Can Creative People Be More
Mentally Healthy but Highly Creative People More Mentally Ill?" *Perspectives on
Psychological Science* 9, no. 5 (2014): 470–80, doi:10.1177/1745691614543973.

[13] Nancy C. Andreasen, "Secrets of the Creative Brain," *The Atlantic,* July/August
2014, 62–75, accessed September 27, 2015, http://www.theatlantic.com/magazine
/archive/2014/07/secrets-of-the-creative-brain/372299/.

[14] Darya L. Zabelina, David Condon, and Mark Beeman, "Do Dimensional Psychopathology Measures Relate to Creative Achievement or Divergent Thinking?"
Frontiers in Psychology 5 (2014): 1029, doi:10.3389/fpsyg.2014.01029.

[15] Scott Barry Kaufman, interview by Gail Saltz, June 23, 2014.

[16] Anna Abraham, "Is There an Inverted-U Relationship Between Creativity and
Psychopathology?" *Frontiers in Psychology* 5 (2014): 750, doi:10.3389/
fpsyg.2014.00750.

[17] Rex Jung, interview by Gail Saltz, June 25, 2014; Rex E. Jung and Richard J. Haler,
"Creativity and Intelligence: Brain Networks That Link and Differentiate the
Expression of Genius," in *Neuroscience of Creativity,* ed. Oshin Vartanian, Adam S.
Bristol, and James C. Kaufman (Cambridge, MA: MIT Press, 2013), 233–54.

[18] Rex Jung, interview by Gail Saltz, June 25, 2014.

1: LEARNING DIFFERENCES

[1] Erica (Schuyler's mother), interview by Gail Saltz, November 14, 2014. All quotations credited to Erica are from this interview.

[2] Mélina Huc-Chabrolle et al., "Psychocognitive and Psychiatric Disorders Associated
With Developmental Dyslexia: A Clinical and Scientific Issue," abstract, *Encephale*
26, no. 2 (April 2010): 172–197, doi:10.1016/j.encep.2009.02.005.

[3] Ibid.

[4] Schuyler, interview by Gail Saltz, December 12, 2014. All quotations credited to
Schuyler are from this interview.

[5] "John Irving, Author," The Yale Center for Dyslexia and Creativity, accessed
November 18, 2015. http://dyslexia.yale.edu/Irving.html.

[6] Matthew Cruger, correspondence with Gail Saltz, August 10, 2015.

[7] Sally Shaywitz, interview by Gail Saltz, October 16, 2014.

[8] "Home," Rudolf Berlin Center, accessed November 18, 2015, http://rudolfberlin-eng
.org/.

[9] W. Pringle Morgan, "A Case of Congenital Word Blindness," *British Medical Journal,* November 7, 1896, accessed November 18, 2015, http://www.ncbi.nlm.nih.gov/pmc/articles/PMC2510936/pdf/brmedj08820-0014.pdf.

[10] Sally Shaywitz et al., "Functional Disruption in the Organization of the Brain for Reading in Dyslexia," *Proceedings of the National Academies of Sciences,* 95, no. 5 (March 1998): 2636–41.

[11] Sally Shaywitz, "Dyslexia," *Scientific American* 275, no. 5 (November 1996): 98–104.

[12] Emilio Ferrer, et al., "Uncoupling of Reading and IQ Over Time: Empirical Evidence for a Definition of Dyslexia," *Psychological Science* 21, no. 1 (2010): 93–101, doi:10.1177/0956797609354084.

[13] Shaywitz interview, October 16, 2014.

[14] Cruger, correspondence, August 10, 2015.

[15] Matthew Schneps, L. Todd Rose, and Kurt W. Fischer, "Visual Learning and the Brain: Implications for Dyslexia," *Mind, Brain, and Education* 1, no. 3 (2007): 128–39; Gadi Geiger et al., "Wide and Diffuse Perceptual Modes Characterize Dyslexics in Vision and Audition," *Perception* 37, no. 11 (2008): 1745–64; Gadi Geiger and Jerome Lettvin, "Peripheral Vision in Persons with Dyslexia," abstract, *The New England Journal of Medicine* 316 (1987): 1238–43, doi:10.1056/NEJM198705143162003.

[16] Shaywitz interview, October 16, 2014.

[17] Geiger et al., "Wide and Diffuse Perceptual Modes."

[18] Annie Murphy Paul, "The Upside of Dyslexia," *The New York Times,* February 2, 2012, www.nytimes.com/2012/02/05/opinion/sunday/the-upside-of-dyslexia.html.

[19] Ulrika Wolff and Ingvar Lundberg, "The Prevalence of Dyslexia Among Art Students," *Dyslexia: An International Journal of Research and Practice* 8, no. 1 (Jan/Mar 2002): 34–42. doi:10.1002/dys.211.

[20] Beryl Benacerraf, interview by Gail Saltz, March 7, 2014.

[21] Carol Greider, interview by Gail Saltz, March 13, 2014.

[22] Sidney (pseudonym), interview by Gail Saltz, October 20, 2014. All quotations credited to Sidney are from this interview.

[23] Barbara Fisher, Rhiannon Allen, and Gary Kose, "The Relationship Between Anxiety and Problem-Solving Skills in Children With and Without Learning Disabilities," *Journal of Learning Disabilities* 29, no. 4 (July 1996): 439–46.

[24] Brent Bowers, "Study Shows Stronger Links Between Entrepreneurs and Dyslexia," *The New York Times,* November 5, 2007, http://www.nytimes.com/2007/12/05/business/worldbusiness/05iht-dyslexia.4.8602036.html.

[25] "Signs of Dyslexia." The Yale Center for Dyslexia and Creativity, accessed December 5, 2015, http://dyslexia.yale.edu/EDU_signs.html.

[26] Julie Logan, "Dyslexic Entrepreneurs: The Incidence, Their Coping Strategies, and Their Business Skills," *Dyslexia: An International Journal of Research and Practice* 15 no. 4 (November 2009): 328–48. doi:10.1002/dys.388.

[27] "John Irving, Author," The Yale Center for Dyslexia and Creativity, accessed November 18, 2015. http://dyslexia.yale.edu/Irving.html.

[28] Evan, interview by Gail Saltz, November 24, 2014.

[29] Robert Cunningham, interview by Gail Saltz, September 17, 2014. All quotations credited to Cunningham are from this interview.

[30] William DeHaven, interview by Gail Saltz, September 18, 2014.

2: DISTRACTIBILITY

[1] Steven Stanley, interview by Gail Saltz, February 5, 2014. All quotations credited to Stanley are from this interview.

[2] "Attention-Deficit/Hyperactivity Disorder (ADHD): Data & Statistics," Centers for Disease Control and Prevention, accessed November 15, 2015, http://www.cdc.gov /ncbddd/adhd/data.html.

[3] Edward M. Hallowell, M.D., and John J. Ratey, M.D., *Driven to Distraction: Recognizing and Coping with Attention Deficit Disorder from Childhood through Adulthood,* rev. ed. (New York: Anchor, 1994), xiv.

[4] Michael P. Millham, interview by Gail Saltz, October 4, 2013.

[5] Harry Kimball, "Hyperfocus: The Flip Side of ADHD?" Child Mind Institute, Sept. 23, 2013, http://www.childmind.org/en/posts/articles/2013-9-23-hyperfocus -flip-side-adhd/.

[6] Francisco X. Castellanos and Erika Proal, "Large-scale Brain Systems in ADHD: Beyond the Prefrontal-striatal Model," abstract, *Trends in Cognitive Science* 16 (January 2012), doi:10.1016/j.tics.2011.11.007.

[7] Caterina Gawrilow et al., "Multitasking in Adults with ADHD," abstract, *ADHD, Attention Deficit, and Hyperactivity Disorders* 3 (September 2011), doi:10.1007/ s12402-011-0056-0; Kimball, "Hyperfocus: The Flip Side of ADHD?"; Millham interview; Castellanos and Proal, "Large-Scale Brain Systems in ADHD."

[8] Lenard Adler et al., "Managing ADHD in Children, Adolescents, and Adults With Comorbid Anxiety in Primary Care," *The Primary Care Companion to the Journal of Clinical Psychiatry* 9, no. 2 (2007): 129–38.

[9] Klaus W. Lange et al., "The History of Attention Deficit Hyperactivity Disorder," abstract, *ADHD, Attention Deficit, and Hyperactivity Disorders* 2, no. 4 (December 2010), doi:10.1007/s12402-010-0045-8.

[10] Edward M. Hallowell, M.D., and John J. Ratey, M.D., *Driven to Distraction: Recognizing and Coping with Attention Deficit Disorder from Childhood through Adulthood,* rev. ed. (New York: Anchor, 1994), xi.

[11] "FDA Permits Marketing of First Brain Wave Test to Help Assess Children and Teens for ADHD," Food and Drug Administration news release, July 15, 2013, http://www .fda.gov/NewsEvents/Newsroom/PressAnnouncements/ucm360811.htm.

[12] Elizabeth R. Sowell et al., "Cortical Abnormalities in Children and Adolescents with Attention-Deficit Hyperactivity Disorder," *The Lancet* 362, no. 9397 (November 22, 2003): 1699–1707, doi:10.1016/S0140-6736(03)14842-8.

[13] Darya Zabelina et al., "Do Dimensional Psychopathy Measures Relate to Creative Achievement or Divergent Thinking?" *Frontiers in Psychology* 5, no. 1029 (2014), doi:10.3389/fpsyg.2014.01029.

[14] Anna Abraham et al., "Creative Thinking in Adolescents with Attention Deficit Hyperactivity Disorder (ADHD)," abstract *Child Neuropsychology* 12, no. 2 (2006). doi: 10.1080/09297040500320691.

[15] Bonnie Cramond, "Attention-Deficit Hyperactivity Disorder and Creativity—What Is the Connection?" *The Journal of Creative Behavior* 28, no. 3 (September 1994): 193–210, doi:10.1002/j.2162-6057.1994.tb01191.x

[16] Holly White and Priti Shah, "Training Attention-Switching Ability in Adults with ADHD," abstract, *Journal of Attention Disorders* 10, no. 1 (August 2006): 44–54.

[17] Kimball, "Hyperfocus: The Flip Side of ADHD?"

[18] Ibid.

[19] Carl C. Gaither and Alma E. Cavazos-Gaither, *Physically Speaking: A Dictionary of Quotations on Physics and Astronomy* (New York: Taylor & Francis, 1997), 310.

[20] Denis Brian, *Einstein: A Life* (New York: Wiley, 1996), 12.

[21] Richard Boada et al., "Understanding the Comorbidity Between Dyslexia and Attention-Deficit/Hyperactivity Disorder," *Topics in Language Disorders* 32, no. 3 (2012): 264–84, doi:10.1097/TLD.0b013e31826203ac; Erik G. Willcutt and Bruce F. Pennington, "Psychiatric Comorbidity in Children and Adolescents with Reading Disability," abstract, *The Journal of Child Psychology and Psychiatry* 41, no. 8 (November 2000): 1039–48, doi:10.1111/1469-7610.00691.

[22] Ethan, interview by Gail Saltz, October 14, 2014. All quotations credited to Ethan are from this interview.

[23] Walter Isaacson, *Einstein: His Life and Universe* (New York: Simon and Schuster, 2008), 12.

[24] Ibid.

[25] Noah, interview by Gail Saltz, October 17, 2014.

[26] Edward Hallowell, interview by Gail Saltz, October 22, 2014. Subsequent quotations credited to Hallowell are from this interview.

[27] Robert Cunningham, interview by Gail Saltz, September 17, 2014. All quotations credited to Cunningham are from this interview.

[28] Mario Livio, interview by Gail Saltz, October 14, 2014. All quotations credited to Livio are from this interview.

[29] Dom, interview by Gail Saltz, October 7, 2014. All quotations credited to Dom are from this interview.

[30] "Daydreaming Boosts Creativity, Study Says," PsychologicalScience.org, published October 23, 2012, http://www.psychologicalscience.org/index.php/news/daydreaming-boosts-creativity-study-suggests.html.

[31] Scott Barry Kaufman, "Mind Wandering: A New Personal Intelligence Perspective," *Beautiful Minds* (blog), September 25, 2013, http://blogs.scientificamerican.com/beautiful-minds/mind-wandering-a-new-personal-intelligence-perspective/.

[32] Scott Barry Kaufman and Jerome L. Singer, "The Origins of Positive-Constructive Daydreaming," *Guest Blog,* December 22, 2011, http://blogs.scientificamerican.com/guest-blog/the-origins-of-positive-constructive-daydreaming/; Jessica Lahey,

"Teach Kids to Daydream," *The Atlantic,* October 16, 2013, http://www.theatlantic
.com/education/archive/2013/10/teach-kids-to-daydream/280615/.

3: ANXIETY

[1] David Sedaris, interview by Gail Saltz, February 11, 2014. Unless otherwise
indicated, all quotations credited to Sedaris are from this interview.

[2] David Sedaris, *Naked* (New York: Little, Brown and Company, 1997), 8-9

[3] Lena Dunham interview, "*Girls* Season 2: Behind the Episode #8," YouTube video,
March 4, 2013, https://www.youtube.com/watch?v=XgWXiiPx-_I. All quotations
credited to Dunham are from this interview.

[4] Katie A. McLaughlin, Evelyn Behar, and T. D. Borkovec, "Family History of
Psychological Problems in Generalized Anxiety Disorder," abstract, *Journal of
Clinical Psychology* 64, no. 7 (July 2008), 905–18; Gayatri Patel and Tonya Fancher,
"Generalized Anxiety Disorder," *Annals of Internal Medicine* 159, no. 11 (2013),
ITC6-1, doi:10.7326/0003-4819-159-11-201312030-01006.

[5] "How Common Is PTSD?" *U.S. Department of Veterans Affairs,* accessed February
6, 2015, www.ptsd.va.gov/public/PTSD-overview/basics/how-common-is-ptsd.asp.

[6] Carolyn Sartor et al., "Common Heritable Contributions to Low-Risk Trauma,
High-Risk Trauma, Posttraumatic Stress Disorder, and Major Depression,"
abstract, *Archives of General Psychiatry* 69, no. 3 (March 2012), 293–99. doi:10.1001/
archgenpsychiatry.2011.1385.

[7] J. David Bremner, Steven Southwick, D. Johnson, Dennis Charney, and Rachel
Yehuda, "Childhood Physical Abuse and Combat-Related Posttraumatic Stress
Disorder in Vietnam Veterans," abstract, *American Journal of Psychiatry* 150, no. 2
(February 1998), 235–39.

[8] Tomohiro Nakao, Kayo Okada, and Shigenobu Kanba, "Neurobiological Model of
Obsessive-Compulsive Disorder: Evidence from Recent Neuropsychological and
Neuroimaging Findings," *Psychiatry and Clinical Neurosciences* 68 (2014): 587–605,
doi:10.1111/pcn.12195.

[9] "Any Anxiety Disorder Among Adults," National Institute of Mental Health,
accessed February 6, 2016, http://www.nimh.nih.gov/health/statistics/prevalence
/any-anxiety-disorder-among-adults.shtml.

[10] Brendan Bradley et al., "Attentional Bias for Emotional Faces in Generalized
Anxiety Disorder," *British Journal of Clinical Psychology* 38, no. 3 (1999): 267–78,
doi:10.1348/014466599162845.

[11] Jeremy D. Coplan et al., "The Relationship Between Intelligence and Anxiety: An
Association With Subcortical White Matter Metabolism," *Frontiers in Evolutionary
Neuroscience* 3, no. 8 (February 2012), doi:10.3389/fnevo.2011.00008.

[12] Ibid.

[13] Ibid.

[14] Barbara Milrod, interview by Gail Saltz, October 22, 2014. All quotations credited to
Milrod are from this interview.

[15] Judy Lin, "Extroverts Promise, but Neurotics Deliver As Team Players," *UCLA Today,* May 2, 2013, http://newsroom.ucla.edu/stories/extroverts-v-neurotics-245761.

[16] Sidney (pseudonym), interview by Gail Saltz, October 20, 2014. All quotations credited to Sidney are from this interview.

[17] Lucia Margari et al., "Neuropsychopathological Comorbidities in Learning Disorders," *BMC Neurology* 13, no. 198 (December 2013), doi:10.116/1471-2377-13-198.

[18] John Walkup, interview by Gail Saltz, February 6, 2015. All quotations credited to Walkup are from this interview.

[19] Ibid.

[20] David Adam, interview by Gail Saltz, February 5, 2015. All quotations credited to Adam are from this interview.

[21] Dan Harris, interview by Gail Saltz, February 6, 2015. All quotations credited to Harris are from this interview.

[22] Lisa (pseudonym), interview by Gail Saltz, November 10, 2014. All quotations credited to Lisa are from this interview.

[23] David Kohn, interview by Gail Saltz, March 3, 2014. Subsequent information about Darwin is from this interview.

[24] Ibid.

[25] Ibid.

[26] Rebecca Stewart and D. L. Chambless, "Cognitive-Behavioral Therapy for Adult Anxiety Disorders in Clinical Practice: A Meta-analysis of Effectiveness Studies," *Journal of Consulting and Clinical Psychology* 77 (2009): 595–606.

[27] A. M. de Souza Moura et al., "Effects of Aerobic Exercise on Anxiety Disorders," *CNS and Neurological Disorders—Drug Targets* 14, no. 9 (November 2015): 1184–93, doi:10.2174/1871527315666151111121259; Kaushadh Jayakody, Shalmini Gunadasa, and Christian Hosker, "Exercise for Anxiety Disorders: Systematic Review," abstract, *British Journal of Sports Medicine* 48, no. 3 (February 2014): 187–96, doi:10.1136/bjsports-2012-091287.

[28] Nick Errington-Evans, "Acupuncture for Anxiety," *CNS Neuroscience Therapy* 18, no. 4 (April 2012): 277–84, doi:10.1111/j.1755-5949.2011.00254.x.

[29] Scott Stossel, *My Age of Anxiety* (New York: Knopf, 2014), 320

4: MELANCHOLY

[1] Andrew Solomon, interview by Gail Saltz, March 31, 2014. All quotations credited to Solomon are from this interview.

[2] Dietmar Winkler, Edda Priek, and Siegfried Kaspar, "Anger Attacks in Depression—Evidence for a Male Depressive Syndrome," *Psychotherapy and Psychosomatics* 74 (2005), 303–07, doi:10.1159/000086321.

[3] "Major Depression Among Adults," National Institute of Mental Health, accessed December 4, 2015, www.nimh.nih.gov/health/statistics/prevalence/major-depression-among-adults.shtml.

[4] "Depression," National Insitute of Mental Health, accessed February 6, 2016, www
.nimh.nih.gov/health/topics/depression/index.shtml

[5] Tiffany Szu-Ting Fu et al., "Confidence Judgment in Depression and Dysphoria:
The Depressive Realism vs. Negativity Hypothesis," *Journal of Behavior Theory and
Experimental Psychiatry* 43, no. 2 (June 2012): 699–704, doi:10.1016/j.
jbtep.2011.09.014.

[6] Joshua Wolf Shenk, *Lincoln's Melancholy: How Depression Challenged a President and
Fueled His Greatness* (New York: Houghton Mifflin, 2005).

[7] Barbara Goldsmith, author of *Obsessive Genius: The Inner World of Marie Curie,*
interview by Gail Saltz, September 29, 2014.

[8] Nassir Ghaemi, interview by Gail Saltz, February 27, 2015. All quotations credited
to Ghaemi are from this interview.

[9] Erin C. Tully et al., "Quadratic Associations Between Empathy and Depression as
Moderated by Emotion Dysregulation," *Journal of Psychology* 7 (January 2015):
1–25.

[10] Erdem Pulcu et al., "Enhanced Subgenual Cingulate Response to Altruistic
Decisions in Remitted Major Depressive Disorder," abstract, *NeuroImage: Clinical* 4
(April 2014): 701–10. doi:10.1016/j.nicl.2014.04.010.

[11] Connie M. Strong et al., "Temperament-Creativity Relationships in Mood Disorder
Patients, Healthy Controls and Highly Creative Individuals," *Journal of Affective
Disorders* 100, no. 1–3 (June 2007): 41–48.

[12] Evan Wright, interview by Gail Saltz, February 13, 2014. All quotations credited to
Wright are from this interview.

[13] Centers for Disease Control and Prevention, "Current Depression Among Adults—
United States, 2006 and 2008," *Morbidity and Mortality Weekly Report* 53, no. 38
(October 1, 2010), 1229–35.

[14] Mary Whooley et al., "Depressive Symptoms, Unemployment, and Loss of Income,"
Archives of Internal Medicine 162, no 22 (2002): 2614–20, doi:10.1001/
archinte.162.22.2614.

[15] Walter F. Stewart, "Cost of Lost Productive Work Time Among US Workers With
Depression," *Journal of the American Medical Association* 289, no. 23 (June 2003):
3135–44.

[16] Ibid.

[17] Robert Leahy, "The Cost of Depression," *The Huffington Post,* October 30, 2010,
www.huffingtonpost.com/robert-leahy-phd/the-cost-of-depression_b_770805.html.

[18] Dom, interview by Gail Saltz, October 7, 2014. All quotations credited to Dom are
from this interview.

[19] "Exercise and Depression," Harvard Health Publications, accessed December 5,
2015, http://www.health.harvard.edu/mind-and-mood/exercise-and-depression
-report-excerpt.

[20] Ibid.

[21] Ibid.

[22] Ibid.

[23] Anne Rice, correspondence with Gail Saltz, June 4, 2014.

[24] Adam Jacques, "Anne Rice: The *Interview with the Vampire* Novelist on Her Daughter's Death, Living Through Her Own Funeral, and the Dangers of Oxford," *Independent* (U.K.), November 2, 2014, www.independent.co.uk/news /people/profiles/anne-rice-the-interview-with-the-vampire-novelist-on-her -daughters-death-living-through-her-own-9829902.html.

[25] Anne Rice, correspondence with Gail Saltz, June 4, 2014.

[26] James Kocsis, interview by Gail Saltz, December 5, 2014. All quotations credited to Kocsis are from this interview.

5: CYCLING MOOD

[1] Emily Martin, interview by Gail Saltz, April 24, 2014. Unless otherwise noted, all quotations credited to Emily Martin are from this interview.

[2] Ibid.

[3] Emily Martin, *Bipolar Expeditions: Mania and Depression in American Culture* (Princeton, NJ: Princeton University Press, 2009),. xv.

[4] Martin interview.

[5] Ibid.

[6] Ibid.

[7] American Psychiatric Association, "Resources and Files," *DSM-5,* accessed February 6, 2016, www.psychiatry.org/psychiatrists/practice/dsm/dsm-5.

[8] James McCabe et al., "Excellent School Performance at Age 16 and Risk of Adult Bipolar Disorder: National Cohort Study," *British Journal of Psychiatry* 196, no. 2 (February 2010): 109–15, doi:10.1192/bjp.bp.108.060368.

[9] Stacey McCraw et al., "Self-Reported Creativity in Bipolar Disorder: Prevalence, Types and Associated Outcomes in Mania Versus Hypomania," *Journal of Affective Disorders* 151, no. 3 (December 2013): 831–36, doi:10.1016/j.jad.2013.07.016.

[10] Jane Collingwood, "The Link Between Bipolar Disorder and Creativity," *PsychCentral* (blog), March 28, 2010, http://psychcentral.com/lib/the-link-between-bipolar -disorder-and-creativity/.

[11] Vabren Watts, "Siblings of Bipolar Patients May Have 'Reproductive Advantages,'" *Psychiatric News* (blog), September 15, 2014, http://psychnews.psychiatryonline.org /doi/10.1176/appi.pn.2014.9b5, doi:10.1176/appi.pn.2014.9b5.

[12] Christopher Ramey and Evangelia Chrysikou, "'Not in Their Right Mind': The Relation of Psychopathology to the Quantity and Quality of Creative Thought," *Frontiers in Psychology* 8, no. 835 (2014), doi:10.3389/fpsyg.2014.00835.

[13] Ibid.

[14] Dean Simonton, interview by Gail Saltz, March 12, 2015.

[15] Margina Ruiter and Sheri L. Johnson, "Mania Risk and Creativity: A Multi-Method Study of the Role of Motivation," *Journal of Affective Disorders* 170 (January 2015): 52–58, doi:10.1016/j.jad.2014.08.049.

[16] Nassir Ghaemi, interview by Gail Saltz, February 27, 2015.

[17] Kay Redfield Jamison, *Touched with Fire: Manic-Depressive Illness and the Artistic Temperament* (New York: Free Press, 1996), 2.

[18] Bill Lichtenstein, interview by Gail Saltz, March 15, 2014. All quotations credited to Lichtenstein are from this interview.

[19] Chuck Nice, interview by Gail Saltz, May 20, 2014. All quotations from Nice are from this interview; National Institute of Mental Health, "Bipolar Disorder in Adults," accessed February 6, 2016, www.nimh.nih.gov/health/publications/bipolar -disorder-in-adults/index.shtml

[20] Jamison, *Touched with Fire,* 73, 105.

[21] Gail Saltz and Susan Beegel, "On Hemingway: Psychobiography," presentation, 92nd Street Y, New York, October 15, 2012, http://92yondemand.org/hemingway -psychobiography-dr-gail-saltz-susan-f-beegel.

[22] Ibid.

6: DIVERGENT THINKING

[1] Elyn Saks, interview by Gail Saltz, January 8, 2015. Unless otherwise noted, all quotations credited to Elyn Saks are from this interview.

[2] Elyn Saks, *The Center Cannot Hold: My Journey Through Madness* (New York: Hyperion, 2007), 35.

[3] Ibid, 136.

[4] Andrea Thompson, "Hearing Voices: Some People Like It," *Livescience,* September 15, 2006, http://www.livescience.com/7177-hearing-voices-people.html.

[5] Thomas Sedlak, interview by Gail Saltz, April 21, 2015. All quotations credited to Sedlak are from this interview.

[6] National Institute of Mental Health, "Schizophrenia," accessed December 6, 2015, http://www.nimh.nih.gov/health/publications/schizophrenia/index.shtml.

[7] Ibid.

[8] Erica Goode, "John Nash, *A Beautiful Mind* Subject and Nobel Winner, Dies at 86," *The New York Times,* May 25, 2015, http://www.nytimes.com/2015/05/25 /science/john-nash-a-beautiful-mind-subject-and-nobel-winner-dies-at-86 .html.

[9] Barnaby Nelson and David Rawlings, "Relating Schizotypy and Personality to the Phenomenology of Creativity," *Schizophrenia Bulletin* 36, no. 2 (2010): 388–99, doi:10.1093/schbul/sbn098.

[10] Scott Barry Kaufman and Elliot S. Paul, "Creativity and Schizophrenia Spectrum Disorders Across the Arts and Sciences," *Frontiers in Psychology* 5, no. 1145 (November 2014), doi:10.3389/fpsyg.2014.01145.

[11] Dean Keith Simonton, "The Mad-Genius Paradox: Can Creative People Be More Mentally Healthy but Highly Creative People More Mentally Ill?" *Perspectives on Psychological Science* 9, no. 5 (September 2014): 470–80; Dean Keith Simonton, interview by Gail Saltz, March 12, 2015.

[12] Margaret Dykes and Andrew McGhie, "A Comparative Study of Attentional

Strategies of Schizophrenic and Highly Creative Normal Subjects," *The British Journal of Psychiatry* 128, no. 1 (January 1976): 50–56, doi:10.1192/bjp.128.1.50.

[13] Andreas Fink et al., "Creativity and Schizotypy from the Neuroscience Perspective," *Cognitive, Affective, and Behavioral Neuroscience* 14, no. 1 (March 2014): 378–87, doi:10.3758/s13415-013-0210-6.

[14] Annukka K. Lindell, "On the Interrelation Between Reduced Lateralization, Schizotypy, and Creativity," *Frontiers in Psychology* 5, no. 813 (2014), doi:10.3389/fpsyc/2014.00813.

[15] Haeme R. P. Park, "Neural Correlates of Creative Thinking and Schizotypy," *Neuropsychologia* 73 (July 2015): 94–107, doi:10.1016/j.neuropsychologia.2015.05.007.

[16] Deanna Barch, interview by Gail Saltz, May 22, 2015.

7: RELATEDNESS

[1] Sarah McMullen, manager for Matt Savage, interview by Gail Saltz, February 17, 2014; Steve Silberman, "The Key to Genius," *Wired,* December 2003, http://www.wired.com/2003/12/genius-2/.

[2] Matt Savage, interview by Gail Saltz, February 19, 2014. All quotations credited to Matt Savage are from this interview.

[3] Diane Savage, interview by Gail Saltz, January 18, 2016. All quotations credited to Diane Savage are from this interview.

[4] Darold Treffert, interview by Gail Saltz, April 7, 2015.

[5] Lawrence Osborne, "The Little Professor Syndrome," *The New York Times Magazine,* June 18, 2000, www.nytimes.com/library/magazine/home/20000618mag-asperger.html.

[6] "Autism Spectrum Disorder (ASD)," Centers for Disease Control and Prevention, accessed December 6, 2015, http://www.cdc.gov/ncbddd/autism/data.html.

[7] Ibid.

[8] Ibid.

[9] Teresa Iuculano et al., "Brain Organization Underlying Superior Mathematical Abilities in Children with Autism," *Biological Psychiatry* 75, no. 3 (February 2014): 223–30, doi:10.1016/j.biopsych.2013.06.018.

[10] David J. Gerlotti et al., "FMRI Activation of the Fusiform Gyrus and Amygdala to Cartoon Characters but Not to Faces in a Boy with Autism," *Neuropsychologia* 43, no. 3 (February 2005): 373–85, doi:10.1016/j.neuropsychologia.2004.06.015.

[11] Emma Ashwin et al., "Eagle-Eyed Visual Acuity: An Experimental Investigation of Enhanced Perception in Autism," *Biological Psychiatry* 65, no. 1 (January 2009): 17–21, doi:10.1016/j.biopsych.2008.06.012.

[12] Fabienne Samson et al., "Enhanced Visual Functioning in Autism: An ALE Metaanalysis," *Human Brain Mapping* 33, no. 7 (July 2012): 1553–81, doi:10.1002/hbm.21307.

[13] Simon Baron-Cohen et al., "Talent in Autism: Hyper-Systemizing, Hyper-Attention to Detail and Sensory Hypersensitivity," *Philosophical Transactions B* 364, no. 1522 (May 2009), doi:10.1098/rstb.2008.0337.

[14] Francesca Happé and Pedro Vital, "What Aspects of Autism Predispose to Talent?" *Philosophical Transactions of the Royal Society B* 364 (2009): 1369–75, doi:10.1098/rstb.2008.0032.

[15] Simon Baron-Cohen et al., "Talent in Autism: Hyper-Systemizing, Hyper-Attention to Detail and Sensory Hypersensitivity," *Philosophical Transactions B* 364, no. 1522 (May 2009), doi:10.1098/rstb.2008.0337. 1378.

[16] Greg Wallace, interview by Gail Saltz, May 15, 2015. All quotations credited to Wallace are from this interview.

[17] Kevin Pelphrey, interview by Gail Saltz, May 27, 2015. All quotations credited to Pelphrey are from this interview.

[18] Darold Treffert, "The Savant Syndrome: An Extraordinary Condition. A Synopsis: Past, Present, Future," *Philosophical Transactions of the Royal Society of London B* 364, no. 2 (May 2009), http://www.ncbi.nlm.nih.gov/pmc/articles/PMC2677584/, doi:10.1098/rstb.2008.0326.

[19] Ron Suskind, "Reaching My Autistic Son Through Disney," *The New York Times Magazine,* March 9, 2014, http://www.nytimes.com/2014/03/09/magazine/reaching-my-autistic-son-through-disney.html.

[20] Treffert interview.

[21] Esther Brokaw, interview by Gail Saltz, April 6, 2015. All quotations credited to Brokaw are from this interview.

[22] Gareth Cook, "The Autism Advantage," *The New York Times Magazine,* December 2, 2012, http://www.nytimes.com/2012/12/02/magazine/the-autism-advantage.html.

[23] Baron-Cohen et al., "Talent in Autism." 1380

8: THE FUTURE OF THINKING DIFFERENTLY

[1] Thomas Insel, interview by Gail Saltz, May 15, 2015. All quotations credited to Insel are from this interview.

[2] Rex E. Jung et al., "Quantity Yields Quality When It Comes to Creativity: A Brain and Behavioral Test of the Equal-Odds Rule," abstract, *Frontiers in Psychology* 6, no. 864 (June 2015), doi:10.3389/fpsyg.2015.00864.

[3] Robert Bilder and Kendra Knudsen, "Creative Cognition and Systems Biology on the Edge of Chaos," *Frontiers in Psychology* 5, no. 1104 (September 2014), doi:10.3389/fpsyg.2014.01104. 1

[4] Simon Kyaga et al., "Mental Illness, Suicide, and Creativity: 40-year Prospective Total Population Study," abstract, *Journal of Psychiatric Research* 47, no. 1 (January 2013): 83–90, doi:10.1016/j.jpsychires.2012.09.010. 83

[5] Ibid.

[6] Bilder and Knudsen, 1.

[7] "Any Mental Illness (AMI) Among Adults," National Institute of Mental Health, accessed December 6, 2015, http://www.nimh.nih.gov/health/statistics/prevalence/any-mental-illness-ami-among-adults.shtml.

[8] David Dobbs, "The Science of Success," *The Atlantic,* December 2009, accessed

December 6, 2015, http://www.theatlantic.com/magazine/archive/2009/12/the
-science-of-success/307761/.

9 Thomas R. Insel and Bruce N. Cuthbert, "Brain Disorders? Precisely," *Science* 348,
no. 6243 (May 1, 2015): 499–500, doi:10.1126/science.aab2358. page 499

10 Harold Koplewicz, interview by Gail Saltz, May 15, 2015.

11 Scott Barry Kaufman, interview by Gail Saltz, June 23, 2014.

12 "Mental Illness Surveillance Among Adults," Centers for Disease Control and
Prevention, accessed February 7, 2016, http://www.cdc.gov
/mentalhealthsurveillance/documents/MentalIllnessSurveillance_FactSheet.pdf.

13 Kevin Pelphrey, interview by Gail Saltz, May 27, 2015.

14 Neil DeGrasse Tyson, interview by Gail Saltz, August 19, 2014.

ACKNOWLEDGMENTS

The Power of Different would never have come into being without my book agent, Trena Keating, who not only understood that without "different" we would never have had the genius creations that make up our history, but who nurtured me with care and intensity exactly the way I needed so that we could grow this book. I so appreciate Trena's curiosity and passionate interest about the mind and brain as well as her supportive enthusiasm for my project and me.

A million thank-yous to Peternelle Van Arsdale, without whose amazing talent, expertise, and professionalism I could not have completed this book. Besides being a highly intelligent and creative thinker, she is a genuinely lovely person who has an amazing ability to empathically tap into other people's worlds and to capture them in writing. I am so grateful for your confidence in this project, even when I was uncertain, and for your beautiful command of language.

A huge thank-you to Whitney Frick and her talented colleagues at Flatiron Books. In a world of faster and less-substantive, you are a beacon of smarter and more-thoughtful. Thank you for seeing what I hoped to accomplish from the very get-go, for believing in this book and what it could deliver to all those who struggle with "different," for painstakingly making this book better at many junctures, and for your never-ending encouragement. You are one very special editor!

This book and its inspiration are completely dependent on the bravery and willingness of so many who shared their stories of struggle with me. Thank you to Andrew Solomon, Emily Martin, Edward Hallowell M.D., Elyn Saks, Beryl Benaceraff M.D., Bill Lichtenstein, Chuck Nice, Dan Harris, David Adam, Esther Brokaw, Evan Wright, Carol Greider M.D., Mario Livio, Anne Rice, David Sedaris, Steven Stanley, Matt Savage. Thank you to Dom, Evan, Ethan, Schuyler, Sidney, and each of their parents. Each of you inspired me with your courage, warmth, and your sparks of genius.

I am indebted to numerous neuroscientists, clinicians, educators, and experts, who work tirelessly to revolutionize our understanding of the brain, mental illness, learning differences, and how we can utilize our understanding in the treatment, education, and development of people with differences. Thank you for the time you spent with me making clearer what we know and what we need to pursue. Thank you to Dr. Harold Koplewicz, Dr. Deanna Barch, Dr. Greg Wallace, Dr. Thomas Sedlak, Mr. William Dehaven, Mr. Bill Cunningham, Dr. Barbara Milrod, Dr. James Kaufman, Dr. Zach Hambrick, Dr. Rex Jung, Dr. Tom Insel, Dr. Kevin Pelphrey, Dr. Scott Barry Kaufman, Dr. Nassir Ghaemi, Drs. Sally and Bennett Shaywitz, Dr. Matthew Cruger, Dr. Michael Millham, Dr. Jim Kocsis, Dr. John Walkup, Dr. Dean Simonton, Dr. Darold Treffert, Dr. David Silbersweig, Dr. Neil deGrasse Tyson.

I would like to thank Henry Timms and the incredible staff of the 92nd Street Y, who supported me and allowed me to grow my Psychobiography series, which in addition to being something I love doing, was one of the original seeds for this book. Thank you to the Weill Cornell Medical Center department of psychiatry, which remains my home and source for brilliant colleagues. Thank you to the New York Psychoanalytic Institute, where I learned how the mind and the brain are one and the same and where I appreciate and admire the work of my colleagues who treat those struggling.

A thank-you to my brother, Adam Riess, and sister-in-law, Nancy Riess, for listening to me go on about this interest and project for many years, and for always being willing to brainstorm and give me great ideas.

Most of all, endless love, appreciation, and thanks to my husband and three incredible daughters, who are my support, my cheering section, my sounding board, my go-to for great judgment, and most of all, my source of daily joy.

INDEX

Acton Jazz Café, 174–75
acupuncture, 105
Adam, David, 94–95, 103
ADD (attention deficit disorder), 1–4,
    13–14, 47–78, 115, 135, 209–10
  anxiety and, 8, 52, 58–59
  attention difficulties in, 49–51, 55
  behavioral therapy for, 66–67, 77–78
  brain and, 13, 51–55, 61, 71, 91
  challenges of living with, 55–62
  characteristics of, 49
  creativity and, 52, 54, 70, 71
  diagnosing, 50, 53
  dyslexia and, 18, 57
  Einstein and, 11, 55–57
  emotional struggles and, 58
  executive function and, 2, 13, 51–52,
    55, 58, 59
  experience of having, 55–74
  flourishing with, 74–78
  gifts of, 68–74
  Hallowell and, 50, 53, 61–65, 70–71, 74
  hyperfocus in, 3
  impulsivity in, 2, 3, 49–51, 53, 54, 59,
    60

Livio and, 68–70, 75, 77
  marital relationships and, 77
  medications for, 2, 48, 66–68, 77–78
  negativity toward children with, 49
  in parents, 8, 77
  partnerships and, 62–63
  prevalence of, 48–49
  reading and, 57–58
  self-esteem and, 49, 52, 67, 77
  Stanley and, 47–48, 50–52, 60–61, 68,
    71, 75, 77
  tests and, 66
  what it means to have, 52–54
  work-arounds for, 62–68
Adderall, 2, 66, 77
ADHD (attention deficit hyperactive
    disorder), 49, 209–10
  see also ADD
adrenaline, 84, 95
agoraphobia, 85
alcoholism, 9, 119, 149
altruism, 114
ambition, 139, 148, 177
American Psychiatric Association (APA),
    5, 53

Andreasen, Nancy, 9
anger, 111
    Wright and, 115–20, 122
angular thinking, 22, 42
anxiety, overuse of word, 81
anxiety disorders, 8, 15, 79–107, 206
    ADD and, 8, 52, 58–59
    agoraphobia, 85
    attention to details and, 99–100
    behavioral therapy for, 82, 87–88, 104,
        105
    brain and, 86, 87
    challenges of living with, 90–95
    Darwin and, 100–101
    diagnosing, 88
    emotions and, 94
    excitement and, 93
    experience of having, 90–103
    familial predisposition to, 82, 85
    flourishing with, 103–7
    generalized anxiety disorder, 84, 88,
        90–103
    gifts of, 99–103
    Harris and, 95–97, 106
    healthy degree of, 106
    hypervigilance and, 88, 90, 95, 96,
        107
    inverted U-shaped curve of, 89–90
    magical thinking and, 87, 105
    medications for, 87–88
    obsessive-compulsive disorder, 11,
        80–83, 86–88, 94–95, 103, 104
    obsessive-compulsive personality
        disorder, 86–88
    panic disorder, 85
    pathological, 93
    phobias, 85, 104
    prevalence of, 82, 87, 104
    schoolwork and, 93–94
    Sedaris and, 79–83, 86, 90–91, 98–103
    as selective advantage, 89
    self-awareness and, 88
    social anxiety disorder, 85–86

    and social component of school, 91
    stress and, 81–84, 92–93, 104
    treatment of, 87–88, 90, 104–5
    what it means to have, 83–90
    work-arounds for, 95–99
Archives of Internal Medicine, 121
Aristotle, 9
Asperger, Hans, 178
Asperger's syndrome, 1, 60, 178, 200
    autism and, 6, 178, 184
    use of term, 178–79
Atlantic, 207
attention, single-minded (hyperfocus), 3
attention difficulties, 49–51, 55
    see also ADD
Auciello, Dominick, 55
auditory integration therapy (AIT), 174,
        189
autism spectrum disorder (ASD), 23,
        173–202, 212
    academic settings and, 186–87
    Asperger's and, 6, 178, 184
    and attention to detail, 181–82
    in boys vs. girls, 179
    brain and, 180–81, 185, 194
    Brokaw and, 195–98
    challenges of living with, 184–89
    diagnosing, 178, 179, 199–200
    experience of having, 182–99
    face recognition and, 180–81, 193,
        194–95
    flourishing with, 185, 199–202
    gifts of, 194–99
    hypersystemizing and, 180–82
    intelligence and, 179, 183, 184
    mathematics and, 180, 184
    memory and, 184–85
    overemphasizing weaknesses in, 193
    pattern recognition and, 195
    perseveration and, 185, 192
    prevalence of, 179
    pushing limits and, 190
    repetitive behaviors and, 185–86

Savage and, 173–78, 183, 185, 186–89,
    191–92, 195, 197, 200–202, 207
savant ability and, 177, 181, 185, 186,
    194–96, 198–99, 201
social interactions and, 176, 177, 184,
    186–91, 193
spatial abilities and, 184
successful life with, 185
uneven performance and, 184
U-shaped curve of, 183
verbal abilities and, 184
visual acuity and, 181
what it means to have, 177–82
work-arounds for, 189–94
autistic disorder, 178

Banacos, Charlie, 191
Barch, Deanna, 166
Beardslee, William, 96
Beautiful Mind, A (Nasar), 161
Beeman, Mark, 9–10, 54
Beethoven, Ludwig van, 136, 138
behavioral therapy:
    for ADD, 66–67, 77–78
    for anxiety, 82, 87–88, 104, 105
    cognitive, 104, 105, 144–45, 171
Benacerraf, Baruj, 29
Benacerraf, Beryl, 29–30, 32, 34–36, 37,
    38, 43, 46
Berlin, Rudolf, 24
Bilder, Robert, 206
Biological Psychiatry, 180, 181
bipolar disorder, 111, 114, 131–51, 155,
    158–59, 206
    challenges of living with, 140–42
    creativity and, 136–39, 142–51
    depression in, 134–36
    experience of, 139–49
    flourishing with, 149–51
    genetics and, 137
    gifts of, 145–49
    Hemingway and, 136, 140, 148–49
    kinetic effect in, 135

Lichtenstein and, 140–42, 144–45,
    147–51
mania and hypomania in, 14, 133–39,
    144–45, 148–51
Martin and, 131–35, 146–51, 216
medications for, 135, 140, 150, 151
mixed state in, 135
Nice and, 142–46
PTSD and, 139
rapid-cycling, 135
sleep and, 134, 135, 142, 145, 149
stigmatization of, 140–42, 148, 151
treatment of, 135, 150
two forms of, 136
vigilance and, 149–50
what it means to have, 134–39
work-arounds for, 142–45
Bipolar Expeditions (Martin), 133
Boyce, Tom, 207
Bradley, Charles, 52–53
brain, 13, 194, 201, 203–5
    ADD and, 13, 51–55, 61, 71, 91
    anxiety and, 86, 87
    ASD and, 180–81, 185, 194
    atypical lateralization in, 165
    capacity of, 192
    cognitive control network in, 14
    cortex of, 91
    creativity and, 164–65
    default network in, 14, 53–54
    depression and, 114
    disorders of, vs. "mental" disorders,
        208
    dyslexia and, 24–29, 91, 210
    executive function in, 2, 13, 51–52, 55,
        58, 59
    face recognition and, 194–95
    and filtering of information, 164
    frontal cortex of, 181
    genius and, 14–15, 165
    gray matter in, 14, 91
    hypomania and, 137–38
    inhibition and disinhibition in, 14, 137

brain (continued)
    plasticity of, 185, 186, 200, 204, 211
    prefrontal cortex in, 137–38
    septal/subgenual cortex in, 114
    subcortical regions in, 137–38
    variations in, 203, 209–11
brain differences, 4–5
    comorbidity and, 91
    flourishing with, 210–18
    future of, 203–18
    genius and, 4, 9–11
    inverted U-shaped curve and, 11–12
    language used to diagnose, 5–6, 7
    negativity and fear surrounding, 8
    overlapping of, 8
    in parents, 8
    treatment of, see treatment
    use of phrase, 211
    work-arounds and, see work-arounds
brain imaging, 194, 204
    ADD and, 51, 53
    anxiety and, 86
    Child Mind Institute and, 209–10
    dyslexia and, 24, 25
    Human Connectome Project and,
        160–61, 166, 203, 204, 208–10
    worry and intelligence and, 89
Brain Research through Advancing
        Innovative Neurotechnologies
        (BRAIN) Initiative, 6–7
Breslin, Jimmy, 140, 141
Brilliant Blunders (Livio), 70
British Journal of Psychiatry, 163
British Medical Journal, 24
Brokaw, Esther, 195–98
Brown, Martha Kay, 117

Cannon, Tyrone, 137
Center Cannot Hold, The (Saks), 154
Centers for Disease Control and
        Prevention, 48, 118, 179
childhood abuse and trauma, 85, 114,
        132–33, 146

childhood disintegrative disorder, 178
Child Mind Institute, 23, 26, 51, 55,
        209–10
Child Neuropsychology, 54
Churchill, Winston, 112
Close, Chuck, 210
Clozapine, 156, 167
cognitive behavioral therapy (CBT), 104,
        105, 144–45, 171
college, 31, 57, 93, 105–6
    depression and, 118–19
Columbia University, 53
comorbidity, 91
compensatory skills, 34
    see also work-arounds
Condon, David, 9–10, 54
convergent thinking, 14
Cook, Gareth, 199
coping strategies, 34
    see also work-arounds
Cramond, Bonnie, 54
creative flow, 162
creativity, 14, 162, 163, 214
    ADD and, 52, 54, 70, 71
    bipolar disorder and, 136–39, 142–51
    brain and, 164–65
    daydreaming and, 76
    depression and, 110, 113, 114, 128, 129
    divergent thinking and, 205–6
    dyslexia and, 28
    impulsivity and, 54
    inverted U-shaped curve and, 11–12
    mental illness and, 9–10, 163
    savant, 195
    and schizophrenia and schizotypal
        thinking, 161–65, 168–70
    and screening out environmental
        input, 163–64
    sculpted, 150, 151
    U-shaped curve and, 205–7
Cruger, Matthew, 23, 26
Csikszentmihalyi, Mihaly, 162
Cunningham, Robert, 41–44, 63, 64, 66

Curie, Marie, 112
Cuthbert, Bruce N., 208, 209
cycling mood, *see* bipolar disorder

dandelion and orchid theory of human
    behavior, 207
Darwin, Charles, 11, 100–101, 107
daydreaming, 53–54, 76
    creativity and, 76
    Einstein and, 74–75
    problem solving and, 75
DeHaven, William, 43
delay aversion, 51
delusions, 158, 159, 166
depression, 15, 109–29, 206, 208
    alcoholism and, 119
    altruism and, 114
    in bipolar disorder, 134–36
    brain and, 114
    challenges of living with, 115–20
    clinical, 111, 135
    college and, 118–19
    creativity and, 110, 113, 114, 128, 129
    cyclical nature of, 114
    drug abuse and, 119
    dysthymia, 111, 114
    empathy and, 13, 113, 114, 126–27
    exercise and, 121–22, 129
    experience of, 115–27
    flourishing with, 127–29
    genetic predisposition for, 116
    gifts of, 13, 113, 124–27
    income and, 118, 119
    intelligence and, 113, 115
    kinetic effect in, 113, 135
    major depression disorder, 111–12
    medical disability caused by, 119
    medications for, 121, 127–28, 129
    in men and boys, 116
    obsessiveness and, 124–25
    pessimism and, 112
    schizophrenia and, 160
    shutdown in, 111

Solomon and, 13, 109–11, 113, 122–29
    suffering and, 111, 113, 128
    suicide and, 119
    treatment of, 113, 119, 127–29
    what it means to have, 111–15
    work-arounds for, 120–24
    see also melancholy
depressive realism, 112, 118, 125
*Diagnostic and Statistical Manual of
    Mental Disorders (DSM)*, 5–6, 7, 15,
    53, 86, 157, 178
Disney, Walt, 193
distractibility, 47–78
    see also ADD
divergent thinking, 14, 153–72, 205
    creativity and, 205–6
    experience of having, 166–70
    flourishing with, 170–72
    gifts of, 168–70
    use of phrase, 157
    what it means to have, 157–65
    see also schizophrenia
Dobbs, David, 207
dopamine, 186
Driven to Distraction (Hallowell), 50, 53,
    61
drug abuse, 119, 206
drug treatments, *see* medications
Duke, Patty, 147–48
Dunham, Lena, 81–82
dyscalculia, 18, 19
dysgraphia, 19, 40
dyslexia, 17–46, 70, 73, 204, 211
    ADD and, 18, 57
    artistic creativity and, 28
    Benacerraf and, 29–30, 32, 34–36, 37,
        38, 43, 46
    brain and, 24–29, 91, 210
    challenges of living with, 28, 29–32
    diagnosing, 26, 43
    empathy and, 37–38
    experience of having, 28–41
    flourishing with, 41–46

forms of and variations in, 18, 19,
    24–25
gifts of, 28–29, 34–41
in girls vs. boys, 19
Greider and, 29–30, 32, 36, 43, 46
as letter and number reversal, 24, 25, 27
memory and, 27, 38
other conditions associated with,
    18–19
peripheral vision and, 26–28, 35
reading and, 25–27, 44–45, 210, 212
self-esteem and, 29, 30, 35, 43, 45–46
tests and, 21–22, 43
undiagnosed, 19
what it means to have, 23–28
work-arounds for, 28, 32–34
dysphoria, 111, 112
dyspraxia, 19
dysthymia, 111, 114

education and school, 78, 211–12
    ASD and, 186–87
    college, *see* college
    cookie-cutter approach to, 211–12
    depression and, 118–19
    expectation of uniformity in, 22
    expertise and, 212
    high school, 93–94
    social component of, 91
    special, 2, 4, 23, 63, 65, 186–87
    testing and, *see* tests
Einstein, Albert, 4, 43, 55–56, 75, 77, 78
    ADD and, 11, 55–57
    daydreaming of, 74–75
    temper of, 59
emotions:
    anxiety and, 94
    stressful, 58
empathy:
    depression and, 13, 113, 114, 126–27
    dyslexia and, 37–38
endorphins, 121
equal-odds rule, 205–6

executive function, 2, 13, 51–52, 55, 58, 59
exercise:
    depression and, 121–22, 129
    stress and, 104–5

face recognition, 180–81, 193, 194–95
family, *see* genetics; parents
Far from the Tree (Solomon), 109, 124–25
fear, 84–85, 86
fight-or-flight response, 84, 95, 105
Fink, Andreas, 164
First-Rate Madness, A (Ghaemi), 113
Fitzgerald, F. Scott, 149
flow, 162
Frances, Allen, 5
Frontiers in Psychology, 10, 54, 162, 165,
    205, 206
Funkhouser, John, 175
future of thinking differently, 203–18
    treatment and, 208–10
Future Project, 212

generalized anxiety disorder (GAD), 84,
    88
    experience of having, 90–103
    see also anxiety disorders
Generation Kill (Wright), 125, 126
genetics, 214
    anxiety and, 82, 85
    bipolar disorder and, 137
    in creativity and brain differences, 206
    depression and, 116
    environment and, 210
    OCD and OCPD and, 86
    panic attacks and, 85
    PTSD and, 85
    schizophrenia and, 158
genius, 4, 77, 114, 168, 169, 216–18
    angular thinking and, 22
    brain and, 14–15, 165
    brain difference and, 4, 9–11
    defined, 4
    mental illness and, 9

Ghaemi, Nassir, 113, 114, 139, 150–51
Girls, 81–82
Goldstein, Joseph, 97
Good Morning America, 95
Goteborg University, 28
grandiosity, 134, 139, 143, 148
Greider, Carol, 29–30, 32, 36, 43, 46
grit, 12, 28, 65, 66, 120, 177

Hallowell, Edward M., 50, 53, 61–65,
    70–71, 74
hallucinations, 159, 166
    auditory, 157–59
    visual, 156, 159
handwriting, 40
Harris, Dan, 95–97, 106
Harvard Medical School Special Health
    Report, 121
hearing voices, 157–59
Hemingway, Ernest, 136, 140, 148–49
high achievers, 4–5
Human Connectome Project, 160–61,
    166, 203, 204, 208–10
Hume, David, 169
hyperactivity, 49, 52–53, 67–68
    see also ADD
hyperfocus, 3
hypergraphia, 136
hypersystemizing, 180–82
hypervigilance, 88, 90, 95, 96, 107
hypomania and mania, 10
    in bipolar disorder, 14, 133–39, 144–45,
    148–51

imagination, 78
impulsivity, 2, 3, 10, 70
    in ADD, 2, 3, 49–51, 53, 54, 59, 60
Insel, Thomas, 5, 7, 15, 203–5, 208–11
intelligence, 183
    ASD and, 179, 183, 184
    depression and, 113, 115
    worry and, 88–89
intelligence tests, 25

ASD and, 184
    impossible figures in, 27–28
Interpreting Interpretation (Saks),
    167–68
Interview with the Vampire (Rice), 123
inverted U-shaped curve, 11–12, 182–83
    anxiety and, 89–90
    ASD and, 183
    creativity and, 205–7
Iowa Writers' Workshop, 9, 145
IQ, 25, 89, 113, 183, 184, 210
    savants and, 185
    see also intelligence tests
irritability, 111
Irving, John, 9, 21, 39, 41, 43
Islands of Genius (Treffert), 195

James, William, 75
Jamison, Kay Redfield, 139–42, 145
Jaques, Elliott, 150
Journal of Affective Disorders, 114, 139
*Journal of Behavioral Therapy and
    Experimental Psychiatry,* 112
*Journal of Consulting and Clinical
    Psychology,* 104
Journal of Frontiers in Psychology,
    137
Journal of Psychiatric Research, 206
Journal of Psychology, 113
*Journal of the American Medical
    Association,* 119
Jung, Rex, 14, 205

Kaufman, Scott Barry, 7–8, 11, 162,
    211–12
kinetic effects:
    in bipolar disorder, 135
    in depression, 113, 135
    in schizophrenia, 160
King's College London, 181–82, 200
Knudsen, Kendra, 206
Kocsis, James, 125, 126
Koplewicz, Harold, 209–10

labeling, 5–8, 15, 128, 170–71
Lamictal, 150
language, 42
Lanza, Ada, 109
Lanza, Peter, 109
learning differences, 17–46
　challenges of living with, 28, 29–32
　experience of having, 28–41
　forms of, 23
　use of term, 22
　what it means to have, 23–28
　see also dyslexia
learning disability, 211
　use of term, 22
Leonardo da Vinci, 4
Lichtenstein, Bill, 140–42, 144–45, 147–51
Life, Animated (Suskind), 92
Lincoln, Abraham, 112, 114
Lincoln's Melancholy (Shenk), 112
Lindell, Annukka K., 164–65
lithium, 135, 140, 150, 151
Livio, Mario, 68–70, 75, 77
Locke, John, 169
Logan, Julie, 34, 39
Lovibond Object Sorting Test, 164

major depression disorder (MDD),
　111–12
mania and hypomania, 10
　in bipolar disorder, 14, 133–39, 144–45,
　148–51
manic-depressive illness, see bipolar
　disorder
Man Who Couldn't Stop, The (Adam), 94
Martin, Emily, 131–35, 144, 146–51, 216
mathematics, 18, 19, 25, 43
　ASD and, 180, 184
McCarten School, 191–92
medications, 8–9
　for ADD, 2, 48, 66–68, 77–78
　Adderall, 2, 66, 77
　for anxiety, 87–88
　for bipolar disorder, 135, 150, 151
Clozapine, 156, 167
　for depression, 121, 127–28, 129, 132
　lithium, 135, 140, 150, 151
　for OCD, 104
　Ritalin, 48, 66–68, 77
　for schizophrenia, 156, 166, 167,
　　171–72
　Zoloft, 121
meditation, 96, 105
melancholy, 9, 15, 109–29
　challenges of living with, 115–20
　dysphoria, 111, 112
　experience of, 115–27
　flourishing with, 127–29
　gifts of, 124–27
　what it means to have, 111–15
　work-arounds for, 120–24
　see also depression
memory:
　ASD and, 184–85
　dyslexia and, 27, 38
　schizophrenia and, 160
mental illness:
　brain disorder vs., 208
　creativity and, 9–10, 163
　DSM and, 5–6, 7, 15
　educating oneself about, 168, 171, 215
　genius and, 9
　inverted U-shaped curve of, see
　　inverted U-shaped curve
　labeling of, 5–8, 15, 170–71
　negativity and fear surrounding, 8
　overlapping of, 8
　prevalence of, 7–8, 206–7, 214
　stigma of, 214, 216–17
　treatment of, see treatment
　vigilance about, 168
Millham, Michael P., 51, 53–54
Milrod, Barbara, 89, 104, 106
mind map, 33
Morgan, W. Pringle, 24
motivation, 139
multiple personality disorder, 169

muscle relaxation, 105
My Age of Anxiety (Stossel), 107

Naked (Sedaris), 80
Nasar, Sylvia, 161
Nash, Alicia, 172
Nash, John, 161, 171, 172
National Institute of Mental Health
    (NIMH), 5, 10
National Institutes of Health (NIH),
    206
    Human Connectome Project, 160–61,
        166, 203, 204, 208–10
neologism, 159
NeuroImage: Clinical, 113–14
neuroimaging, *see* brain imaging
Neuropsychologia, 165, 180
New England Journal of Medicine, 27
Newton, Isaac, 4
New York Times, 34
New York Times Magazine, 199
Nice, Chuck, 131, 142–46
92nd Street Y, 12
Nobel Prize, 9, 29, 161, 171, 217–18
nonsense words, 159
norepinephrine, 121
NPR, 147

Obama, Barack, 6–7, 203
obsessive-compulsive disorder (OCD), 11,
    80–83, 86–88, 94–95, 103, 104
obsessive-compulsive personality disorder
    (OCPD), 86–88
obsessiveness, depression and, 124–25
orchid and dandelion theory of human
    behavior, 207
Oregon State University, 137
originality, 77, 78, 115, 138, 162, 164
    ADD and, 52, 54
    see also creativity
Orygen, 161
Oxford-Liverpool Inventory of Feelings
    and Experiences (O-LIFE), 165

panic attacks, 85
    Darwin and, 100
    Harris and, 95
panic disorder, 85
paranoid delusions, 158, 159
parents, 63–64
    ADD in, 8, 77
    of high school students, 93–94
Patchett, Ann, 9
pattern recognition, 195
Paul, Elliot S., 162
Pelphrey, Kevin, 173, 184–86, 192–94,
    215
perfect pitch, 182
perseveration, 185, 192
persistence, 169
Perspectives on Psychological Science,
    163
pessimism, 112
phobias, 85, 104
Plato, 9
play, 76
post-traumatic stress disorder (PTSD),
    84–85, 114
    bipolar disorder and, 139
Psychiatric News, 137
Psychobiography series, 12
Psychological Science, 25
Psychology Today, 5
psychotic episodes, 157–58
psychoticism, 10
psychotic thinking, 157

reading, 25, 26, 42
    ADD and, 57–58
    dyslexia and, 25–27, 44–45, 210, 212
relatedness, *see* autism spectrum
    disorder
reporters, 125
resilience, 28
Rice, Anne, 122–23
risk-taking, 136, 139, 143, 148, 169
Ritalin, 48, 66–68, 77

Rosenthal, Michael, 55
Royal College of Psychiatry, 163

Saks, Elyn, 153–62, 166–72, 216
Saks Institute for Mental Health Law,
     Policy, and Ethics, 155
Savage, Diane, 174–75, 190, 197, 200
Savage, Matt, 173–78, 183, 185, 186–89,
     191–92, 195, 197, 200–202, 207
savants, 177, 181, 185, 186, 194–96,
     198–99, 201
schizoaffective disorder, 158–59
schizoid personality disorder, 158–60
schizophrenia, 153–72, 206
     creativity and, 161–65, 168–70
     disorganized thinking in, 159
     experience of having, 166–70
     flourishing with, 170–72
     genetics and, 158
     kinetic effect in, 160
     medications for, 156, 166, 167, 171–72
     memory and, 160
     Nash and, 161, 171, 172
     paranoid, 158, 159
     "positive" and "negative" symptoms of,
          159–60
     prevalence of, 158
     Saks and, 153–62, 166–72, 216
     and screening out environmental
          input, 163–64
     spectrum of, 167
     stigmatization of, 166–68
     treatment of, 166–68, 171–72
     what it means to have, 157–65
Schizophrenia Bulletin, 161
schizotypal thinking, 157, 158, 162
     creativity and, 162, 164, 168–70
     gifts of, 168–70
school, see education and school
Science, 208
Scientific American, 7
Sedaris, David, 79–83, 86, 90–91,
     98–103

Sedlak, Thomas, 157, 167, 168–69, 171
self-awareness, 62
     anxiety and, 88
self-confidence, 112
self-esteem, 121
     ADD and, 49, 52, 67, 77
     dyslexia and, 29, 30, 35, 43, 45–46
     inflated (grandiosity), 134, 139, 143,
          148
Sexton, Anne, 136, 140
Shaywitz, Bennett A., 25
Shaywitz, Sally, 24, 25, 38, 43, 44–46
Shenk, Joshua Wolf, 112
Sherwood, Ben, 106
Silverstein, Steve, 175
Simonton, Dean Keith, 138, 163
Singer, Jerome L., 76
skill development and progression, 42
sleep, 105
     bipolar disorder and, 134, 135, 142, 145,
          149
social anxiety disorder, 85–86
Solomon, Andrew, 13, 109–11, 113,
     122–29
Sonne, Lars, 199
Sonne, Thorkil, 199
special education, 2, 4, 23, 63, 65,
     186–87
Specialisterne, 199
SSRIs, 104
Stanford University, 180
Stanley, Steven, 47–48, 50–52, 60–61, 68,
     71, 75, 77
Stossel, Scott, 107
Strength of Mind series, 12
stress, 58
     anxiety and, 81–84, 92–93, 104
     exercise and, 104–5
substance abuse, 9, 119, 149, 206
suffering, 65, 216
     depression and, 111, 113, 128
suicide, 119, 135, 159, 206
Suskind, Owen, 192–93, 199

Suskind, Ron, 192–93, 199
synesthesia, 74, 120
systemizing, 180–82

tenacity, 169
tests, 21–22, 31, 43–44, 78, 212
    ADD and, 66
    anxiety about, 81
    dyslexia and, 21–22, 43
    intelligence, *see* intelligence tests
    time limits on, 43, 44, 66
*Touched with Fire: Manic-Depressive
    Illness and the Artistic Temperament*
    (Jamison), 139–40, 145
trauma:
    childhood, 85, 114, 132–33, 146
    PTSD and, *see* post-traumatic stress
    disorder
treatment, 77, 168, 205, 211, 214–15
    behavioral therapy, *see* behavioral
        therapy
    future of, 208–10
    medications, *see* medications
    of symptoms vs. diagnoses, 15
    see also specific conditions
Treffert, Darold, 195, 198, 201
Tyson, Neil DeGrasse, 215

University of California, Santa Barbara,
    75
University of Iowa Writers' Workshop, 9,
    145
University of Melbourne, 161
University of Mexico, 205
University of Montreal, 181
University of Wisconsin, 27

Uptown Mood Disorder Support Group
    of New York, 141–42
U-shaped curve, *see* inverted U-shaped
    curve

van Gogh, Vincent, 215–16
Vinet, Will, 172
Voices of an Illness, 142

walking, 121
Walkup, John, 92–94, 105
Wallace, Greg, 183, 184, 190–91,
    194–95
White, Holly, 54
Woman in the Body, The (Martin), 131
Woolf, Virginia, 136
word salad, 159
work-arounds, 32
    ADD and, 62–68
    anxiety and, 95–99
    ASD and, 189–94
    bipolar disorder and, 142–45
    dyslexia and, 28, 32–34
    melancholy and, 120–24
    self-awareness, 62
World Health Organization, 208
worry, 84, 95–97, 107
    intelligence and, 88–89
Wright, Evan, 115–20, 122, 124–26, 128,
    129
writers, 9, 145

Yale University, 24, 25, 45, 137

Zabelina, Darya L., 9–10, 54
Zoloft, 121